SUBSTANCE ABUSE

Selected Titles in ABC-CLIO's
CONTEMPORARY
WORLD ISSUES
Series

For a complete list of titles in this series, please visit
www.abc-clio.com.

Books in the Contemporary World Issues series address vital issues in today's society, such as genetic engineering, pollution, and biodiversity. Written by professional writers, scholars, and nonacademic experts, these books are authoritative, clearly written, up-to-date, and objective. They provide a good starting point for research by high school and college students, scholars, and general readers as well as by legislators, businesspeople, activists, and others.

Each book, carefully organized and easy to use, contains an overview of the subject, a detailed chronology, biographical sketches, facts and data and/or documents and other primary-source material, a directory of organizations and agencies, annotated lists of print and nonprint resources, and an index.

Readers of books in the Contemporary World Issues series will find the information they need to have a better understanding of the social, political, environmental, and economic issues facing the world today.

SUBSTANCE ABUSE

A Reference Handbook

David E. Newton

**CONTEMPORARY
WORLD ISSUES**

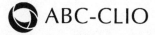 ABC-CLIO

Santa Barbara, California • Denver, Colorado • Oxford, England

Library of Congress Cataloging-in-Publication Data

Newton, David E.
Substance abuse : a reference handbook / David E. Newton.
    p. cm. — (Contemporary world issues)
  Includes bibliographical references and index.
    ISBN 978-1-59884-509-9 (hard copy : alk. paper) —
ISBN 978-1-59884-510-5 (ebook)
1. Substance abuse—Handbooks, manuals, etc. I. Title.
HV4998.N488   2010
362.29—dc22   2010007451

ISBN: 978-1-59884-509-9
EISBN: 978-1-59884-510-5

14 13 12 11 10   1 2 3 4 5

This book is also available on the World Wide Web as an eBook.
Visit www.abc-clio.com for details.

ABC-CLIO, LLC
130 Cremona Drive, P.O. Box 1911
Santa Barbara, California 93116-1911

This book is printed on acid-free paper (∞)

Manufactured in the United States of America

*For Ed Semeyn and Tom Littell
and all the young men and women of Wilcox Park
for the great honor their friendship has done me;
thanks for the memories!*

Contents

List of Tables and Figures

Tables

Preface

Nature has provided the human race with a dazzling variety of plants, from which an endless number of useful products have been produced. Some of these products are essential for the very survival of animal life on the planet. Others are so toxic that minuscule amounts are sufficient to cause almost immediate death. Somewhere within this array of plant products are substances that have very special effects on an animal's nervous system, so-called psychoactive substances. Some of the best known psychoactive substances are caffeine, found in the coffee, tea, and chocolate drinks consumed around the world; nicotine, a component of tobacco products; opium and its derivatives, such as codeine, heroin, and morphine; marijuana and other products of the cannabis family of plants; cocaine and other products of the coca plant; psilocybin; peyote and mescaline; cathinone and other products of the khat plant; and an almost uncountable number of synthetic products not derived from plants, but similar in their psychoactive effects on humans and other animals. These so-called *designer drugs* include amphetamine and methamphetamine and their analogs (chemical relatives); the barbiturates; flunitrazepam; gamma-hydroxybutyric acid (GHB); phenylcyclidine (PCP) and its analogs; and meperidine and its analogs.

Many of these substances have been known to and used by humans almost since the beginnings of civilization. Archaeologists have found representations of their use in cave paintings, artwork on stone walls, and even remnants of the substances themselves in ancient dwellings, all dating back thousands of years. These traditions survive today in a number of different religions, where the consumption of psychoactive substances is still an integral part of many religious and cultural ceremonies. In fact, those ceremonies often make explicit reference to the role that opiates, coca products, and derivatives of cannabis (for example) played in the earliest stages of Chinese, Indian, South American, Oceanic, and other cultures. The essential role of psychoactive substances in these traditions is reflected in a variety of ways in modern society: in India, the psychoactive material bhang (a cannabis product) is openly sold through government-owned and operated shops; in parts of Africa, khat is sold commercially through shops no different from those that offer fruits and vegetables; and in the United States, special legal exemptions are provided for Native American tribes that have long incorporated peyote or psilocybin into their traditional ceremonies.

Evidence suggests that humans may also have been using psychoactive substances for non-religious, non-medical purposes for thousands of years. Men and women enjoy smoking opium or chewing coca leaves for no other reason that just to "get high," to relax, or to enjoy some type of "out-of-body" experience. And it is this recreational use of psychoactive substances that is of such great concern throughout the world today, and it is the subject of this book.

The use of these substances is seldom an entirely positive or benign experience; it may often be followed by a harmful or destructive episode or series of episodes, which may include psychological or mental disturbances, as well as physical ailments affecting the circulatory, nervous, and other systems. Individuals who become addicted to a psychoactive substance may also find themselves spiraling into a life of crime, required in order to support their expensive drug habit. For people who lose control of their ability to use psychoactive substances on a moderate and safe basis, then, these substances can easily ruin a person's life. They can also create social, political, legal, medical, economic, and psychological problem of enormous scope for society as a whole.

It is hardly surprising, then, that human cultures have long attempted to provide legal mechanisms for keeping substance abuse under control in the general population. In their harshest forms, these mechanisms may include penalties as severe as life imprisonment or even death for what some viewers would say are mild abuses of a psychoactive substance. More commonly, penalties involve shorter prison terms and/or fines. Increasingly, societies are attempting to deal with the problems of substance abuse with programs of prevention and treatment for consumers of psychoactive substances and massive programs of interdiction for the producers and purveyors of these drugs.

This book attempts to provide a general overview of the extensive and complex problem of substance abuse. Chapter 1 is devoted to a brief review of the major psychoactive substances and their background and history in human culture. Chapter 2 focuses on a number of issues that the United States faces with regard to substance abuse, issues such as methods that have been devised for controlling the use of illegal substances; drug testing in the workplace, in schools, and in athletic programs; prevention and treatment programs; and the legalization (or decriminalization) of drugs. Chapter 3 refers the status of substance abuse worldwide, reviewing not only the extent of the problem in various regions and nations around the world, but also the variety of drug laws that have been developed to deal with this problem.

Chapter 4 provides a chronology of the use of psychoactive substances by humans and of the mechanisms that societies have developed to deal with problems of drug abuse. Chapter 5 includes biographical sketches of a number of individuals who have been involved in the attempt to deal with substance abuse in the United States and other parts of the world. Chapter 6 is a collection of portions of important documents dealing with substance abuse, including laws and treaties, reports and recommendations, and decisions in court cases. The chapter also provides data and statistics on topics such as drug schedules, drug use by various substance, cigarette consumption, and alcohol-related vehicle accidents. Chapter 7 provides a list of organizations that are concerned with one aspect or another of the use of illegal substances as well as legal psychoactive substances, such as tobacco and alcohol. Chapter 8 is an annotated bibliography of print and nonprint resources. The book concludes with a glossary of important terms used in a discussion of substance abuse.

1

Background and History

Introduction

In June 2009, the U.S. Congress passed and President Barack Obama signed the Family Smoking Prevention and Tobacco Control Act, instituting a number of new controls on the sale of cigarettes. For the first time, the Food and Drug Administration (FDA) was given authority to regulate tobacco products, just as it oversees a host of foods, pharmaceuticals, and other products sold in the country. The act allows the FDA to ban certain types of advertising for tobacco products and to prohibit the use of certain chemicals in cigarettes. It also prohibits the use of certain terms about tobacco products, such as "mild" and "light," and it requires cigarette packages to contain graphic images of the harm caused by smoking on at least half of their front and back panels. This legislation raises new questions about the status of tobacco users in the United States. Are such individuals now to be thought of as "drug addicts" or "substance abusers"? Should they be classified with people who use marijuana (or cocaine or heroin), or are they just another group of Americans, like those who drink alcoholic beverages, who enjoy a legal product with detrimental side effects? These questions are more complex than they may at first appear, and they pose the primary challenge for this book. Who is the substance abuser? What personal mental and physical challenges do such individuals face? Of what concern is substance abuse to society in general, and what regulations, if any, should be applied to the use of body- and mind-altering substances?

A Brief History of Substance Use and Abuse

The use of natural and synthetic products that alter one's consciousness has been part of human culture as far back as records exist. In some instances, it even predates any written or pictorial accounts that humans left behind. In 1992, for example, Jan Lietava, of Comenius University in Bratislava, reported on the discovery of a number of natural herbs with mind-altering properties, including ephedra, at a Neanderthal burial site in the Shandihar region of Iraq dating to at least 50,000 BCE. Lietava wrote that the substances found at the site had "marked medical activity" (Lietava 1992). The discovery is thought to be the earliest evidence of drug use by humans.

Most other drugs with which humans are familiar today have long histories also. The first references to the cultivation of the cannabis plant, from which marijuana is produced, date to at least 10,000 BCE. The precise use of these plants is not clear, however, as the plant is used not only for the production of marijuana, but also for the manufacture of hemp, a valuable fiber used to make cloth. The earliest evidence of a cannabis product, in fact, is a piece of cord attached to pottery dating to about 10,000 BCE in China. The first reliable evidence that the plant was also used to make a product that could be smoked dates to somewhat later, about the first or second century CE, also in China. Myths dating to the period claim that the Chinese deity Shen Nung tested hundreds of natural products, including marijuana, to determine their medical and pharmacological properties (Iversen 2000, 18–19). These myths form the basis for a very early Chinese pharmacopeia, which describes the hallucinogenic properties of marijuana, which is called *ma*, a Chinese pun for "chaotic." (Iversen 2000, 19).

The use of marijuana as an intoxicant also has a long history in Indian culture, where its first mention dates to about 2000–1400 BCE in the classic work *Science of Charms*. According to legend, the Indian god Shiva became embroiled in a family argument that so angered him he wandered off into the fields, where he lay down and fell asleep under a leafy cannabis plant. When he awoke, he tasted a leaf of the plant and found that it so refreshed him that it became his favorite food. Thus was born the tradition of making and consuming a concoction of the cannabis plant known as *bhang* in honor of the Lord Shiva at many religious ceremonies, a tradition that continues today (Booth 2003, 24; also see Society for the Confluence of Festivals in India 2009).

The history of opium and other opiates (derivatives or chemical relatives of opium) is similar to that of marijuana and other psychoactive substances. Although there is some evidence that the poppy was cultivated and used by the Neanderthals, the first concrete, written evidence of its use dates to about 3500 BCE in lower Mesopotamia. Tablets found at the Sumerian spiritual center at Nippur describe the collection and treatment of poppy seeds, presumably for the preparation of opium. The Sumerians gave the name of Hul Gil, or "joy plant," to the poppy, almost certainly reflecting the sensations it produced when eaten (Kritikos and Papadaki 1967). Thereafter, the plant and the drug are mentioned commonly in almost every civilization of antiquity, where they were used for medical and, apparently, psychoactive reasons, probably in association with religious ceremonies. Interestingly, opium was almost universally ingested by mouth rather than by smoking. In fact, the first mention of the drug's use by smoking is not found until about 1500, when the Portugese introduced the practice, then thought by the residents of all other nations as being a "barbaric and subversive" custom ("A Brief History of Opium," 2009).

Although marijuana and opium were apparently not known in the New World, the Western Hemisphere had its own psychoactive drugs of choice, one of which was mescaline, derived from the peyote cactus (*Lophophora williamsii*). As in the Old World, this drug was apparently popular thousands of years ago, although it became known to Europeans only with the Spanish conquests of South America in the sixteenth century. One of the early chroniclers of the history of peyote was a Spanish priest, Bernardino de Sahagun, who estimated from extant documents that the drug had been in use for at least 1,800 years before the Spanish arrived in the New World. De Sahagun's estimate is problematic, however, partly because the conquistadors so aggressively destroyed all historical documents of the natives on which they could lay their hands. Later ethnologists and archaeologists think his estimates are conservative, and that the drug was used at least a thousand years earlier. One writer has placed the first use of peyote in the New World of at least 8,000 years ago (Spinella 2001, 344). In any case, it was still being widely used for both religious and recreational purposes when the Spaniards arrived, and the conquerors' efforts to abolish this practice were largely unsuccessful. One of the most thorough and detailed observers of native practices in the region, Danish ethnologist Carl Lumholtz, described peyote ceremonies he observed during an extended trip to Mexico:

> The plant, when taken, exhilarates the human system and allays all feeling of hunger and thirst. It also produces colour-visions. . . . Although an Indian feels as if drunk after eating a quantity of hikuli [native name for peyote], and the trees dance before his eyes, he maintains the balance of his body even better than under normal circumstances (Lumholtz 1902, 364).

The other psychoactive plant native to the New World is the coca plant, *Erythroxylum coca*. Recent studies have shown that the plant was being used at least 3,000 years ago. Two of eleven mummies from a burial area in northern Chile contained small quantities of the drug, whose age was determined by carbon-14 dating. Historically, archaeologists had previously set 600 CE as the earliest date for which good evidence of the use of coca has been set. That evidence consists of mummies that had been buried with a supply of coca leaves and whose cheeks were deformed by a bulge characteristic of those who chew leaves of the plant (Peterson 1977, 17). As with peyote, the Spaniards attempted to abolish the practice of coca use but were entirely unsuccessful. As they discovered, coca provides the chewer with energy and stamina, qualities of considerable benefit especially to those who lived in the thin air of the high Andes, and also of use for the exhausting manual labor in mining and other occupations to which the natives were assigned by the conquistadors.

The use of psychoactive substances has often been the subject of dispute within nations and regions. Indeed, Chapters 2 and 3 of this book discuss in some detail some of the issues surrounding the use of such substances in the United States and the rest of the world today. An example of the historical controversies about the use of psychoactive substances is the Opium Wars of the mid-nineteenth century between China and Great Britain. Although opium had been known in China and used for medical purposes for hundreds of years, by 1800 it had been banned for recreational use. Coincidentally, however, Great Britain had just come into control of the world's largest source of opium with its conquest of the Indian subcontinent. That situation was a tinderbox, with the British eagerly searching for a market for the massive amounts of opium they now controlled and the Chinese determined not to permit the importation of the drug to their country.

The British took advantage of this opportunity in 1836 when they bribed officials at the port of Canton to allow them to bring opium into the country. Before long, the drug was widely available throughout China, and the number of people addicted to its use rose to an estimated two million (Chrastina 2009). The Chinese government finally decided to take vigorous action against the smuggling of opium into their country by the British in 1839. Emperor Tao-kuang appointed a trusted bureaucrat named Lin Tse-hsü to lead an anti-opium campaign across the country. Lin was especially aggressive against British merchants in China who trafficked in opium and against merchant ships who were attempting to deliver the drug at the port of Canton. As the year progressed, skirmishes between the Chinese and British increased in number and severity, and war between the two nations broke out in mid-1840. The result of the conflict was a foregone conclusion, with the British then having one of the largest and strongest military establishments in the world. In 1842, the Chinese sued for peace, which was confirmed by the Treaty of Nanjing, signed on August 29 of that year. The treaty called for China to open five ports to foreign trade, to pay significant reparations to Great Britain, and to cede Hong Kong to the British. The treaty settled matters temporarily, but discord between the two nations continued, and war broke out again in 1856. As before, the British prevailed, and the war ended with the Treaty of Beijing in 1860. Again, the Chinese were required to open more ports to foreign trade (10 this time) and to pay very large reparations to Great Britain and its ally, France. (For an excellent overview of the Opium Wars, see Beeching 1975)

Controversies over the use of psychoactive substances have extended to every material that might fit that description. Even a substance that hardly attracts opprobrium today—coffee—has been the subject of controversy at a number of times in the past. In 1511, for example, the governor of Mecca banned all coffee-houses within his district. His action was based on the belief that coffee is an intoxicant and therefore forbidden by Islamic law. To his misfortune, the governor was later overruled by his superior, the Sultan of Cairo, and paid with his own life. After a coffee craze swept through Europe in the seventeenth century, similar concerns about its use arose in a number of locations. In 1600, for example, a number of Christian clerics asked Pope Clement VIII to ban coffee because it came from the land of the infidels (the Islamic world) and it would cause drinkers to lose their souls. After tasting the new drink, however, Clement had a somewhat different take on the issue. He could not believe, he said, that such a delicious drink could be evil. Instead, he decided to "fool the devil" by baptizing coffee and allowing its free use among all Christians (Grierson 2009).

The pope's decision did not, however, resolve the controversy over the use of coffee in many parts of Europe. The disputes that arose illustrate that such controversies may or may not arise solely out of the medical or health effects of a substance. In some cases, for example, objections to the rapid spread of coffeehouses were raised by tavern owners, who probably cared little one way or another about the psychoactive effects of coffee, and a great deal more about the competition coffeehouses posed to their businesses. Like earlier Christian leaders, they argued that coffee was a product of unbelievers, and that good Christian men should drink only the brew that had been prepared traditionally by monks: beer. Other efforts to close coffeehouses did focus on their supposed health risks. Perhaps the most famous of these efforts was the "Women's Petition against Coffee," published in 1674 in London. In this petition, a group of women asked the authorities to close coffeehouses because the drink was harming their sexual lives with their husbands. They complained of the "Grand INCONVENIENCIES accruing to their SEX from the Excessive Use of that Drying, Enfeebling LIQUOR" (Clarkson and Gloning 2003). (Some critics have observed that women's greatest complaint about coffeehouses, to the contrary, was that they were not permitted to enter such establishments [Grierson 2009].) The Women's Petition drew a comparable response from men, or at least a man purporting to represent the male position on coffeehouses. The "Men's Answer to the Women's Petition against Coffee" was a long harangue that insisted that the coffeehouse is "the citizen's academy, where he learns more wit than ever his granmum taught him [and that] ... 'Tis Coffee that ... keeps us sober." He continues: "[Let] all our wives that hereafter shall presume to petition against it, be confined to lie alone all night, and in the day time drink nothing but bonny clabber" (Svensk 2009). If there is any lesson to be learned from this contretemps, and the longer history of coffee itself, it is that virtually any substance with some effect on a person's mental or physical condition is likely to be the subject of controversy at some point in history.

The above review provides only a modest introduction to the earliest history of drug use in the Old and New Worlds. Similar stories could be told for other naturally occurring psychoactive plants and their products, such as tobacco, alcohol, caffeine, and psilocybin, as well as a host of synthetic products developed in the last century, such as amphetamine, the barbiturates, lysergic acid diethylamide (LSD), and MDMA (3,4-Methylenedioxyme-thamphetamine). Those stories would require a series of books much larger than this work, however, although salient points in that history will be discussed in this and following chapters.

Speaking of Drugs

Any discussion of substance abuse makes use of a number of terms whose definitions are essential to a clear understanding of the subject. Some of the most important of these terms are the following:

Drug is probably the most fundamental term used in talking about substance abuse, but it is also the term with the greatest variety of meanings. According to Merriam-Webster's Dictionary, for example, the two major definitions of the term refer to its medical use and its recreational use. In the former instance, *drug* is defined as

> (1) a substance recognized in an official pharmacopoeia or formulary (2) a substance intended for use in the diagnosis, cure, mitigation, treatment, or prevention of disease (3) a substance other than food intended to affect the structure or function of the body (4) a substance intended for use as a component of a medicine but not a device or a component, part, or accessory of a device." In the latter instance, the term is defined as "something and often an illegal substance that causes addiction, habituation, or a marked change in consciousness (Merriam-Webster's Online Dictionary 2009).

Legal and *illegal* are terms that describe substances that are or are not permitted by law to be manufactured, transported, sold, and consumed. The term *legal drugs* refers both to prescribed drugs, that is, drugs that can be obtained only with a medical professional's prescription, and over-the-counter (OTC) drugs, which are freely available to any consumer without a prescription. A number of substances that produce psychoactive effects are also legal in the United States. These substances include amyl nitrite, betal nuts, caffeine, catnip, henbane, hops, a variety of inhalants, kava kava, ketamine, mandrake, nitrous oxide, nutmeg, and tobacco. Illegal drugs cannot be obtained legally except by clearly specified medical applications. Legal and illegal drugs are also known as licit and illicit drugs, respectively.

Substance abuse is a term now more widely used than the formerly popular *drug abuse*. The term has become more common at least partly because it can be used for a wider variety of materials that are not in and of themselves illegal, such as alcohol, tobacco, and caffeine, which may also be abused in much the same way as illegal drugs, such as marijuana, cocaine, and heroin.

The term *substance abuse* itself is somewhat vague, since it can refer to a variety of conditions ranging from relatively harmless to life-threatening. In his book *Illegal Drugs*, Paul Gahlinger describes four levels of drug abuse (Gahlinger 2004, 90). The first level he calls "experimental use," because it involves the first exposure people have to drugs. They "try out" a glass of beer, a cigarette, or a lid of marijuana. For some people, that is as deeply as one becomes involved in "substance abuse." They do not enjoy the experience or decide not to go any further. (Although, as Gahlinger points out, even this level of drug abuse is an illegal act for substances such as marijuana and cocaine, although not for alcohol and tobacco.) The next level of drug use is one that Gahlinger labels "recreational use." It refers to cases in which a person takes a drink, has a cigarette, or uses an illegal drug from time to time "just for the fun of it." The person's life is not disrupted in any way by this occasional, low-key use of a substance.

Gahlinger calls the next level of drug use "circumstantial use," because it includes those occasions when substance use develops into a certain pattern: a person uses a drug to deal with a personal problem, because of the feelings the drug produces, or just to be sociable with others. Again, drug use at this level is not necessarily harmful, but it may be the gateway to the fourth level, "compulsive use," or, as most people would describe the situation, an *addiction*. Addiction is a medical and psychiatric condition that typically involves both physiological and psychological elements. It is more commonly known among many professionals as *substance depen-dence*. The *Diagnostic and Statistical Manual of Mental Disorders, 4th edition* (DSM-IV) defines substance dependence as a "maladaptive pattern of substance use" that is characterized by at least three of seven symptoms: (1) tolerance of the substance, meaning that an individual gradually becomes able to consume the substance with-out unpleasant side effects; (2) withdrawal, meaning that depriva-tion of the substance causes significant physical and emotional stresses; (3) increased consumption of the substance over time; (4) a lack of desire or ability to stop using the substance; (5) large amounts of time devoted to finding ways to obtain amounts of the substance needed to achieve a desired effect; (6) abandonment of otherwise typical social, occupational, and recreational activities because of the time needed for substance use; and (7) continued use of the substance in spite of an individual's knowledge of its deleterious effects (First, Frances, and Pincus 2004, 128).

Narcotics is a term that was traditionally used for opioids, drugs that are derivatives of or similar to opium. The word *narcot-ics* comes from the Greek term "narkōsis," which means "to make numb." Today, the term is used more generally for any substance that cause numbness or stupor, induces sleep, and relieves pain.

Psychoactive is an adjective used for any substance that acts on the central nervous system and alters one's consciousness or mental functioning. The word *psychotropic* is sometimes used as a synonym for "psychoactive." A number of other terms with the prefix *psycho-* are also used to describe certain specific types of psychoactive drugs. Psychotomimetic drugs, for example, are compounds that produce symptoms similar to ("mimic") those of a psychosis. Psychedelic drugs are those that produce altered sense of consciousness or distorted sensory perceptions. One large class of psychoactive drugs are the *hallucinogens*, which, as their name suggests, causes hallucinations, or perceptions of images and events for which there is no real stimulus. Psychoac-tive drugs have been used throughout history for a number of purposes: as medicines, as recreational drugs, and as a means for achieving spiritual experiences in religious ceremonies. Drugs used for the last of these purposes are sometimes called *entheogen* substances, from the Greek words for "to create", "the divine", and "within."

Generic is a term used to describe a particular form of a drug, or the name given to such a drug. Most drugs have at least two names, and often, they have three. The first name is its systematic, or scientific, name. For example, the systematic name for the compound that we commonly call *aspirin* is sodium acetylsalicylic acid. The systematic names for compounds are derived from rules established by the International Union of Pure and Applied Chemistry (IUPAC) and have the advantage of unambiguously identifying every different compound in the world. Such names are essential for researchers because they prevent any confusion whatsoever as to the substance about which a person is talking. The practical difficulty with IUPAC names is that they can be long and quite beyond the understanding of the ordinary person. The systematic name for the drug known as Ecstasy, for example, is (RS)-1-(benzo[d][1,3]dioxol-5-yl)-N-methylpropan-2-amine.

The generic name for a compound does not necessarily follow rules like those established by IUPAC. It is a simpler,

TABLE 1.1
Some Street Names for Illegal Drugs

Generic Name	Street Names
Amphetamine	Black Dex, Bennies, Black and White, Black Bombers, Bumblebees, Dexies, Fives, Footballs, French Blue, Horse Heads, Jolly Beans, Lid Poppers, Lightning, Oranges, Pep Pills, Rhythm, Rippers, Snap, Sparkle Plenty, Sweets, Thrusters, Uppers
Cocaine	All-American Drug, Aunt Nora, Bazulco, Bernie, Big C, Bolivian Marching Powder, Burese, C, Carrie Nation, Cecil, Charlie, Chloe, Double Bubble, Dream, Flake, Florida Snow, Happy Trails, Henry VIII, Merck, Monster, Powder Diamonds, Scorpion, Snow White
Heroin	Al Capone, Antifreeze, Aunt Hazel, Big H, Big Harry, Blow, Bozo, Brown Sugar, Dead-on-Arrival, Dr. Feelgood, Galloping Horse, Good and Plenty, Him, Joy Flakes, Old Steve, Rambo, Rawhide, Smack
Marijuana	Acapulco Red, Black, Boo, Canadian Black, Crying Weed, Don Juan, Flower Tops, Giggle Weed, Grass, Indian Hemp, Jane, Kentucky Blue, Locoweed, Magic Smoke, Muggles, Pot, Rainy Day Woman
MDMA	Adam, Batmans, Bermuda Triangles, Care Bears, E, Ecstasy, Four Leaf Clover, Hug Drug, Igloo, Lover's Special, Orange Bandits, Pink Panthers, Smurfs, Tom and Jerries, Tweety Birds, Wafers
Methamphetamine	Beannies, Black, Boo, Blue Devils, Chicken Feed, Clear, Cris, Hot Ice, Mercedes, Meth, Motorcycle Crack, Pink, Po Coke, Scootie, Sketch, Speckled Birds, Spoosh, Tick Tick, Wash
PCP	Angel Dust, Black Dust, Busy Bee, Crazy Coke, Crystal Joint, Dipper, Elephant Tranquilizer, Green Tea, Heaven & Hell, K, Lemon 714, Soma, Super, Tic Tac, Wack
Peyote	Half Moon, Hikori, Hikuli, Hyatari, Nubs, Seni, Tops

A much more complete list of street names can be found on the Internet at: White House Office of National Drug Control Policy. "Street Terms." http://www.whitehousedrugpolicy.gov/streetterms/Default.asp.

shorter name to which one can more easily refer. The compound officially known as (±)-1-phenylpropan-2-amine, for example, is more commonly known by the generic name of *amphetamine*. Proprietary formulations of drugs always carry a specific *brand name* also that associates that formulation with the company that makes the drug. Some brand names for amphetamine (sometimes mixed with other compounds) are Dexedrine, Adderall, Biphetamine, Desoxyn, and Vyvanse.

Finally, illegal drugs almost always have a number of *street names*, nicknames by which they are known among substance abusers, professionals, and the general public. The list of street names is very long indeed. Table 1.1 shows only a sample of some of these names and the drugs for which they are used.

Classifying Drugs

In many cases (as in the last part of this chapter), it may be useful to discuss the specific characteristics of individual drugs, such as cocaine, heroin, and PCP. In other cases, it is helpful to focus on the common properties of large classes of drugs. Drugs can be classified in a number of ways: on the basis of their chemical structures, as to their medical uses, by the mental and physical effects they produce, and on the basis of their legal status. A chemical system of classification organizes drugs according to their chemical structures. One might speak, for example, about the amphetamines, which are all derivative of the specific compound, amphetamine; barbiturates, which are all derivatives of barbituric acid; and the benzodiazepines, which are all derivatives of the chemical compound by that name. Figure 1.1 shows three members of the barbiturate family with its parent compound, barbituric acid.

A more common system of classification is based on the effects produced by drugs. The most common categories included in such as system are depressants, stimulants, and hallucinogens. The first group of substances, the *depressants*, get their name from the fact that they depress the central nervous system, reducing pain, relieving anxiety, inducing sleep, and, in general, calming a person down. Some common depressants are opium and its relatives, cannabis, alcohol, the barbiturates, the benzodiazepines, muscle relaxants, antihistamines, and antipsychotics. Depressants are commonly referred to as "downers" because they reduce the activity of the central nervous system.

FIGURE 1.1A
Barbituric acid

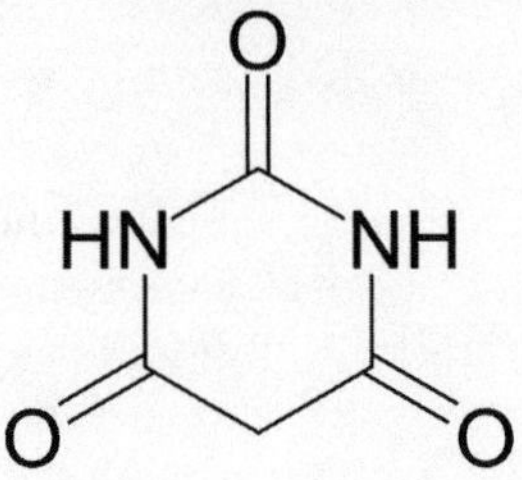

FIGURE 1.1B
Phenobarbital

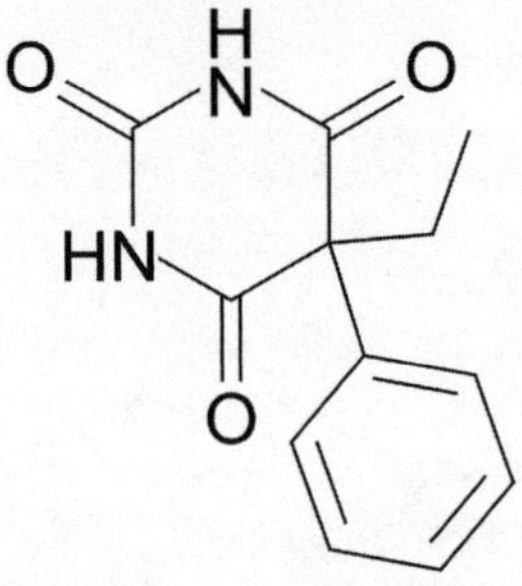

FIGURE 1.1C
Amobarbital

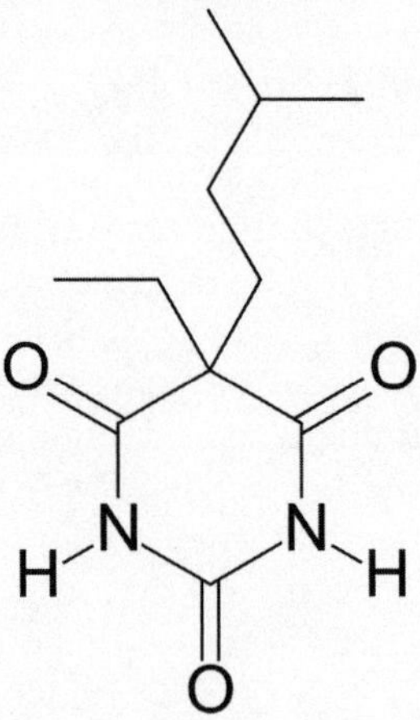

FIGURE 1.1D
Pentobarbital

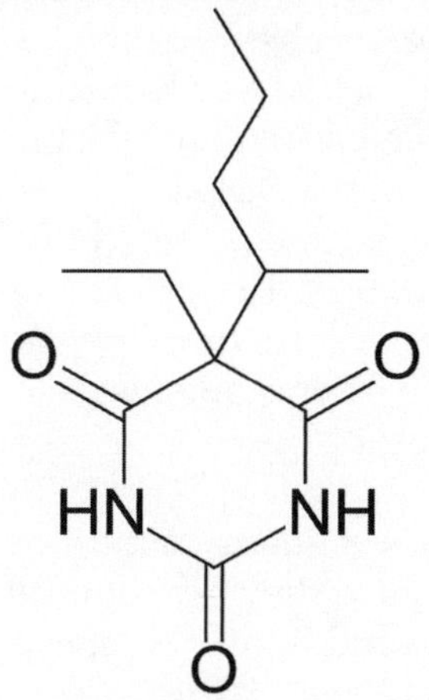

Stimulants have just the opposite effect. They increase the activity of the central nervous system, promoting physical and mental activity. Stimulants are used medically to treat a number of conditions that are characterized by depression, such as sleepiness, lethargy, and fatigue; to improve attentiveness and concentration; to promote weight loss by decreasing appetite; and to treat attention deficit hyperactivity disorder (ADHD) and clinical depression. Because of their effects, compounds in this category are sometimes called "uppers." Some common stimulants are amphetamine and its chemical analogs, caffeine, cocaine, Ecstasy (ethylenedioxymethamphetamine), and nicotine. (In chemistry, analogs [or analogues]) are chemical compounds similar in structure and function to other chemical compounds.)

Hallucinogens differ from stimulants and depressants in one important way. The latter classes of drugs amplify normal mental conditions, increasing those conditions in the case of stimulants and decreasing them in the case of depressants. Hallucinogens, by contrast, produce qualitatively different mental conditions, such as the perception of objects and events that do not, in fact, actually exist. The experiences produced by hallucinogens are, in some respects, similar to other kinds of so-called out-of-body experiences, such as those experienced during dreaming, meditation, and trances. Ironically, the one effect that is *not* produced by hallucinogens is hallucination, an experience in which a person completely accepts as real an event or object that has no basis whatsoever in reality. To someone who has taken a hallucinogen, by contrast, there is almost always some realization that the bizarre experiences he or she is having do have at least some basis in reality.

Hallucinogens can be subdivided into three groups: psychedelics, dissociatives, and deliriants. The term *psychedelic* comes from two Greek words, *pysche*, meaning "soul," and *delos*, meaning "to reveal." The term thus suggests a chemical that allows a person to look into her or his innermost self to discover one's authentic person. For this reason, psychedelics (as well as other hallucinogens) have a very long history of use in religious and mystical ceremonies since they are thought to allow a person to go beyond the simple (and limited?) reality of everyday life. Dissociatives are chemicals that disrupt normal nerve transmissions in the brain so that one loses touch, to a greater or lesser extent, with the physical world. He or she literally "disassociates" from that world with the result, as with psychedelics, that one can focus on one's innermost soul without the distraction of physical reality. Deliriants are a form of dissociative that have even more extreme effects on an individual. A person who takes a dissociative may be aware of the mental changes he or she is experiencing, while someone who has taken a deliriant is probably not aware of these changes. Of all hallucinogens, deliriants are most likely to produce true hallucinations.

Some categories of drugs in addition to stimulants, depressants, and hallucinogens are antipsychotics, used to treat psychoses because of their calming effects; antidepressants, used to treat depression and similar mood disorders; inhalants, abused by some individuals as a way of achieving some type of altered mental states, such as a "high"; and marijuana, which is often listed as a drug group in and of itself.

Finally, drugs can be categorized on the basis of their legal status in any particular nation. This method of categorization is of special interest and concern, of course, because it clarifies which substances are legal for individuals to use and which are not. The basis for classifying the legal status of drugs in the United States was established by the Controlled Substances Act of 1970. That law created five classes, or "schedules," of drugs according to their medical use and potential for abuse. Drugs placed in Schedule I, for example, currently have no approved legitimate medical use in the United States and a high potential for abuse. Some Schedule I drugs include the stimulant cathinone, the depressant methaqualone (Quaalude), the psychedelic 3,4-methylenedioxymethamphetamine (MDMA), and most opiates. Schedule II drugs include a number of substances that, while strongly subject to use as recreational drugs, do have some legitimate medical uses. These drugs include the amphetamines, most barbiturates, cocaine, morphine, opium, and phencyclidine (PCP). An excerpt of the law creating the drug schedules and a list of drugs in each schedule are to be found in Chapter 6 of this book.

How Do Drugs Work?

The transmission of a nerve impulse within the central nervous system (CNS) is a two-step process, one of which is an electrical mechanism, and one of which is chemical. A nerve impulse passes along a neuron (nerve cell) by means of a constantly changing electrical charge on the membrane of that cell. When that electrical impulse reaches the outermost edge of the cell structures known as *axons*, it initiates the release of chemicals from the axon into the space between that neuron (the *presynaptic neuron*) and some other adjacent neuron (the *postsynaptic neuron*), a space known as the *synapse*, or *synaptic gap*. These "message-carrying" chemicals are known as *neurotransmitters*. Some examples of neurotransmitters are acetylcholine, epinephrine (adrenaline), γ-aminobutyric acid (GABA), dopamine, serotonin, and nitrous oxide. After a neurotransmitter has crossed the synaptic gap, it attaches itself to a section of the dendrite on a receiving cell. A dendrite is a short projection in a neuron designed for the acceptance of neurotransmitters from another neuron. The point at which a neurotransmitter docks is called a *receptor site*. A specifically designed receptor site exists for each different type of neurotransmitter. Once a neurotransmitter has bonded to a receptor site on a dendrite, it stimulates the dendrite to initiate an electrical impulse, similar to the one that traveled through the first neuron. That electrical impulse then passes through the dendrite and into the neuron cell body, repeating the process of nerve transmission from the presynaptic neuron. Meanwhile, the neurotransmitter is released from the dendrite, travels back across the synaptic gap to the presynaptic neuron, and is available for reuse in transmission of the nerve message.

Most drugs exert their effects on the CNS by interrupting the action of neurotransmitters at some point in the process described above. Stimulants, for example, tend to prevent the reuptake of a neurotransmitter at the very end of the process. As a result, neurotransmitters tend to accumulate in the synaptic gap and reinsert themselves into receptor cells on the second neuron which is, as a result, restimulated over and over again. This repetitious stimulation is responsible for the increased activity observable in the brain after the ingestion of a stimulant.

Other stimulants have other modes of action. Nicotine, for example, causes its effects because its structure is somewhat similar to that of the neurotransmitter acetylcholine. Just as acetylcholine works by stimulating an acetylcholine receptor in a dendrite, so nicotine exerts its influence by stimulating a receptor similar to that for acetylcholine, called the nicotinic receptor. Caffeine operates in yet another way on the nervous system. It exerts its effects by acting as antagonist at a dendrite receptor site for the neuromodulator adenosine. A neuromodulator is substance that affects the rate at which nerve messages pass through the brain. In the case of adenosine, the effect is to slow down this process. Thus, whenever an adenosine molecule locks onto one of its receptor sites in a dendrite, no other neurotransmitter can enter that site, and a nerve message is interrupted. The brain's reaction rate slows down as a result of this event. If caffeine is present in the bloodstream, it may also enter the brain and dock at a receptor site normally reserved for adenosine molecules. A molecule that is able to act in a manner similar to some other molecule to produce a diminished response is said to be an *antagonist* for the second molecule. (By contrast, a molecule that acts like another molecule to produce an augmented response is called an *agonist*.) Thus, caffeine is an antagonist for adenosine. The only difference between the two substances is that caffeine has no effect on the rate at which nerve messages are transmitted. When it docks at an adenosine receptor, it prevents an adenosine molecule from docking there also, preventing a slowdown in the brain's activity. A person who has had a cup of coffee, then, does not experience the "slow down" responses, such as drowsiness, that might typically result from the action of adenosine in the brain.

As one might expect, the action of depressants on the nervous system is quite different from that of stimulants. In most cases, the neurotransmitter most commonly affected is γ-aminobutyric acid, generally known as GABA. GABA is a somewhat unusual neurotransmitter in that it tends to reduce the rate at which nerve transmission takes place. (Most neurotransmitters increase brain activity.) That is, as the flow of GABA from the presynaptic neuron to the postsynaptic neuron causes changes in the structure of the latter, that tends to reduce the rate at which nerve transmission continues. Depressants tend to enhance this effect. For example, members of the benzodiazepine family, a group of depressants, are able to bind to GABA receptor sites on postsynaptic neurons, increasing the efficiency with which those receptors work. Thus, with benzodiazepine molecules present in the brain, GABA neurotransmitters operate more efficiently and tend to significantly slow down brain activity, resulting in drowsiness and slower mental activity.

Another process by which depressants work takes advantages of the body's natural system for dealing with pain. Neurons contain receptor cells especially adapted to a group of natural opiate neurotransmitters called endorphins, enkephalins, and dynorphin. These neurotransmitters are often called *endogenous opiates* or *endogenous opioids* because they are opium-like compounds that occur naturally within ("endo-") the body. By contrast, the class of drugs generally known simply as "opiates" are more correctly called *exogenous opiates* (or *exogenous opioids*) because they occur naturally outside of ("exo-") the body (as in plants). Endogenous opiates exert their effect on a receptor in the presynaptic neuron that controls the release of GABA from that neuron. When an opiate neurotransmitter docks at this receptor site, it reduces the release of GABA. Fewer GABA molecules flow through the synaptic gap and stimulate the postsynaptic neuron.

The importance of this change is that the amount of GABA in a neuron affects the amount of a second neurotransmitter, dopamine, also present in the neuron. Specifically, the more GABA, the less dopamine (recall that GABA is an inhibitory neurotransmitter). Thus, with less GABA present in the postsynaptic neuron, the greater the amount of dopamine. The significance of this change is that one of the primary effects of dopamine is the production of feelings of elation and well-being. The effect in an endogenous opiate on the presynaptic neuron, then, is to produce a sense of euphoria. Scientists now believe that this system, beginning with the release of endogenous opiates from the pituitary gland, has evolved as a way for the body to deal with pain.

The action of depressants (exogenous opiates) is simply to enhance this process. If one ingests heroin, for example, there are simply more opiate molecules in the bloodstream, some of which reach the brain. Once in the brain, the heroin molecules act in a virtually identical fashion to the way endogenous opiates work. A person who has taken heroin, then, feels the same sense of pleasure and rapture that comes from the action of endogenous opiates.

The above discussion might be taken to mean that scientists have now essentially solved the puzzle as to how drugs affect the CNS. Such is not the case. In fact, the mechanism(s) by which some drugs affect mental and physical behavior is still largely a mystery. The case of lysergic diethylamide (LSD) is a case in point. For some time, scientists have known that LSD has a chemical structure similar to that of the neurotransmitter serotonin. Serotonin itself is a bit of a puzzle for neuroscientists because there are so few cells that produce the chemical in the brain (only a few thousand), but its influence is widespread, with each serotonergic (serotonin-making) cell activating at least 500,000 other neurons (Frederickson 2002). The presence of LSD molecules in the brain almost certainly means that the substance will dock with serotonin receptor sites, either in the presynaptic or postsynaptic neuron, exerting either an agonistic or antagonistic effect. Theories have been developed around all of four these possibilities, with a number of variations. Thus far, however, no one theory has been shown to explain the bizarre physical and mental effects that occur as the result of the ingestion of LSD.

A Survey of Legal and Illegal Drugs

The rest of this chapter is devoted to a review of some of the most common and most important substances involved in substance abuse problems. Each section deals, where appropriate, with a brief history of the use of the drug in the United States, current and historical patterns of drug consumption, and health effects associated with each substance. Other considerations, such as legal, political, social, moral, and other issues for each substance are discussed in Chapter 2 for the United States, and Chapter 3 for the rest of the world. To provide a perspective on the relative popularity of some legal and illegal substances, Table 1.2 provides a general summary of the consumption of these substances within three contexts: lifetime use (used at least once in a person's lifetime); past year (used at least once in the year before the survey was conducted); and past month (used at least once in the month before the survey was conducted.)

TABLE 1.2
Consumption of Certain Legal and Illegal Substances by Persons Aged 12 and Older in 2008 (in thousands)

Substance	Lifetime Use	Past Year Use	Past Month Use
Marijuana and hashish	102,404	25,768	15,203
Cocaine	36,773	5,255	1,855
Heroin	3,788	453	213
Hallucinogens	35,963	3,678	1,060
Inhalants	22,274	2,047	640
Nonmedical use of legal prescription drugs	51,970	15,166	6,224
Tobacco products	173,927	84,370	70,868
Alcohol	205,404	165,071	128,974

Source: Results from the 2008 National Survey on Drug Use and Health: National Findings, Tables 1.1A and 2.1A. Washington, D.C.: Department of Health and Human Services, Substance Abuse and Mental Health Services Administration, Office of Applied Studies, September 2009.

Tobacco

Tobacco is a product obtained from the leaves of plants belonging to the genus Nicotiana, the most widely cultivated of which is the species *Nicotiana tabacum*. When dried and cured, tobacco leaves are used to make a variety of products including cigarettes, cigars, snuff, chewing tobacco, dipping tobacco, and snus, a moist form of the powder placed under the lip. Tobacco was first grown in the New World, where it was used almost exclusively for religious ceremonies and other special occasions, such as the signing of treaties and the celebration of important life events such as birth and marriages. Tobacco was used for these purposes largely because of its mild hallucinatory effects. Europeans who arrived in the New World in the fifteenth century and later were introduced to the product and began using it for purely recreational purposes. When they returned home, they brought with them samples of tobacco, which soon became widely popular for chewing, smoking, and for use as snuff.

Chemically, tobacco is a very complex substance, with at least 4,000 discrete components having been identified as constituents. The most important of these components is probably nicotine, a toxic stimulant that produces the "high" for which tobacco is used and which also produces the substance dependence that results from tobacco use. The health effects of tobacco use were largely unknown or ignored until the second half of the twentieth century. At that point, a number of scientific studies began to show that tobacco and tobacco smoke contain a number of ingredients with possible health effects, ranging from respiratory disorders, to diseases of the eyes and nose, to heart problems, to cancer. Table 1.3 lists some of the most important constituents of tobacco smoke, with the health risks they pose.

Although the health effects of tobacco use were ignored for most of its history, such is no longer the case. Public health agencies, private groups, and nonprofit organizations now work diligently to advertise the harmful effects of tobacco products on the

TABLE 1.3
Some Constituents of Tobacco Smoke and Their Health Risks

Constituent	Concentration in Smoke[1,2]	Health Risk to Humans
Acrolein	60–140 μg	Toxin
4-Aminobiphenyl	2–5.6 ng	Carcinogen
Ammonia	10–130 μg	Respiratory irritant
Arsenic	40–120 μg	Carcinogen
Benzene	20–70 μg	Carcinogen
Benzo(a)pyrene	20–40 ng	Carcinogen
Cadmium	7–350 ng	Carcinogen
Carbon monoxide	10–23 mg	Toxin
Chromium (VI)	4–70 ng	Carcinogen
Ethylene oxide	7 μg	Carcinogen
Hydrogen cyanide	400–500 μg	Toxin
Hydrogen sulfide	10–90 μg	Respiratory irritant
Maleic hydrazine	1.16 μg	Mutagen
Methanol	100–250 μg	Toxin
2-Naphthylamine	1–334 ng	Carcinogen
Nickel	0–600 ng	Carcinogen
Nicotine	1–3 mg	Toxin
Nitrogen oxides (NO_x)	100–600 μg	Respiratory irritant
Polonium-210	0.03–1.0 pCi	Carcinogen
Prussic acid	400–500 μg	Toxin
Pyridine	16–40 μg	Respiratory irritant
Vinyl chloride	11–15 ng	Carcinogen

[1]As measured by a standard cigarette-smoking machine.
[2]ng = nanograms; μg = micrograms; mg = milligrams; pCi = picocuries.
Source: Adapted from Knut-Olaf Haustein and David Groneberg, *Tobacco or Health?: Physiological and Social Damages Caused by Tobacco Smoking*, 2nd ed. Berlin, New York: Springer, 2009, 35–37, Tables 3.1, 3.2, 3.3.

human body. In its most recent announcements about the health effects of smoking, the Office of Smoking and Health of the U.S. Centers for Disease Control and Prevention (CDC) pointed out that tobacco use is responsible for an estimated 438,000 deaths in the United States every year, about one out of every five deaths in the nation. That total is greater than the total number of deaths from human immunodeficiency virus (HIV), illegal drug use, alcohol use, motor vehicle injuries, suicides, and murders combined (Centers for Disease Control and Prevention 2009). The CDC report went on to note that tobacco use is responsible for cancer of a number of organs, including the bladder, blood (leukemia), oral cavity, pharynx, larynx, esophagus, cervix, kidney, lung, pancreas, and stomach. In fact, tobacco use is now implicated in about 90 percent of all cases of lung cancer in men and 80 percent of all cases of lung cancer in women in the United States (Center for Disease Control and Prevention 2009). In addition, many diseases of the respiratory system are caused by the use of tobacco products, with an estimated 90 percent of all case of chronic obstructive lung diseases based on the use of tobacco.

In recent years, health authorities have become increasingly concerned about the effects of tobacco use—especially smoking— even among those individuals who do not use tobacco. Research has shown that the smoke emitted by cigarette use can affect individuals in close proximity to a smoker, and even, in some cases, those who are at some distance from a smoker. Evidence now suggests that up to 50,000 deaths in the United States annually can be attributed to secondhand smoke, with an addition 3,400 cases of lung cancer and 22,700 to 69,600 cases of heart disease attributable to secondhand smoke. Secondhand smoke, also referred to as environmental tobacco smoke (ETS), is a special problem for children, partly because their immune systems may not be fully developed, and partly because they may be less able to remove themselves from locations in which they are exposed to smokers (as when their parents smoke). According to some estimates, secondhand smoke may be responsible for as many as 150,000 to 300,000 cases of lower respiratory tract infections among children in the United States each year, and between 400,000, and 1,000,000 children with asthma may have their conditions aggravated by exposure to secondhand smoke (American Lung Association 2009).

The considerable health risks posed by tobacco use have led to increased regulation of the product and more aggressive campaigns to discourage smoking and other tobacco use in the United

States and other parts of the world, a topic discussed in more detail in Chapters 2 and 3. The results of these efforts have begun to bear fruit in the United States, where the percentage of smokers has continued to drop over the past 40 years from a maximum of about 42 percent of the general population (52% of men and 34% of women) in 1965 to less than 21 percent of the general population in 2007 (24% of men and 19% of women) (Health, United States, 2008–2009, 116). The only group for which this trend did not hold was high school students, among whom the proportion of smokers rose from 27.5 percent in 1991 (the first year for which data were available) to 36.4 percent in 1997, before falling back to a recent low of 20.0 percent in 2007, in line with patterns for older Americans.

Alcohol

The production and use of alcoholic beverages dates to the earliest periods of human civilization. The first evidence of jugs designed to hold alcoholic beverages dates to about 10,000 BCE, while the first record of the use of wine appears in Egyptian pictographs dating to about 4,000 BCE (Patrick 1952, 12–13; Lucia 1963, 216). The production of alcoholic beverages is generally thought to be one of the first chemical processes discovered by humans, at least partly because the fermentation of fruit and vegetable matter, a process that results in the production of alcohol, occurs naturally and commonly. It is not difficult to imagine early humans discovering that the taste and effects of fermented plant products was pleasant enough to prompt them to find ways of making such beverages artificially.

Today, alcoholic beverages of one kind or another are a part of every human culture of which we know. In some cases, they are used for religious or ceremonial purposes, but most commonly, they are enjoyed solely for recreational purposes. In the United States, the annual consumption of alcohol per person has tended to remain at 2.0–2.5 gallons for more than 150 years. In 1850, for example, the average consumption for all alcoholic beverages was 2.10 gallons, the largest proportion of which consisted of hard liquor (1.88 gal), with much smaller amounts of beer (0.14 gal) and wine (0.08 gal). In 2006, average consumption was 2.27 gallons annually, although the proportions of beverages had changed, with consumption of beer at 1.19 gallons, wine at 0.37 gallons, and hard liquor at 0.71 gal). Except for a number of years that include World War II and the years following

Prohibition, when alcoholic beverage consumption fell significantly, Americans' consumption of beer, wine, and hard liquor has remained remarkably constant (National Institute on Alcohol Abuse and Alcoholism 2009a).

Studies of people who drink alcoholic beverages often divide subjects into about six categories: abstainers, who have never had an alcoholic beverage; former drinkers; light drinkers, defined as having three drinks or less per week; moderate drinkers, defined as having three to seven drinks a week for women and fewer than 14 drinks per week for men; and heavy drinkers, which includes women who have more than one drink per day and men who have more than two drinks per day. Based on these definitions, the number of Americans who can be classified in each category has changed relatively little over the past decade. The percentage of lifetime abstainers in the population has remained at about 14 to 17 percent, with an upward trend from 1997 to 2007. The number of former drinkers has remained at about 14.5 to 15.5 percent, with essentially no change over time. The number of current drinkers, at all levels, has also remained about the same, dropping only from 70.5 percent in 1997 to 68.4 percent in 2007. The percentages of light drinkers (39.8–42.0%), moderate drinkers (21.1–22.4%), and heavy drinkers (5.1–6.1%) have also remained relatively constant from 1997 to 2007 (National Institute on Alcohol Abuse and Alcoholism 2009b).

A form of alcohol consumption that has become of increasing concern in recent years is so-called binge drinking. The National Institute of Alcohol Abuse and Alcoholism (NIAAA) defines binge drinking as consumption of alcohol that brings a person's blood alcohol concentration (BAC) to 0.08 percent or above, which typically happens when a man consumes five or more drinks or a woman consume four or more drinks in about two hours ("NIAAA Council Approves Definition of Binge Drinking 2004, 3). Binge drinking has often been associated with younger drinkers, particularly men and women of college age. And there is some reason for this focus. The proportion of binge drinkers is highest in the 18–20 years age group, and 90 percent of the alcohol consumed by those under the age of 21 is used for binge drinking (Naimi et al. 2008). Nonetheless, almost three-quarters (70%) of all binge drinking episodes occur among individuals (men twice as often as women) over the age of 25.

Binge drinking is of concern not only because of the health problems associated with all forms of alcohol use, but also because of the additional likelihood of other events associated with the stupor that accompanies binging. These additional risk factors include many kinds of accidents, such as falls, drowning, automobile accidents, and burns; intentional injuries, such as attacks on other individuals, sexual assaults, and suicide attempts; an increased possibility of sexually transmitted infections; loss of control over one's own health problems, such as care for diabetic symptoms; and unintended pregnancy.

Alcohol consumption has been implicated in a number of life-threatening diseases and conditions. One study found that it is the third leading lifestyle-related cause of death in the United States, after tobacco use and overeating. In 2000, alcohol was found to be responsible for 85,000 deaths in the United States, or about 3.5 percent of all mortalities in 2000 (Mokdad, Marks, Stroup, and Gerberding 2004, 1238). Some of the medical and psychiatric problems that are associated with alcohol use include liver disease, pancreatitis, cardiovascular disease, malignant neoplasms, depression, dysthymia, mania, hypomania, panic disorder, phobias, generalized anxiety disorder, personality disorders, schizophrenia, suicide, neurologic deficits, brain damage, hypertension, coronary heart disease, ischemic stroke, and cancers of the esophagus, respiratory system, digestive system, liver, breast and ovaries (Cargiulo 2007, S5).

Some researchers have found that moderate consumption of alcohol may have some health benefits, such as reducing the risk of coronary disease, dementia, and diabetes (Alcohol Problems and Solutions 2009). This evidence appears to be strong enough that the U.S. Department of Health and Human Services and the U.S. Department of Agriculture included a comment in their *2005 Dietary Guidelines for Americans* the statement that "Alcohol may have beneficial effects when consumed in moderation" (U.S. Department of Health and Human Services and U.S. Department of Agriculture 2006, 43). Given the very serious health problems associated with alcohol consumption, however, most statements like this one are followed by a warning that overconsumption of alcohol can pose a serious risk to human health and, for some people, even moderate amounts of alcohol can be harmful.

Marijuana

As indicated earlier in this chapter, marijuana and related substances (such as hashish) have been used in some parts of the world for many centuries. The use of the drug in the United States, however, appears to have been relatively limited until the 1960s. Prior to that time, marijuana was largely the drug of choice of certain small, specialized groups, such as jazz musicians (Harrison, Backenheimer, and Inciardi 1995). Surveys conducted by various agencies of the federal government found that marijuana use among the general population was relatively low, with an estimated 553,000 persons between the ages of 12 and 25 having reported that they tried marijuana in 1965 ("Marijuana Use and Drug Dependence," 2002, [2]). That number changed fairly dramatically over the next decade, however, largely as the result of a rebellion by young people against the adult culture, according to some observers (Harrison, Backenheimer, and Inciardi 1995). By 1970, the number of first-time marijuana users had risen to about five times the 1965 rate, peaking at about 1.25 million college-age individuals. The number continued to rise for high school-age respondents, however, until it peaked at about 1.75 million new users in 1978 ("Marijuana Use and Drug Dependence," 2002, [2]). The number of new users for both age groups continued to decline after these peak years before increasing once again between 1990 and 2000. Another decline occurred during the first decade of the twenty-first century until the number of first-time users of marijuana between the ages of 12 and 25 reached just over four million (1.1 million ages 12 through 17 and 2.9 million ages 18 through 25) in 2007, the last year for which data are available (government agencies have changed from reporting raw numbers to percentages of first-time users; these numbers are estimated from Substance Abuse and Mental Health Services Administration 2009b, Table B5, and U.S. Census Bureau 2009).

One of the most controversial issues in the field of substance abuse concerns the health effects of consuming marijuana. Even though literally thousands of studies on the topic have been conducted, experts still disagree as to the precise effects that result from consuming marijuana and the severity of these effects. In its own review of the research, the National Institute of Drug Abuse has listed the following acute and chronic effects of marijuana ingestion:

- impairment of short-term memory;
- impairment of attention, judgment, and other cognitive functions;
- loss of coordination and balance;

- increase in heart rate;
- reduction and memory and learning skills in a medium time range;
- increased risk of cough, bronchitis, emphysema, and cancer of the head, neck, and lungs;
- increased risk of addiction (National Institute of Drug Abuse 2009).

In addition to the risks of ingesting marijuana, there may be some health benefits to the practice. Thus far, research seems to suggest that these benefits derive from ingesting by mouth (as a pill) the primary constituent of marijuana, a chemical called delta-9-tetrahydrocannabinol (Δ^9-THC). In fact, the FDA has approved the use of a product called Marinol® (dronabinol) for two specific purposes only: treatment of nausea for cancer chemotherapy patients and as an appetite stimulant for persons with AIDS suffering from wasting. The FDA has not approved any medical use of marijuana that involves smoking the product.

Cocaine

Cocaine is obtained from various plants belonging to the genus Erythroxylum, most commonly the coca plant *E. coca*. Residents of the South American Andes Mountains have used the leaves of the coca plant for religious, recreational, and medical reasons for many hundreds (or thousands) of years. In Bolivia and Peru, for example, people chew coca leaves as a way of dealing with the lassitude that results from living in very thin air at altitudes of 3,000 meters or more.

Once the plant was introduced to Europe by early Spanish conquerors, it became widely popular for medical applications and as a recreational drink. One preparation was a coca-infused wine, Vin Mariani, which apparently was a favorite of Pope Leo XIII (Vintage Wine 2009). Coca products were also imported to the United States, where they appeared in any number of preparations, ranging from toothache remedies to a popular soft drink (Coca-Cola) to pills, liquids, and even an injectable solution from the drug firm of Parke-Davis (Parke-Davis Cocaine Injection Kit 2009; Sure Cure Antiques 2009).

By 1900, evidence of the health consequences of cocaine use had become widely known, and legal prohibitions on the drug's use were being instituted. Illegal cocaine was still readily available, however, usually in the form of the salt cocaine hydrochloride, in the form of a white powder which users inhaled or dissolved in water and injected. Reports of serious damage to the nasal passages as a result of cocaine "snorting" appeared as early as 1910, although these studies appear not to have much effect on the use of the drug for recreational purposes (Erowid 2009).

Until the 1970s, powder cocaine was the drug of choice among many substance abusers, especially among well-to-do individuals. Its cost was usually too high for low- or moderate-income persons, accounting for its common name "the champagne of drugs" (Gahlinger 2004, 242). In the mid-1970s, a new form of cocaine became available, so-called freebase cocaine. The name comes from the method by which the product is made: cocaine hydrochloride is treated with a base, such as sodium bicarbonate, which neutralizes the acidic cocaine hydrochloride, leaving behind free cocaine. The cocaine is extracted from the reaction mixture with ether, which is then allowed to evaporate, leaving behind pure cocaine crystals, which can then be smoked. (The one serious risk here is smoking crystals that still contain some ether, resulting in a fire when the product is lighted.) Freebase cocaine rapidly became very popular because it was generally purer than powder cocaine and, as a result of being smoked, reached the brain more rapidly.

About a decade after the discovery of freebasing, yet another form of cocaine was developed: crack cocaine. The process for making crack cocaine is essentially the same as that for making freebase cocaine. Powder cocaine is neutralized with sodium bicarbonate, sodium hydroxide, or another base and heated. When the excess water in the mixture has evaporated, pure cocaine and additional by-products remain in the form of a rock-like crystalline substance. The substance gets its name of "crack" from the sound it makes during the chemical reaction by which it is formed. Because it is much safer and cheaper to make than freebase cocaine, crack cocaine soon became very popular among low- and middle-income individuals, resulting in an epidemic that peaked between 1984 and 1990 in the United States.

Determining the prevalence (the number of users) of crack cocaine in the United States is difficult because so many individuals who fall into this category are likely to be missed by traditional survey methods. Instead, some researchers have developed a *crack index*, which estimates the number of crack users based on secondary data, such as the number of emergency room visits, number of arrests, and number of newspaper citations (Fryer, Heaton,

Levitt, and Murphy 2005, 2). This index shows a remarkable surge in the apparent use of crack cocaine during the second half of the 1980s, when the crack index rose from essentially 0 in 1984 to almost 1.5 in 1987 to 3.0 in 1989. The index then leveled off at between 2.5 and 3.0 until 1995, when it gradually began to decline (Fryer, Heaton, Levitt, and Murphy 2005, 44, Figure 4). In its most recent report on the prevalence of crack cocaine, the Substance Abuse and Mental Health Services Administration reported that 73 percent of all emergency room admissions for cocaine-related problems were caused by smoking (i.e., crack), 22 percent by inhalation (i.e., powder), and 5 percent by some other means of administration. During the period of study (1995 through 2005), the number of smoking admissions decreased slightly, from 79 percent to 73 percent, while the number due to inhalation increased slightly, from 14 percent to 22 percent (Substance Abuse and Mental Health Services Administration 2009a, 2, Figure 1).

Users of cocaine do so because of the heightened feelings of sensation they experience, which may be described as an increased sense of energy and alertness, a feeling of supremacy, an elevated mood, and a sensation of euphoria. These feelings may not be entirely positive, as they can be accompanied by more unpleasant reactions, such as a sense of anxiety or irritability or a sensation of paranoia. As with any drug, however, these short-term feelings are balanced by longer-term physiological and psychological effects such as an increase in heart rate, that may lead to cardiovascular problems; irritation of the upper respiratory tract and lungs among those who inhale the drug; constriction of blood vessels in the brain, which may lead to seizures or stroke; disruption of the gastrointestinal system, which can results in perforation of the inner walls of the stomach and intestines; kidney damage that can be serious enough to lead to kidney failure; and impairment of sexual function among both men and women.

Amphetamines

Amphetamine was first synthesized in 1887 by the Romanian chemist Lazăr Edeleanu while conducting research on ephedrine, one of the oldest psychoactive stimulants known to humans. Edeleanu's discovery was largely ignored for four decades before British chemist Gordon Alles, working at the time at the University of California at Los Angeles (UCLA), repeated Edeleanu's work and decided to explore the effects of amphetamine on humans (using himself as a subject). Alles found that amphetamine worked as a stimulant, much as does ephedrine, but even more effectively. He decided to continue and expand his research, eventually synthesizing and studying the effects of two amphetamine analogs, 3,4-methylenedioxyamphetamine (MDA) and 3,4-methylenedioxymethamphetamine (MDMA). Alles soon realized the potential medical benefits of amphetamine and its analogs and sold the process for making the drugs to the pharmaceutical company of Smith, Kline, and French, who first marketed amphetamine for the control of high blood pressure and the symptoms of asthma under the commercial name of Benzedrine in 1932.

The potential use of the amphetamines for recreational use did not escape the attention of many individuals, and the drugs soon became widely popular for this purpose in the mid-twentieth century (Rasmussen 2008). Even national governments realized their potential benefits as stimulants during World War II, when the armed forces of both Allied and Axis nations distributed amphetamines in large quantities to improve the endurance and aggression of their troops (Borin 2003). One problem was that the end of the war did not mean a loss of interest in amphetamines by former members of the armed services, and amphetamine abuse became a major public health problem in the late 1940s and 1950s. Eventually, the U.S. government attempted to solve the problem by banning the over-the-counter sale of amphetamine products in 1953.

Although these efforts at controlling the production and use of amphetamines was moderately successful at first, it was only the beginning of a long war between users of the drugs and drug enforcement agencies, a history that will be told in more detail in Chapter 2 of this book. Suffice to say that the abuse of methamphetamine and its analogs still poses one of the most serious problems of substance abuse in the United States and some other parts of the world. A recent study by the National Association of Counties, for example, found that 87 percent of 500 law enforcement agencies conducted for the study reported an increase in arrests for methamphetamine-related crimes over the preceding three years. Those agencies also reported that methamphetamines are by far the most serious drug problem in their counties, with 58 percent listing them as their number one priority, compared to 19 percent for cocaine, 17 percent for marijuana, and 3 percent for heroin (*The Meth Epidemic in America*, 2005, 2).

The immediate results of taking amphetamines result from stimulation of the central nervous system and include increased heart rate and blood pressure, a sense of euphoria, increased wakefulness and need for physical activity, increased respiration, and decreased appetite. An excessive dose of an amphetamine can lead to irregular heartbeat, respiratory problems, cardiovascular collapse, and death. Some long-term effects of amphetamine use are related to these short-term effects, as overstimulation of the body may result in more serious respiratory and cardiac problems. It may also result in the onset of psychotic episodes that may include anxiety, confusion, insomnia, mood disturbances, violent behavior, feelings of paranoia, visual and auditory hallucinations, and delusions.

Other Drugs and Their Effects

The preceding review covers only a few of the most important substances abused by individuals today. Table 1.4 provides a brief summary of some other substances of abuse, their classification, and their long-term health effects.

TABLE 1.4
Some Substances of Abuse and Their Health Effects

Substance	Type of Drug	Long-Term Health Effects
Barbiturates	Derivatives of barituric acid; depressants	Chronic tiredness, loss of coordination, vision problems, dizziness, slowed reflexes, sexual dysfunction, menstrual irregularities, breathing disorders
LSD	Derivative of the ergot fungus (Claviceps genus); synthetic compound primary form of consumption	Depression, HPPD[1], anxiety, panic attacks, depression, disorientation; no confirmed physical effects
Mescaline	Obtained from the peyote cactus, *Lophophora williamsii*; hallucinogen	Psychological dependence, depression, anxiety, HPPD[1], schizophrenic and paranoid episodes, depression, panic attacks, miscarriage, birth defects, liver damage (from ingestion of the wrong cactus)
Opiates	Narcotic alkaloids found in the opium plant *(Papaver somniferum)* and their synthetic analogs; analgesics and sedatives	Minor health effects from pure drugs; health effects from ancillary factors, such as the use of needles (clean or dirty) for injection; presence of impurities in drugs; substance dependence
PCP	Synthetic compound; dissociative anesthetic	Severe psychotic episodes that may develop after a single use and persist for days, weeks, months, or years

[1]HPPD is Hallucinogen Persisting Perception Disorder; continual presence of visual disturbances reminiscent of those experienced during an earlier ingestion of hallucinogenic substances; also known as flashbacks.

References

Alcohol Problems and Solutions (2009). "Alcohol and Health." http://www2.potsdam.edu/hansondj/alcoholandhealth.html. Accessed on September 19, 2009.

American Lung Association (2009). "Secondhand Smoke Fact Sheet." http://www.lungusa.org/site/pp.asp?c=dvLUK9O0E&b=35422. Accessed on September 19, 2009.

Beeching, Jack (1975). *The Chinese Opium Wars*. New York: Harcourt Brace Jovanovich.

BLTC Research (2009). "A Brief History of Opium." http://www.opioids.com/timeline/. Accessed on September 15, 2009.

BLTC Research (2009). Photograph, "Parke-Davis Cocaine Injection Kit." http://cocaine.org/parkedavis-works.htm. Accessed on September 21, 2009.

BLTC Research (2009). "Vintage Wine." http://cocaine.org/cocawine.htm. Accessed on September 21, 2009.

Booth, Martin (2003). *Cannabis: A History*. New York: Thomas Dunne Books/St. Martin's Press.

Borin, Elliott (2003). "The U.S. Military Needs its Speed." http://www.wired.com/medtech/health/news/2003/02/57434. Accessed on September 22, 2009.

Cargiulo, Thomas (2007). "Understanding the Health Impact of Alcohol Dependence." *American Journal of Health-System Pharmacy* 64 (1, March): S5–S11.

Centers for Disease Control and Prevention (2009). *Health, United States, 2008*. Hyattsville, MD: U.S. Department of Health and Human Services.

Centers for Disease Control and Prevention (2009). "Smoking and Tobacco Use." http://www.cdc.gov/tobacco/data_statistics/fact_sheets/health_effects/effects_cig_smoking/. Accessed on September 19, 2009.

Chrastina, Paul (2009). "Emperor of China Declares War on Drugs." http://opioids.com/opium/opiumwar.html. Accessed on September 16, 2009.

Clarkson, Janet, and Thomas Gloning (2003). "The Women's Petition Against Coffee (1674)." http://www.uni-giessen.de/gloning/tx/wom-pet.htm. Accessed on September 16, 2009.

Erowid (2009). "Cocaine Timeline." http://www.erowid.org/chemicals/cocaine/cocaine_timeline.php#Note2. Accessed on September 21, 2009.

First, Michael B., Allen Frances, and Harold Alan Pincus (2004). *DSM-IV-TR Guidebook*. Washington, D.C.: American Psychiatric Association.

Frederickson, Anne (2002). "Mechanisms of LSD: a Glimpse into the Serotonergic System." http://serendip.brynmawr.edu/bb/neuro/neuro98/202s98-paper3/Frederickson3.html. Accessed on September 17, 2009.

Fryer, Roland, Paul S. Heaton, Steven D. Levitt, and Kevin M. Murphy (2005). "The Impact of Crack Cocaine." NBER Working Paper No. W11318. http://ssrn.com/abstract=720405. Also available in preliminary form at http://www.internationalpolicy.umich.edu/edts/pdfs/NBER%20SI%20crack%20paper.pdf. Accessed on September 21, 2009.

Gahlinger, Paul (2004) *Illegal Drugs: A Complete Guide to Their History, Chemistry, Use and Abuse*. New York: Plume.

Grierson, James (2009). "The History of Coffee." http://www.mrbreakfast.com/article.asp?articleid=26. Accessed on September 16, 2009.

Harrison, Lana D., Michael Backenheimer, and James A. Inciardi (1995). "Cannabis Use in the United States: Implications for Policy." In Peter Cohen and Arjan Sas, eds. *Cannabisbeleid in Duitsland, Frankrijk en de Verenigde Staten*. Amsterdam: Centrum voor Drugsonderzoek, Universiteit van Amsterdam, 81–197. Available in English at http://www.cedro-uva.org/lib/harrison.cannabis.01.html#prev.

Iversen, Leslie L. (2000). *The Science of Marijuana*. New York: Oxford University Press.

Kritikos, P. G., and S. P. Papadaki (1967). "The History of the Poppy and of Opium and Their Expansion in Antiquity in the Eastern Mediterranean Area." *Bulletin on Narcotics* 19 (3): 17–38 and 19(4): 5–10.

Lietava, Jan (1992). "Medicinal Plants in a Middle Paleolithic Grave." *Journal of Ethnopharmacology*. 35(3; January): 263–266.

Lucia, Salvatore P. (1963). *A History of Wine as Therapy*. Philadelphia: J. B. Lippincott.

Lumholtz, Carl (1902). *Unknown Mexico*. 2 vols. New York: Charles Scribner & Sons.

Merriam-Webster Online Dictionary (2009). http://www.merriam-webster.com/dictionary/drug. Accessed on September 16, 2009.

Mokdad, Ali H., James S. Marks, Donna F. Stroup, and Julie L. Gerberding (2004). "Actual Causes of Death in the United States, 2000." *Journal of the American Medical Association* 291 (10, March 10): 1238–1245.

Naimi, Timothy S., et al. (2003). "Binge Drinking among US Adults." *JAMA* 289 (13, April 2): 70–75.

National Association of Counties (2005). *The Meth Epidemic in America*. Washington, D.C.: National Association of Counties.

National Household Survey on Drug Abuse (2002). "Marijuana Use and Drug Dependence." *NHSDA Report.*

National Institute on Alcohol Abuse and Alcoholism (2009a). "Apparent per Capita Ethanol Consumption for the United States, 1850–2006." http://www.niaaa.nih.gov/Resources/DatabaseResources/QuickFacts/AlcoholSales/consum01.htm. Accessed on September 18, 2009.

National Institute on Alcohol Abuse and Alcoholism (2004). "NIAAA Council Approves Definition of Binge Drinking." *NIAAA Newsletter* No. 3.

National Institute on Alcohol Abuse and Alcoholism (2009b). "Percent Distribution of Current Drinking Status, Drinking Levels, and Heavy Drinking Days by Sex for Persons 18 Years of Age and Older." http://www.niaaa.nih.gov/Resources/DatabaseResources/QuickFacts/AlcoholConsumption/dkpat25.htm. Accessed on September 18, 2009.

National Institute on Drug Abuse (2009). "Research Report Series—Marijuana Abuse." http://www.nida.nih.gov/researchreports/marijuana/Marijuana3.html. Accessed on September 21, 2009.

Patrick, Charles H. (1952). *Alcohol, Culture, and Society.* Durham, NC: Duke University Press.

Peterson, Robert C. (1977). "History of Cocaine." In Robert C. Peterson and Richard C. Stillman, *Cocaine: 1977.* NIDA Research Monograph #13. Rockville, MD: Department of Health, Education, and Welfare.

Rasmussen, Nicolas. 2008. "America's First Amphetamine Epidemic 1929–1971: A Quantitative and Qualitative Retrospective With Implications for the Present." *American Journal of Public Health* 98 (6, June): 974–985.

Society for the Confluence of Festivals in India (2009). "Tradition of Bhang." http://www.holifestival.org/tradition-of-bhang.html. Accessed on September 15, 2009.

Spinella, Marcello (2001). *The Psychopharmacology of Herbal Medicine: Plant Drugs That Alter Mind, Brain, and Behavior.* Cambridge, MA: MIT Press.

Substance Abuse and Mental Health Services Administration (2009a). *Cocaine Route of Administration Trends: 1995–2005.* Drug and Alcohol Information Services. http://www.oas.samhsa.gov/2k7/crackTX/crackTX.pdf. Accessed on September 21, 2009.

Substance Abuse and Mental Health Services Administration (2009b). *Results from the 2008 National Survey on Drug Use and Health: National Findings.* Rockville, MD: Office of Applied Studies, NSDUH Series H-36, HHS Publication No. SMA 09-4434.

Sure Cure Antiques (2009). Photograph, "Lloyd's COCA COCAINE for Insanity, Hysteria & Migraine." http://www.surecureantiques.com/catalog30.html. Accessed on September 21, 2009.

Svensk, Hallock (2009). "Bonny Clabber, Convivial Solitude, and the Rationalization of the Public Sphere." *Universal Journal: The Association of Young Journalists and Writers.* http://ayjw.org/articles.php?id=582284. Accessed on September 16, 2009.

U.S. Census Bureau (2009). "2007 Population Estimates." http:// factfinder.census.gov/servlet/QTTable?_bm=y&geo_id=01000US &qr_name=PEP_2007_EST_DP1&ds_name=PEP_2007_EST&_lang=en &_caller=geoselect&state=qt&format=. Accessed on September 18, 2009.

U.S. Department of Health and Human Services and U.S. Department of Agriculture (2006). *2005 Dietary Guidelines for Americans.* Washington, D.C.: U.S. Government Printing Office.

2

Problems, Controversies, and Solutions

Introduction

We believe that the possession offense [for marijuana] is of little functional benefit to the discouragement policy and carries heavy social costs, not the least of which is disrespect and cynicism among some of the young. Accordingly, even under our policy of discouraging marihuana use, the better method is persuasion rather than prosecution. Additionally, with the sale and use of more hazardous drugs on the increase, and crimes of violence escalating, we do not believe that the criminal justice system can afford the time and the costs of implementing the marihuana possession laws. Since these laws are not mandatory in terms of achieving the discouragement policy, law enforcement should be allowed to do the job it is best able to do: handling supply and distribution (National Commission on Marihuana and Drug Abuse 1971).

As noted in Chapter 1, the use of psychoactive substances has been the subject of considerable dispute for much of human history in many parts of the world. These disputes are not based on the question as to whether or not individuals should use alcohol, tobacco, marijuana, cocaine, heroin, and other psychoactive substances to the point where they become addicted or where their physical and/or mental health begins to deteriorate significantly. Almost no one would dispute that these consequences of substance use are undesirable, and they should be prevented or treated. In the vast majority of instances, the real debate over the use and abuse of psychoactive substances concerns the extent to which they should be legal, if at all. The paragraph with which this chapter opens, for example, comes from a report issued to President Richard M. Nixon in 1971 on the legal status of marijuana. Marijuana had been illegal or closely taxed for almost half a century before this report was issued. Continued aggressive action against drugs such as marijuana, cocaine, and heroin was a key element in President Nixon's domestic program. But the committee reporting to him, the National Commission on Marihuana and Drug Abuse, suggested a new approach to the problem of marijuana use in the United States: decriminalization for possession of small amounts of the drug, and a more vigorous program of prevention to reduce its use. Nixon rejected this and other recommendations made by the committee. As a Schedule 1 drug, marijuana use continues to be illegal today.

This chapter reviews the ongoing debate about the legal status of alcohol, tobacco, marijuana, and other substances abused by some individuals. First, however, the chapter reviews a discussion of the alternatives posed by the National Commission on Marihuana and Drug Abuse, and by many other expert committees and commissions, professionals in the field of substance abuse, and interested citizens and organizations: the role of prevention and treatment in reducing substance abuse.

Substance Abuse Prevention

No matter how one feels about the legality of alcohol, tobacco, marijuana, and other drugs as substances available for use by the general public, nearly everyone agrees that efforts should be made to prevent people from using these products to a point where their lives are disrupted and to provide treatment for such individuals for the worst effects of substance abuse and addiction. Individuals and agencies at every level—from the federal government to state government to local government to small groups and individuals—have been and are involved in programs of drug prevention. Some groups focus on one part of the problem of substance abuse, targeting alcohol, tobacco, or other drugs for their efforts, while others think that drug prevention programs must include some reference to all substances of abuse.

Literally hundreds of drug abuse prevention programs (also called simply *drug education* programs) are in existence in the United States today. No brief summary can do justice to the variety of goals, activities, and accomplishments of these programs, but many subscribe to a few general principles. One of the best statements of those principles can be found in a 2003 publication of the National Institute of Drug Abuse (NIDA), *Preventing Drug Use among Children and Adolescents: A Research-Based Guide for Parents, Educators, and Community Leaders* (Robertson, David, and Rao 2003). The authors of that report list 16 general principles that should guide prevention programs, such as:

- Prevention programs should enhance protective factors or reduce risk factors;
- Prevention programs should address all forms of substance abuse, including alcohol, tobacco, and other drugs;
- Prevention programs should be designed to address specific characteristics of the target population, such as age, sex, and ethnicity;
- Family-based programs should focus on strengthening family ties, including classes in parenting where necessary;
- Prevention programs are appropriate at every age level, from preschool to adult, and must be tailored to meet the needs of each specific group;
- Programs that involve more than one type of group, such as family and a community organization, tend to be more effective than those that focus on a single type of group;
- Prevention programs should make use of the best information available from research on substance abuse and its prevention; and
- Programs should have a long-term focus, with repetition of key concepts constituting the program (adapted from Robertson, David, and Rao 2003, 2–5).

One of the lead federal agencies dealing with drug prevention education is the Center for Substance Abuse Prevention

(CSAP) of the Substance Abuse and Mental Health Services Administration (SAMHSA). The mission of CSAP is to work with local communities to develop programs of substance abuse prevention that are appropriate for that community and its specific problems in this area. CSAP uses a five-step approach in achieving this mission, beginning with an assessment of the specific substance abuse issues faced by a community, an analysis of the resources available within that community to develop a program of prevention, planning and development of such a program, implementation of the program, and an evaluation of its successes and failures (SAMHSA's Center for Substance Abuse Prevention 2009).

A number of for-profit and non-profit organizations have also been established to assist schools and communities in the development and implementation of substance abuse prevention programs. Perhaps one of the best known of these organizations is D.A.R.E., the Drug Abuse Resistance Education. D.A.R.E. was established in 1983 by Los Angeles police chief Darryl Gates and one of his deputy chiefs, Glenn Levant, as a way of trying to deal with the problem of substance abuse, especially among teenagers, in Los Angeles. D.A.R.E.'s drug prevention program consists of a series of classes run by police officers who have had at least 80 hours of training in drug prevention programs. The organization claims to have a presence in 75 percent of all American school districts and in 43 foreign countries ("About D.A.R.E" 2009).

An important question about D.A.R.E.—and all other drug prevention programs—is how effective they are. Does participation in a D.A.R.E. class, or any other drug prevention program, actually reduce the likelihood that individuals will become involved in substance abuse? A number of studies have been conducted to answer this question. One of the best known of these studies was prepared by the Office of the Surgeon General of the United States in 2000. Among its many objectives, that report attempted to identify substance abuse programs that were and were not effective. It classified a number of programs as "model programs," because there was sound scientific evidence that the programs significantly reduced the likelihood that participants would become involved in substance abuse; as "promising," because they showed evidence of achieving this goal; and as "does not work," because available evidence did not support the goal of reducing substance abuse and, in some cases, actually increased the likelihood that participants would become involved in substance abuse (*Youth Violence: A Report of the Surgeon General* 2001, 102–109). Table 2.1 below shows some of the programs that fell into each of the three categories.

It is interesting that D.A.R.E. is one of only two programs classified as Does Not Work in the report (the other being a program called "Scared Straight"). Authors of the report acknowledged the widespread popularity of D.A.R.E., but explained that

TABLE 2.1
Effectiveness of Selected Drug Prevention Programs

Category	Program
Model	
Violence Prevention	Seattle Social Development Project
	Prenatal and Infancy Home Visitation by Nurses
	Functional Family Therapy
	Multisystemic Therapy
	Multidimensional Treatment Foster Care
Risk Prevention	Life Skills Training
	The Midwestern Prevention Project
Promising	
Violence Prevention	School Transitional Environmental Program
	Montreal Longitudinal Study/Preventive Treatment Program
	Syracuse Family Development Research Program
	Perry Preschool Program
	Striving Together to Achieve Rewarding Tomorrows
	Intensive Protective Supervision Project
Risk Prevention	Promoting Alternative Thinking Strategies
	I Can Problem-Solve
	Iowa Strengthening Families Program
	Preparing for the Drug-Free Years
	Linking the Interests of Families and Teachers
	Bullying Prevention Program
	Good Behavior Game
	Parent-Child Development Center Programs
	Parent-Child Interaction Training
	Yale Child Welfare Project
	Families and Schools Together
	The Incredible Years Series
	Preventive Intervention
	The Quantum Opportunities Program
Does Not Work	Drug Abuse Resistance Education
	Scared Straight

Source: Youth Violence: A Report of the Surgeon General. Washington, D.C.: Department of Health and Human Services. U.S. Public Health Service, 2001: 109, Box 5–2.

it was classified as Does Not Work because "numerous well-designed evaluations and meta-analyses . . . consistently show little or no deterrent effects on substance use. Overall, evidence on the effects of the traditional DARE curriculum, . . . shows that children who participate are as likely to use drugs as those who do not participate (*Youth Violence: A Report of the Surgeon General* 2001, 110)."

Substance Abuse Treatment

Patterns of substance abuse among Americans are closely monitored by a number of federal agencies, probably the most important of which is the Office of Applied Studies (OAS) of the Substance Abuse and Mental Health Services Administration (SAMHSA) of the U.S. Department of Health and Human Services. In its most recent survey, OAS found that an estimated 23.2 million individuals over the age of 12 needed treatment for some type of substance abuse in 2007, a number largely unchanged from previous years. However, only 10.4 percent of those who might have benefitted from treatment (2.4 million individuals) actually received the care they needed at a specialty facility, such as a hospital, drug or alcohol rehabilitation center, or mental health center ("Treatment Approaches for Drug Addiction" 2009, 1).

As is the case with substance abuse prevention programs, a number of organizations and agencies have developed principles upon which programs of substance abuse treatment should be based. The National Institute on Drug Abuse (NIDA) has provided one such set of guidelines in one of the newsletters in its *NIDA InfoFacts* newsletters. Among the general principles the NIDA suggests are the following:

- No single treatment is appropriate for everyone.
- Effective treatment attends to multiple needs of the individual, not just his or her drug abuse.
- Remaining in treatment for an adequate period of time is critical.
- Counseling—individual and/or group—and other behavioral therapies are the most commonly used forms of drug abuse treatment.
- Medications are an important element of treatment for many patients, especially when combined with counseling and other behavioral therapies.

- An individual's treatment and services plan must be assessed continually and modified as necessary to ensure that it meets his or her changing needs.
- Many drug-addicted individuals also have other mental disorders.
- Medically assisted detoxification is only the first stage of addiction treatment and by itself does little to change long-term drug abuse.
- Treatment does not need to be voluntary to be effective (quoted from "Treatment Approaches for Drug Addiction" 2009, 2).

As these guidelines suggest, treatment for substance abuse and addiction usually make use of two approaches: medication and behavioral therapies. Medications are sometimes the first line of attack for individuals who have actually become addicted to a substance. Such is most often the case with opiate addictions, in which case four medications are generally available for use: methadone, levo-acetyl methadol (LAAM), naltrexone, and buprenorphine. For some substances, such as cocaine and marijuana, no medications are available for assisting a person with withdrawal and treatment of a dependence or addiction. After a person has gone through the worst stage of recovery— withdrawal from use of a substance—then personal and group counseling are often helpful in weaning him or her entirely from the substance.

One might reasonably ask which types of treatment work best for each type of substance abuse and addiction for which individuals and under what circumstances. In fact, researchers have conducted many studies on just such issues. Because of the many variables involved, it is not possible to make simple assessments as to any one part of this complex equation. There is, however, an abundance of information about specific types of treatment for specific situations. One of the best resources for that information is a Web site operated jointly by the National Institute on Drug Abuse; the National Development and Research Institutes, Inc.; the University of California at Los Angeles Integrated Substance Abuse Program; and the Texas Institute of Behavioral Research at Texas Christian University. The Web site is called Drug Abuse Treatment Outcome Studies (DATOS). Readers interested in learning more about the effectiveness of various types of treatments for individuals of various ages dealing with specific types of substance abuse under specific types of conditions should refer to this Web site at http://www.datos.org/.

Drug Testing

As noted at the beginning of this chapter, the abuse of psychoactive substances, such as alcohol, tobacco, marijuana, and other drugs has been a matter of concern in the United States for at least a century. Individuals, private organizations, and government agencies have searched for ways of dealing with this problem, with prevention and treatment programs being viewed as two possible solutions. A number of other ways of dealing with substance abuse have also been developed. One of these methods is drug testing.

The 1960s and 1970s saw a dramatic increase in substance abuse in the United States. In some cases, as discussed for the use of marijuana in Chapter 1 of this book, that increase may have represented a general rejection of moral standards by some younger members of society. But increased substance abuse was also directly linked to the Vietnam conflict of the early 1960s to 1975. Many men and women who served in Vietnam sought relief from the horrible conditions they faced there by turning to alcohol and other drugs. By the end of the war, very large numbers of personnel had either used drugs from time to time or had become addicted to them (see, for the most comprehensive study on this issue, Robins 1973). To track the severity of this problem, the Department of Defense ordered that returning veterans be randomly tested for drug use before being discharged from the service ("A Timeline of Drug Testing in the United States," 2009).

Drug Testing in the Workplace

For a variety of reasons, President Richard M. Nixon soon overturned the Pentagon's drug testing plan. But the idea of identifying substance abusers in the society as a whole, but especially in the workplace, had already begun to set in. Many studies have been done on the prevalence of drug testing in the workplace over the past three decades, but most seem to suggest that businesses began to see value in screening job applicants (and, less commonly, current employees) for illegal drug use as early as the 1970s. During the 1980s, however, the number of businesses that had adopted such programs increased dramatically, from about

20 percent at the beginning of the decade to more than twice that number at the end of the decade (Hartwell, Steele, and Rodman 1996, 35). The longest continuous series of studies on drug testing in the workplace is one conducted by the American Management Association (AMA), which has collected data on the topic for more than two decades. AMA surveys show that the percentage of businesses contacted that require preemployment drug testing rose to a peak of 81 percent in 1996. It then began to fall off fairly rapidly until it reached a new low of 62.6 percent in 2004, the last year for which data are available (American Management Association 2001; American Management Association 2004). Throughout this period, the number of companies that tested current employees in addition to new hires was consistently much less, usually by a factor of one-half, than those who screened for preemployment purposes.

Proponents of drug testing in the workplace offer a number of arguments in support of their position. First, they point out that workers who are under the influence of illegal substances are more likely to have or cause accidents in the workplace, causing injuries and deaths to coworkers, innocent bystanders, and themselves, and costing the company significant amounts of money in property loss. A number of studies appear to confirm this position. For example:

- About 40 percent of deaths in the workplace and 47 percent of the injuries have been correlated with alcohol use or alcoholism.
- Anywhere from 38 to 50 percent of all workplace accidents involve substance abuse involving alcohol or drugs.
- A 1998 study found that 19 percent of the individuals killed in workplace accidents had alcohol and/or drugs in their bloodstream during a postmortem examination.
- Companies that have adopted drug testing programs have experienced a decrease of more than half (51%) in the number of workplace-related accidents within a two-year period of instituting the program.
- Companies that have instituted drug testing programs have also experienced a decline in workmen's compensation rates of more than 10 percent (Judge 2007, 14).

Proponents of workplace drug testing also pose a number of other arguments in favor of the practice. For example, they point to data that suggest that workers who are drug-free tend to be more productive at their jobs. They also suggest also that the use of illegal substances in the workplace may affect general morale and reduce the ability of coworkers to do their own jobs efficiently. Finally, they believe that testing programs may be an important factor in helping to reduce the problem of substance abuse overall, since workers will have to reduce or discontinue use of illegal substances if they are to be hired for or retain a job (Newton 1999, 31–38).

Opponents of drug testing have their own counterarguments. They point out, in the first place, that drug testing can be a significant intrusion on a person's privacy, which is protected in the United States by the Fourth Amendment to the U.S. Constitution's ban on "unreasonable searches and seizures." Since the vast majority of drug tests are conducted randomly and are not based on some illegal or improper act on the part of the testee, they would appear to violate this constitutional protection. Second, opponents note that drug tests tend to be notoriously unreliable with high percentages of false positives (a positive test when a person has not actually used a drug) and false negatives (a negative test when a person *has* been using a drug). The authority most often cited in defense of this position is a study conducted by the National Research Council (NRC) in 1994, which concluded that "[d]espite beliefs to the contrary, the preventive effects of drug-testing programs have never been adequately demonstrated" (Normand, Lempert, and O'Brien 1994, 11). This finding still forms the basis of some strong arguments in opposition to workplace drug testing, such as the comment in a 2009 blog on workplace drug testing which quoted an opinion that "urinalysis has been imposed on millions of American workers involuntarily without so much as a single scientifically controlled study to show that it is a safe or effective means of promoting workplace safety" (Stepper 2009).

In fact, a number of studies conducted since the 1994 NRC report suggest that that study might not be the definitive word on the effectiveness of workplace drug testing. A 2007 study by Christopher S. Carpenter at the University of California at Irvine, for example, reviewed three large national studies and summarized Carpenter's own research on the topic. For all four studies, Carpenter came to the conclusion that drug testing is, to some extent, effective in reducing the probability that substance abuse will occur in the workplace. He concluded that "[t]he overall pattern of results remains largely consistent with the hypothesis that workplace drug testing deters worker drug use" (Carpenter 2007, 795).

Opponents of workplace drug testing also argue that such programs are not cost-effective. In a 1991 study of the use of drug testing in federal agencies, for example, the cost of identifying a single substance abuser was estimated to be about $77,000 (cited in Zimmer 1999, 14). That number may be a gross underestimate, however, if one assumes (probably correctly) that only one out of 10 individuals who tests positive is a serious substance abuser. In such a case, the actual cost of identifying a single individual likely to be a risk in the workplace may range from $700,000 to $1.5 million (Donohoe 2005, 72). Given a number of options for locating potential substance abuser risks in the workplace, some critics say, other options to drug testing should be considered. (An excellent review of the issues involved in workplace drug testing on the Internet is this pair of Web sites: Olson 2004a and Olson 2004b.)

Finally, opponents of drug testing in the workplace sometimes point to the fact that most testing programs ignore the one drug—alcohol—responsible for by far the greatest proportion of accidents in the workplace.

Drug Testing in Schools

Businesses are by no means the only place where drug testing has become somewhat routine and, at the same time, controversial. The practice is also carried out now in many schools, colleges, and universities, and in professional sports. In fact, the debate over the use of drug testing in schools began just at the nexus of these two issues when a number of school districts in the late 1980s and early 1990s decided to institute mandatory drug tests for students who wished to participate in sports at the schools. Drug testing in schools was initiated among athletic teams for a number of reasons, one being that illicit drug use was sometimes thought to be (correctly or not) especially common among student athletes. In addition, participation in athletics is a voluntary activity, unlike school attendance itself, and so boys and girls can choose whether or not to submit to drug tests. Finally, some school districts felt that student athletes should be presentable as desirable role models for the rest of the student body.

In any case, mandatory drug testing for student athletes was met in some instances by objections from individuals who objected to the practice for one reason or another. The case that eventually drew the most attention nationwide involved a decision by the Vernonia School District in Oregon in 1991 to require student athletes to be tested for a number of illicit drugs. One student, James Acton, objected to the policy and filed suit to have the district's policy declared unconstitutional. That case worked its way through the courts and was eventually decided four years later by the U.S. Supreme Court, which ruled in favor of the district by a vote of 6 to 3. That decision served as an important precedent for lower courts, who eventually issued decisions allowing drug testing of students who participate in any extracurricular activity and even of students who drive to school. The most recent Supreme Court decision on school drug testing came in 2002 in the case of *Board of Education of Independent School District No. 92 of Pottawatomie Cty v. Earls* (536 U.S. 822), when the court ruled by a 5 to 4 vote that schools could require drug tests from students who participate in any extracurricular activity. Writing for the majority, Justice Clarence Thomas made the point that "[g]iven the nationwide epidemic of drug use, and the evidence of increased drug use in Tecumseh schools, it was entirely reasonable for the School District to enact this particular drug testing policy" (U.S. Supreme Court 2002, 836).

Today, drug testing in schools may take a number of different forms. It may involve student athletes only, participants in other types of extracurricular activities, a random sample of the student body, or all members of the student body on either a voluntary or required basis. A recent study on this variety of programs found that about 20 percent of all schools (containing about 20% of all students in the country) had one or another of these programs (Yamaguchi, Johnston, and O'Malley 2003, 22–23, Table 2). The most popular program was one in which testing was required only when there was specific cause or reason to suspect illicit drug use, with about 13.0 percent of all schools (and 13.4% of all students) involved in this type of program. The pattern of drug testing programs in about 170 schools from 1998 to 2002 is shown in Table 2.2.

As with workplace drug testing, arguments both in support of and in opposition to drug testing in schools have been presented, and, in many cases, the arguments are similar to those used in the workplace controversy. Most importantly, proponents of testing say, schools should do something to stem the tide of substance abuse in the nation, and carefully controlled testing of

TABLE 2.2
Drug Testing Programs in U.S. Schools, 1998–2002, Percent of Schools/Students

Category	1998	1999	2000	2001	2002
Any program	14.4/16.2	19.5/21.1	23.4/24.0	15.9/15.6	20.7/20.1
Athletes	n/a	2.9/4.6	7.0/7.4	5.0/5.7	6.5/6.9
Other extracurricular	n/a	0.6/1.6	2.9/3.1	3.3/2.8	3.0/2.9
Cause/Suspicion	n/a	14.4/15.2	15.8/15.7	12.1/11.2	13.0/13.4
School probation	n/a	4.0/3.4	4.1/3.4	2.8/1.4	1.2/1.1
Volunteered	n/a	4.6/5.7	3.5/3.9	3.3/3.0	3.0/2.5
Random	0/0	1.7/1.0	1.2/1.3	0/0	1.2/1.1
Routine	2.5/3.3	3.4/3.4	6.5/5.5	4.4/4.1	3.6/4.2
Mandated	5.6/5.2	2.3/2.0	5.9/4.6	5.5/5.3	4.1/3.3

Source: Yamaguchi, Ryoko, Lloyd D. Johnston, and Patrick M. O'Malley. *Drug Testing in Schools: Policies, Practices, and Association With Student Drug Use.* Occasional Paper No. 2. Ann Arbor, MI: University of Michigan Institute for Social Research, 2003, 22–23, Table 2.

all or certain groups of students is one way to do that. Besides, students who do not use drugs have nothing to fear from substance testing. Opponents disagree, pointing out that less invasive methods of drug prevention are available, and students should not have to give up their right of privacy for the purposes of drug testing (see, for example, Jones 2009).

Drug Testing in Amateur and Professional Sports

While interest in drug testing in the workplace and schools appears to have diminished somewhat (in the first instance) or remained about constant (in the second), it has increased quite significantly in one other situation: professional sports. Some modest efforts to limit the use of illegal substances by athletes go as far back as 1970, when the National Collegiate Athletic Association (NCAA) first established a Drug Education Committee to provide information about drug use among college athletes. It took more than 10 years, however, for the NCAA to authorize a study of the use of drugs by college athletes and 16 years before the association actually began testing athletes. That program was initiated for championship and bowl games in the fall of 1986, based on a list of banned substances adopted a year earlier by the NCAA. Today the NCAA bans thousands of drugs that fall into eight major categories: stimulants, anabolic agents, alcohol and beta blockers, diuretics and other masking agents, street drugs, peptide hormones and analogues, anti-estrogens, and beta-2 agonists ("2009–10 NCAA Banned Drugs," 2009). Most of these substances have short-term effects and must be taken just prior to an activity or in an effort to mask the use of an illegal substance (masking agents). They are, therefore, relatively easy to detect by standard drug tests.

The exception to that statement is the anabolic agents, also known as anabolic-androgenic steroids (AAS), substances that are chemically similar to the male sex hormone testosterone. Anabolic-androgenic steroids are popular among athletes because they produce weight gain, which occurs almost entirely in the form of muscle mass, increasing an individual's strength, speed, and endurance. AAS compounds also have a number of troubling side effects, however, which provide an important argument against their use. These side effects include increased blood pressure and blood cholesterol levels along with increased risk for cardiovascular disease, acne, and liver damage. A number of mental conditions have also been associated with steroid use, including aggression and violence (sometimes called "roid rage"), mania, and psychosis.

Anabolic agents are the primary cause of concern among both amateur and professional sports associations because athletes value their effects so highly and they are more difficult to detect than are stimulants, masking agents, and other drugs. In many cases, it is difficult to know if an athlete is bigger, stronger, and faster as the result of training or because he or she has been taking AAS drugs. Probably the most dramatic example of this dilemma has been the revelation that many of the best known and most successful professional baseball players achieved their physical superiority not just by training, but by the use of substances that have long been banned in most sports, although not in professional baseball until 2004 ("Steroids," 2009).

Today, nearly all amateur and professional sports organizations have drug testing programs for a number of illegal substances. National Football League (NFL) regulations, for example, call for a four-game suspension after a first positive test, a six-game suspension after a second positive test, and a one-year suspension after a third positive test. A policy adopted by Major League Baseball in 2005 calls for counseling of a player who tests positive for an illegal substance the first time; a 15-day suspension and maximum fine of

$10,000 after a second positive test; a 25-day suspension and a maximum fine of $25,000 after a third positive test; a 50-day suspension and a maximum fine of $50,000 after a fourth positive test; and a one-year suspension and maximum fine of $100,000 after a fifth positive test. Of all major sports, only the National Hockey League (NHL) has no drug testing program ("Anabolic Steroids: Road to the Gold or Road to the Grave," 2009).

Controlling the Use of Drugs

As discussed in Chapter 1, many countries have, at one time or another in their histories, struggled with the question of how to control the use of one psychoactive substance or another within their boundaries. Three approaches have frequently been used in such efforts: education, taxation, and outright prohibition. Educational efforts are based on the assumption that the more people know about the deleterious effects of a substance, the less likely they are to use those substances for recreational purposes. One of the classic examples of this approach to dealing with a psychoactive substance in the United States has been the Women's Christian Temperance Union (WCTU). The WCTU was founded in Cleveland, Ohio, in November 1874 as the outgrowth of an 1873–1874 campaign known as the Woman's Crusade. During this campaign, a number of ordinary housewives decided to rebel against what they saw as the evils of drinking alcohol that they had experienced in their communities firsthand. They organized "sit-ins" and "pray-ins" at local taverns, demanding that the sale of liquor be discontinued. Within the first three months of their campaign, these women had driven more than 250 establishments out of business ("Women's Christian Temperance Union," 2009).

One of the WCTU's earliest programs was an effort to introduce anti-alcohol education into public schools. In 1879, the organization created a permanent committee, a year later to become the WCTU Department of Scientific Temperance Instruction in Schools and Colleges, for this purpose. WCTU members were encouraged to appear before their local school boards of education to demand that anti-alcohol classes be included in the regular curriculum, and the organization itself began to produce materials to be used in such classes, including a textbook called *Alcohol and Hygiene*. When these efforts proved to be only moderately successful, the organization aimed its sights higher: at state legislatures. It lobbied for the introduction of bills that would require local districts to adopt anti-alcohol curricula, an effort that was first successful in the state of Vermont in 1882. The pressure from WCTU members was so great that Vermont legislators passed the bill by large majorities in both houses (Hanson 2009). This success was replicated elsewhere in the country, and by the end of the century, some form of anti-alcohol education law had been adopted by almost every state, the District of Columbia, and all U.S. possessions (Hanson 2009).

The success of educational efforts like those of the WCTU is difficult to determine. On the one hand, the average annual consumption of alcohol in the United States actually increased in the years in which the WCTU was most successful in passing legislation on anti-alcohol education. That number increased from 1.72 gallons of alcohol per person per year in the decade of 1871–1880 to 2.06 gallons in 1896–1900 to 2.56 in 1911–1915, a 49 percent increase in consumption in about 40 years (Nephew et al. 2002, 18, Table 1). Average alcohol consumption among Americans was not to reach that level again until the 1970s.

On the other hand, the efforts of the WCTU have generally been credited with providing the momentum that eventually culminated in the great "noble experiment" to ban alcohol completely in the United States with the Eighteenth Amendment to the U.S. Constitution in 1919. That amendment did not actually ban the consumption of alcoholic beverages, although it did prohibit the manufacture, sale, and transportation of such beverages within the United States. The educational efforts originally promoted by the WCTU and other temperance organizations thus evolved over time into a very different type of effort to restrict the consumption of alcohol: legal remedies, the strongest of which, of course, was an amendment to the U.S. Constitution.

Many books and untold numbers of scholarly papers have been written about the American prohibition movement, the name given to the effort to stamp out the drinking of alcoholic beverages in the United States between 1919 and 1933 (the year in which the Twenty-first Amendment to the Constitution, rescinding the Eighteenth Amendment, was adopted). Experts in the area have drawn conclusions from across the board, from the experiment's having been a great success in terms of reducing the consumption of alcohol among Americans, to its having been a nearly total failure, on the basis not only of no change in drinking habits, but also in terms of the explosion of crime engendered by the need to supply drinkers with alcoholic beverages illegally. Of course, statistical data about alcohol consumption during the period of 1919–1933 is unavailable, since alcoholic beverages were illegal at the time. A number of studies suggest, however, that the Eighteenth Amendment had, at best, only limited success in reducing the consumption of alcohol. These studies show that the number of deaths from alcohol-related problems, the age at which males and females began drinking, and the number of arrests for drunkenness and other alcohol-related problems all suggest a significant increase in the amount of alcohol consumption during the period ("Did Alcohol Prohibition Reduce Alcohol Consumption and Crime?" 2009).

Taxation of Drugs

World history is replete with examples of efforts to control the use of psychoactive substances by means of taxation or methods that fall short of actual, total prohibition. Probably the earliest example in American history of such an effort was the whiskey tax of 1791, imposed by the federal government on the producers of that beverage. The tax was imposed by the young U.S. government for a number of reasons, perhaps the most important of which was the dire financial status of the government. Under provisions under which the federal government was established, that government was required to assume all of the debts accumulated by the states in association with the Revolutionary War. The government began operation, then, with a huge debt. The first Secretary of the Treasury, Alexander Hamilton, envisioned a modest tax on alcoholic spirits (whiskey, in particular) as being a possible lucrative source of income for paying down this debt. Even before the new government had formed, Hamilton presaged this idea in his earlier writings. In the Federalist Papers, for example, he had written that "[t]he single article of ardent spirits, under federal regulation, might be made to furnish a considerable revenue" (Hamilton 1787, 280). Interestingly, Hamilton's interest in a tax on spirits was motivated by more than just a concern about revenue. He concluded the paragraph from which the above quotation is taken with the observation that "[t]hat article [spirits] would well bear this rate of duty; and if it should tend to diminish the consumption of it, such an effect would be equally favorable to the agriculture, to the economy, to the morals, and to the health of the society. There is, perhaps, nothing so much a sub-ject of national extravagance as these spirits" (Hamilton 1787, 280).

In 1791, then, Hamilton was able to convince the Congress to impose a tax on alcohol, based in part on the size of the manufac-turing operation: large companies paid six cents a gallon in tax, while small companies paid nine cents a gallon, a system that was almost guaranteed to produce strong opposition from the lat-ter, most of whom were then located on the western frontier. That opposition eventually boiled over into the so-called Whiskey Rebellion of 1794, with armed uprising breaking out in many of the colonies. That rebellion continued for more than five years and was met with considerable force by federal troops, whose action was necessitated at least in part by the government's desire to establish a strong central government within the new nation. Even though the federal troops prevailed in armed conflict on the field, opposition to the tax was so strong that it was eventually repealed in 1802.

The U.S. government has sometimes taken somewhat circui-tous routes—short of outright bans—to the control of psychoactive substances other than alcohol. Such was long the case with cocaine and opiates. During the second half of the nineteenth century, these substances were generally available to the public and unregu-lated by the government. The Sears, Roebuck catalogs of the late nineteenth century, for example, carried advertisements for "coca wine" that was recommended for the treatment of neuralgia, sleep-lessness, and despondency ("Vintage Wine," 2009). Some catalogs also listed small quantities of cocaine accompanied by a syringe with which to inject the drug, sold for $1.50 (Buxton 2006, 16–17). Perhaps the best known everyday use of cocaine, however, was as an ingredient in a popular new soft drink invented by Atlanta pharmacist John Pemberton in 1885, Coca-Cola. Originally sold as a patent medicine, the drink soon became widely popular as a refreshing soft drink. As its name clearly announces, the drink originally contained cocaine. By 1903, however, the drug was removed, largely in response to growing concerns about its harm-ful and addictive effects.

By the turn of the century, pressures for some kind of control over the use of cocaine and opiates began to grow from both national and international sources. The first factor of importance was the annexation by the United States of the Philippine Islands, one of the penalties paid by Spain following its defeat in the Spanish-American War of 1898. Along with the many natural resources provided by the Philippines, the United States inherited a very large population of residents of the island who had become addicted to cocaine. The federal government was forced to develop some program for dealing with these individuals. The decision was finally reached that addiction to cocaine and other drugs, such as opiates, was really an international problem, rather than one restricted to the Philippines. As a consequence, President Theodore Roosevelt called for an international conference, called the International Opium Commission, to be held in Shanghai in February 1909. That meeting was followed by a second international conference, held at The Hague, Netherlands, in May 1911. The Hague conference adopted the first international treaty for the control of psychoactive substances, calling for all signatories to do whatever they could to "control, or to cause to be controlled, all persons manufacturing, importing, selling, distributing, and exporting morphine, cocaine, and their respective salts, as well as the buildings in which these persons carry such an industry or trade" (International Opium Convention Signed at The Hague January 23, 1912, Article 10). The treaty provided a powerful impetus for the U.S. government to adopt measures for the control of cocaine and opiates within its own borders.

Domestic issues also contributed to the increasing pressures for regulation of psychoactive substances. By the first decade of the twentieth century, medical studies began to show possible health issues associated with the use of these substances, for example, an increase in respiratory diseases in connection with the use of cocaine. Law enforcement officers also pointed to the legal problems created by addicts needing the money required to support their drug habits. And a number of religious and social leaders grew increasingly concerned about the moral effects of the apparent spread of cocaine and heroin use among Americans.

As perhaps to be expected, much of the blame for the nation's growing substance abuse problem fell on minority groups. A committee appointed to study this problem in 1903, for example, singled out Chinese immigrants as a major factor in the substance abuse problem faced by Americans. In its report, the Committee on the Acquirement of the Drug Habit noted that opium use was rife among Chinese immigrants and concluded somewhat ominously that "[i]f the Chinaman cannot get along without his dope we can get along without him" (Drug Policy Alliance 2001). Accusation increasingly fell on the African

American community also. A number of legislators, law enforcement personnel, and experts in the field of substance abuse pointed out that cocaine and heroin use were especially common among Blacks, often with terrible social consequences. A leading advocate for stricter controls on drugs, Hamilton Wright, the first Opium Commissioner of the United States, said at the Shanghai convention in 1909 that "cocaine is often the direct incentive to the crime of rape by the Negroes of the South and other sections of the country" (Musto 1987, 43–44). (Somewhat ironically, no credible evidence existed for Wright's claim, or for any of the other similar warnings raised about the special problems that Blacks created by their abuse of illegal substances [Courtwright 1995, Chapter 10].)

The confluence of international and domestic pressures led in 1914 to the adoption of the Harrison Act, the first federal legislation designed specifically to control the consumption of cocaine and opiates in the United States. (The act was actually written by Wright, although introduced by Representative Francis Burton Harrison of New York.) The main provision of the act was the requirement that all individuals who "produce, import, manufacture, compound, deal in, dispense, sell, distribute, or give away opium or coca leaves, their salts, derivatives, or preparations, and for other purposes" register with federal officials and pay a tax on all their proceedings. The practical effect of the Harrison Act was to make the possession and consumption of cocaine and opiates illegal for any use other than medical applications. As an attempt to solve the nation's substance abuse problems, however, it was a failure, producing almost the opposite result. Individuals who had become dependent on cocaine or an opiate could no longer obtain their drug of choice legally and found it necessary to find ways of getting it on the black market and, in many cases, to commit crimes to get the money they needed for the increasingly expensive product.

Recognizing this disturbing trend, the Secretary of the Treasury, William Gibbs McAdoo, appointed a committee to evaluate the effects of the Harrison Act. The committee reported a number of trends as a result of the act's passage, perhaps most significant of which was that (1) the use of cocaine and opiate had actually increased since adoption of the act and (2) a thriving new community of "dope peddlers" had arisen, bringing drugs illegally into the country from Canada and Mexico (Brecher 1972, Chapter 8). To remedy this situation, the committee recommended more of the same, that is, amendments to the Harrison Act that would increase penalties for illegal use of cocaine and opiates. Within a year of adoption of the new amendments in 1924, signs appeared that stricter enforcement of the Harrison Act was not working either. An editorialist for the *Illinois Medical Journal* wrote in 1926 that "[t]he Harrison Narcotic law should never have been placed upon the Statute books of the United States . . . instead of stopping the [drug] traffic, those who deal in dope now make double their money from the poor unfortunates upon whom they prey" (Brecher 1972, Chapter 8).

The "tax and regulate" approach to controlling cocaine and opiates has also been used with other psychoactive substances. The 1937 Marihuana Tax Act is an example. (Note that the modern spelling of the substance, marijuana, is of relatively recent origin, with an "h" instead of a "j" being more common historically.) Marijuana is obtained from the cannabis plant, of which three species are of commercial significance, *Cannabis sativa*, *C. indica*, and (less commonly), *C. ruderalis*. The plant is an annual dioecious (one type of gamete per plant) flowering herb that grows to a height of about three meters (10 feet). It has historically been utilized primarily for two purposes. First, the soft, flexible fibers obtained from its stalk—known as *hemp*—are used in the manufacture of more than 25,000 industrial products, including paper, cloth, construction materials, medicines, and biofuels (North American Industrial Hemp Council, Inc. 1997). Second, the dried flowers and leaves of the plant are smoked to produce a "high" for recreational and religious purposes.

For the first 300 years of American history, hemp was a very popular commercial crop. As early as 1619, the Virginia Assembly passed a law requiring every farmer to grow at least some hemp to be used both for domestic purposes and for exportation and foreign trade. Hemp was also used as legal tender at the time in Maryland, Pennsylvania, and Virginia. The fiber became especially popular during the Civil War when it was used as a substitute for cotton and other natural materials by both sides in the war (Frontline 2008). Largely because of its association with marijuana, hemp largely disappeared as a commercial crop in the United States for many years. Recently, however, a number of states have passed laws allowing the farming of cannabis plants for the production of industrial hemp. As of early 2010, 16 states had passed such laws (Guard 2009).

The use of cannabis products for purely recreational purposes appears to have had its beginning in the United States in the 1910s, when immigrants fleeing the Mexican Revolution arrived in this country, often bringing with them a long-standing recreational habit: the smoking of marijuana. The marijuana used for this purpose comes from cannabis plants botanically different from those used for the production of hemp. The latter have been developed to contain the lowest possible amount of Δ^9-tetrahydrocannabinol (THC), the chemical responsible for the psychoactive effects of ingesting marijuana plant products. By contrast, other types of cannabis plants have been developed with relatively high concentrations of THC which, in general, have stalks that yield poor-quality hemp unsuitable for commercial use.

By the early 1930s, the use of marijuana for recreational purposes had become relatively widespread in some parts of the United States, producing a reaction among law enforcement officials, governmental officials, and many private organizations and individuals. In many cases, the objections to the use of marijuana appear to have had their basis in a general fear and dislike of the immigrants who first brought the product to the United States (*Frontline* 2008). In any case, by 1931, 29 states had outlawed the use of marijuana and the federal government had begun to consider ways of banning its use nationwide (*Frontline* 2008).

The first step in this direction occurred in 1937 when the U.S. Congress passed and President Franklin Delano Roosevelt signed the Marihuana Tax Act. Justification for the legislation was based to a considerable extent on some questionable statements about the effects of marijuana on the human personality. In his testimony before Congress as it considered the marijuana bill, for example, Commissioner of Narcotics Harry J. Anslinger said that, while the drug first produces feelings of "well-being [and] a happy, jovial mood," that euphoria is soon replaced by must less salubrious emotions, including:

> a more-or-less delirious state ... during which [users] are temporarily, at least, irresponsible and liable to commit violent crimes ... [and] releases inhibitions of an antisocial nature which dwell within the individual ... Then follow errors of sense, false convictions and the predominance of extravagant ideas where all sense of value seems to disappear.

The deleterious, even vicious, qualities of the drug render it highly dangerous to the mind and body upon which it operates to destroy the will, cause one to lose the power of connected thought, producing imaginary delectable situations and gradually weakening the physical powers. Its use frequently leads to insanity ("Taxation of Marihuana," 1937).

The bill that was finally passed by Congress did not specifically outlaw the production, sale, or consumption of marijuana, but it did impose a somewhat complex system of taxes and regulations. Anyone involved in any of these activities had to register with the federal government and to pay a tax for each type of activity. For example, anyone who grew or processed a cannabis product had to pay a tax of $24 annually (equivalent to $360 in 2009 dollars). The tax for sale of a cannabis product to anyone who already held a license was $1 per transaction ($15 in 2009 dollars), but $100 ($1,500 in 2009 dollars) to anyone who did not hold such a license ("Marihuana Tax Act of 1937" 2009). Federal authorities did not take long to put the Marihuana Tax Act into effect. On October 1, 1937, they arrested two men in Denver, Colorado, for possession (Moses Baca) and selling (Samuel Caldwell) marijuana. Judge Foster Symes sentenced Baca to 18 months in jail and Caldwell to four years at hard labor and a $1,000 fine (Uncle Mike 2008).

Assessing the effectiveness of the 1937 legislation is difficult, of course, because marijuana has been, for all practical purposes, illegal since passage of the act. However, substantial evidence is available from arrests for marijuana-related crimes and other sources to suggest that the act was somewhat less than totally successful. A 1998 study found, for example, that the percent of individuals surveyed who reached the age of 21 in the decades following 1937 and who first used marijuana increased from 0 percent in the 1940s to 2 percent in the 1950s to 6 percent in the 1961–1966 period to 21 percent in the 1967–1971 period to 40 percent in the 1972–1976 period (Johnson and Gerstein 1998, 29, Table 2). Official government statistics available since 1965 also suggest similar trends, with a gradual increase in the number of marijuana users from that year to a peak in the late 1970s, falling off then to a fluctuating but relatively constant level from that point to the present day ("Trends in Marijuana Incidence," 2008, Table 3.3).

Outright Bans on Substances

The first federal law designed to outlaw the consumption of a psychoactive substance entirely was the Eighteenth Amendment ban on alcohol, certified in 1919 and discussed earlier in this chapter. Similar laws against other psychoactive substances had been enacted much earlier, however, by individual states and municipalities. Probably the first of these laws was the prohibition of the smoking of opium in opium dens, adopted by the city of San Francisco in 1875. That law was very limited, designed to deal almost entirely with Chinese immigrants who brought the habit of opium smoking with them when they immigrated to the United States. All other uses of opium were excluded from the law, and the substance was still widely used by the non-Chinese population for medical and recreational purposes (Gieringer 2000). (Hawaii had passed a similar law in 1856, but had not yet been admitted to the Union as a state [Forbes 1998–2003, 169, #2163].) A number of other California cities soon followed San Francisco's example, including Oakland, Sacramento, Stockton, and Virginia City. In 1881, the state legislature enacted a similar law applying to all parts of the state (Gieringer 2000).

The first laws prohibiting the consumption of marijuana were enacted in the Rocky Mountain and Southwestern states toward the end of World War I. At the time, a number of Mexicans were fleeing the Mexican Revolution of 1910–1920 and entering the United States. Many of them brought with them the habit of smoking marijuana, a practice largely unknown in this country at the time. As with the San Francisco law, laws prohibiting the consumption of marijuana usually reflected the dislike and disapproval of foreigners as much as it did opposition to the use of psychoactive substances. Somewhat ironically, however, the first law banning the use of marijuana had a somewhat different motivation. By the mid-1910s, a number of Mormon missionaries returning from assignments to Mexico brought with them the practice of smoking marijuana, a practice that was quickly condemned by the Church as opposed to doctrine (as was and is the use of all other kinds of psychoactive substances). In August 1915, the synod of the Mormon Church banned the use of marijuana among all church members, and two months later, Utah state legislature passed similar legislation, as was commonly the case with other church prohibitions at the time in the state (Whitebread 1995b).

In the 20 years following adoption of the Utah law, a total of 27 states passed similar legislation, banning the use of marijuana. Although most of those states were west of the Mississippi, some were located in the Northeast, where there were few or no Mexicans. In these states, the justification for the laws was that individuals who had become dependent on alcohol, cocaine, and opiates and who were now deprived of those drugs because of the Eighteenth Amendment and the Harrison Act were likely to turn to marijuana as their new "drug of choice" (Whitebread 1955).

Thus, as has often been the case with the American federalist system for much of our history, individual states made their own decisions as to how they would deal with psychoactive substances, whether they would ban them outright, and, if so, which substances would be prohibited. The federal government itself took a number of piecemeal actions, many (as noted above) that fell short of outright bans on substances. During the mid-twentieth century, some of the legislation that was adopted to deal with the nation's substance abuse problem were the following:

Food, Drug, and Cosmetic Act of 1938 was a comprehensive revision of the nation's laws dealing with foods, drugs, and cosmetics. Among its many provisions was the recognition that the definition of a "drug" could include substances that could be used for purposes other than therapeutic applications. It assigned to drug manufacturers the responsibility for deciding whether a product could be sold freely to the general public (over-the-counter use) or required a prescription.

Opium Poppy Control Act of 1942 banned the growing of opium poppies without a federal license, supposedly to guarantee a dependable supply of opiates for the federal government during World War II.

Durham-Humphrey Amendment of 1951 established two general categories of drugs: prescription (also called *legend*) drugs and over-the-counter (OTC) drugs. Legend drugs were defined as substances that were unsafe to use without supervision of a medical professional. They could be purchased only with a prescription from a medical professional and were required to carry the statement: "Caution: Federal law prohibits dispensing without a prescription."

1951 Boggs Amendment to the Harrison Narcotic Act was passed by the U.S. Congress in an atmosphere of increasing national concern about the spread of substance abuse, especially among teenagers. The Boggs amendment was significant in a number of ways, primarily in the dramatic increase in penalties it provided for drug possession and use. It established a minimum mandatory sentence of 2 years for simple possession of marijuana, cocaine, or heroin, with a maximum sentence of 5 years; a minimum of 5 years and a maximum of 10 years for a second offense; and a minimum of 10 years and a maximum of 15 years for a third offense. In addition, the Boggs amendment was significant in that it was the first time that marijuana, cocaine, and opiates had been included with each other in a single piece of federal legislation.

The Boggs amendment was important not only as a piece of federal legislation, but also because it served as a model that the federal government urged states to use for their own state laws. Many states took up the suggestion. Between 1953 and 1956, 26 states passed "mini-Boggs" bills, some of which carried penalties significantly more severe than those in the federal bill. The law in Louisiana, for example, provided for a 5-to-99-year sentence without the possibility of parole, probation, or suspension of sentence for sale or possession of any illegal substance (Bonnie and Whitebread 1974, 210). Similarly, Virginia adopted a mini-Boggs law that made possession of marijuana the most severely punished crime in the state. While first-degree murder earned a mandatory 15-year minimum sentence and rape, a mandatory 10-year sentence, possession of marijuana drew a mandatory minimum of 20 years, and sale of the drug a mandatory minimum of 40 years (Whitebread 1995a).

Narcotics Control Act of 1956 was yet another attempt by the U.S. Congress to solve the nation's drug problem with harsher legislation. Coming on the heels of the widely-popular Kefauver hearings on crime in the United States, the Narcotics Control Act of 1956 provided for very stiff penalties on the sale of and trafficking in illegal substances, with a mandatory minimum sentence of 5 years and a mandatory 10-year sentence for all subsequent violations. In addition, judges were prohibited from suspending sentences or providing probation for convicted offenders.

Drug Abuse Control Amendments of 1965 was yet another piece of legislation designed to bring under control the spread of illegal drug use in the United States. Among its many provisions was one designed to deal with a new and growing problem, the use of psychoactive substances other than marijuana, cocaine, and heroin. Amateur drugmakers had become increasingly skillful in learning how to make products previously available only from drug manufacturers (such as methamphetamines and LSD), as well as analogs of drugs already banned by the federal government. For the federal government, the effort was a bit like trying to grab hold of a balloon. No sooner had some control been achieved over one part of the nation's drug problem when another issue arose elsewhere. Instead of having to deal with three, four, or a handful of illegal substances, the federal government was faced with restricting the use of dozens upon dozens of modifications of these drugs and entirely new drugs invented by imaginative amateur chemists. The Drug Abuse Control Amendments of 1965 attempted to deal with this problem by giving the Secretary of Health, Education, and Welfare authority to regulate any substance whatsoever that might have the potential for abuse because of its stimulant, depressant, or hallucinogenic effects. Although penalties against these drugs were less severe than those for marijuana, cocaine, and heroin, they represented the first concerted effort by the federal government to stem the growth of this new arm of the nation's substance abuse problem.

Controlled Substances Act of 1970 (CSA) was an effort by the federal government to update and revise the various bills previously passed in an effort to control substance abuse in the nation. It was designed to be a comprehensive, overriding statement of federal policy about illegal substance use, along with guiding principles for prosecution and punishment. The act was enacted as Title II of the Comprehensive Drug Abuse Prevention and Control Act of 1970. Arguably the most important part of the CSA was Section 812, in which five "schedules" of drugs are established. The schedules are based on three features of any given substance: (1) its potential for abuse, (2) its value in accepted medical treatment in the United States, and (3) its safety when used under medical supervision. Thus, substances placed in Schedule I are those that (1) have a high potential for abuse, (2) have no currently accepted use for medical treatments in the United States, and (3) cannot be safely used even under appropriate medical supervision. Examples of Schedule I drugs are heroin, LSD, marijuana, mescaline, peyote, and psilocybin. By contrast, substances listed in Schedule V (1) have minimal potential for abuse, (2) have accepted medical applications in the United States, and (3) are generally regarded as safe to use under medical supervision (although they may have the potential to lead to addiction). Examples of Schedule V drugs are certain cough medications that contain small amounts of codeine and products used to treat diarrhea that contain small amounts of opium.

In the first announcement of scheduled drugs in the Federal Register in 1971, 59 substances were listed in Schedule I, 21 in Schedule II, 22 in Schedule III, 11 in Schedule IV, and five in Schedule V (Title 21—Food and Drugs, 7803–7805). Since that time, about 160 substances have been added to and dropped from one or more of the schedules (Office of Diversion Control 2009).

The Comprehensive Drug Abuse Prevention and Control Act (CDAPCA) also included a perhaps unexpected provision that repealed all mandatory minimum sentences for substance abuse. As noted above, these sentences were first established in the Boggs amendment in 1951, and increased in later legislation. By 1970, however, the Congress had become convinced that minimum sentencing had had little or no effect on the problem of substance abuse and decided to repeal all minimum mandatory sentences. A report to the U.S. Senate Committee on the Judiciary, which was considering the CDAPCA, noted that:

> It had also become apparent that the severity of penalties including the length of sentences does not affect the extent of drug abuse and other drug-related violation. The basic consideration here was that the increasingly longer sentences that had been legislated in the past had not shown the expected overall reduction in drug law violations. The opposite had been true notably in the case of marihuana. Under Federal law and under many State laws marihuana violations carry the same

strict penalties that are applicable to hard narcotics, yet marihuana violations have almost doubled in the last 2 years alone (Committee on the Judiciary, U.S. Senate 1969, 2).

Federal Legislation since the Controlled Substances Act, 1970–2010

For almost a century, state, local, and federal legislators have been concerned about a substance abuse problem in the United States that seems not to have been amenable to control by prevention and treatment, educational programs, or punitive legislation. Since adoption of the Controlled Substances Act in 1970, the U.S. Congress has continued to pass law after law, attempting to deal with this issue. State and local legislative bodies have generally followed suit, often acting even more aggressively than the federal government.

On one front, the U.S. Congress has continued to pass laws increasing penalties for substance abuse and expanding the scope of such laws. In 1984, for example, the U.S. Congress changed its views on the effectiveness of harsh penalties for the control of substance abuse, reversing the stand its predecessors had taken in the CDAPCA of 1970. In the Federal Sentencing Reform Act of 1984, it ordered the Federal Sentencing Reform Committee to establish new minimum mandatory sentences for convictions for various types of substance abuse. It also established new mandatory minimum sentences for drug offenses committed near schools, mandated prison sentences for serious drug felonies, and created probationary penalties for less serious offenses. Two years later, the Congress followed up on its new, harder line against substance abuse convictions by establishing new sentences for cocaine possession. Continuing a historical trend that singles out minorities in legislation of this kind, the Anti-Drug Abuse Act of 1986 provided for a mandatory minimum sentence of 5 to 40 years for cocaine possession, a sentence that could not be suspended nor was it subject to parole. The inequity in the law was based on the fact that the mandatory minimum sentence was required for possession of 500 grams of powder cocaine (by far the drug of choice among middle- and upper-class whites), or five grams of crack cocaine (much more popular among blacks and lower-income men and women) (Gahlinger 2004, 67–68). Two years later, Congress extended this policy in the Omnibus Drug Abuse Act of 1988 by imposing a five-year mandatory sentence for possession of three grams of crack cocaine for second-time offenders and for possession of one gram of crack cocaine for third-time offenders (U.S. Code 2009c, 416–417).

While Congress has apparently remained convinced of the effectiveness of strong penalties against substance abuse, it has also had to deal with a change in the nature of that problem, specifically with the expansion of the number of chemicals similar in chemical structure and psychoactive properties to cocaine, heroin, and other traditional drugs of abuse, now available to the general public. These chemicals are often called *designer drugs*.

The term *designer drugs* has at least two meanings. First, it is used to describe new kinds of medications being developed for the treatment of a variety of specific diseases. The field of study out of which such drugs develop is called *pharmacogenomics*, a combination of two terms referring to the study of drugs (*pharmacy*) and the study of genetics (*genomics*). Second, the term *designer drugs* is used to refer to a number of synthetic chemicals that are derivatives of legal drugs developed for use in recreational settings. Chemists (usually amateur chemists) who synthesize designer drugs usually do so primarily for the purpose of avoiding legal restrictions on the production and sale of compounds that have been declared illegal by the U.S. government. Such compounds have generally been classified by the government as Schedule I or Schedule II drugs, that is, drugs that have high potential for abuse, that have some or no currently accepted medical use in treatment in the United States, and that lack any accepted safety for use under medical supervision. Table 2.3 outlines the major classes of designer drugs that have been developed over the past few decades.

The federal government first became interested in controlling the production and use of designer drugs used for recreational purposes in the early 1980s when it became apparent that existing legislation was ineffective against the many new psychoactive compounds being produced by amateur chemists. In order to deal with this issue, the Congress included a provision in the Comprehensive Crime Control Act of 1984 that allowed the administrator of the Drug Enforcement Agency to place analogs of banned substances on Schedule I or Schedule II for a period of up to one year, with a six month extension if necessary. The law was somewhat

TABLE 2.3
Major Classes of Designer Drugs and Their Analogs

Class of Drugs	Examples	Street Names
Fentanyl analogs	Alpha-methylfentanyl Benyzlfentanyl Carfentanil Remifentanil Thenyfentanyl Thiofentanyl	Apache China Girl China Town China White Good Fellas Great Bear Tango & Cash
Phenylethylamine analogs	3,4-methylenedioxyamphetamine (MDA) 3,4-methylenedioxymethylamphetamine (MDMA) 3,4-methylenedioxyethylamphetamine (MDEA) 4-bromo-2,5-dimethoxyphenethylamine 4-methylthioamphetamine (4-MTA)	Ecstasy Adam Eve Eden Flatliner Death Drug Chicken Powder Bromo Shamrock
Meperidine analogs	1-methyl-4-phenyl-4-propionoxypiperidine (MPPP) l-(2-phenethyl)-4-phenyl-4-acetoxypiperidine (PEPAP)	New Heroin Synthetic Heroin
Flunitrazepam (Rohypnol)	(single compound)	Rowies Roachies Roofies Ropies Circles Forget-Me-Pill Mexican Valium (also known as "date rape" pill)
Gamma-hydroxybutyric acid (GHB)	(single compound)	G Liquid E Fantasy Georgia Home Boy Liquid Ecstasy Easy Lay Salty Water Cherry Meth Organic Quaalude
Methaqualone	Quaalude	Ludes Mandrex Quad Quay

unusual in that no evidence of a compound's properties or possible risks was needed for such an action; the administrator's concerns about a substance were sufficient for listing. Two years later, Congress moved to make its ban on analogs even broader and more comprehensive in the Controlled Substances Analogue Enforcement Act of 1986. It provided, first of all, that:

> A controlled substance analogue shall, to the extent intended for human consumption, be treated, for the purposes of any Federal law as a controlled substance in schedule I (U.S. Code 2009b, 388).

It then defined a "controlled substance analog" as any substance as:

1. the chemical structure of which is substantially similar to the chemical structure of a controlled substance in schedule I or II;
2. which has a stimulant, depressant, or hallucinogenic effect on the central nervous system that is substantially similar to or greater than the stimulant, depressant, or hallucinogenic effect on the central nervous system of a controlled substance in schedule I or II; or
3. with respect to a particular person, which such person represents or intends to have a stimulant, depressant, or hallucinogenic effect on the central nervous system that is substantially similar to or greater than the stimulant, depressant, or hallucinogenic effect on the central nervous system of a controlled substance in schedule I or II (U.S. Code 2009a, 374).

As with other illegal substances, designer drugs have been the subject of a number of other pieces of legislation since the mid-1980s. Most of these acts deal with specific substances, such as methamphetamine (Comprehensive Methamphetamine Control Act of 1996, Children's Health Act of 2000, and Combat Methamphetamine Epidemic Act 2005) and MDMA (ecstasy; Illicit Drug Anti-Proliferation Act of 2003).

Since the mid-1980s, the U.S. Congress has also begun to focus on other aspects of the nation's substance abuse problem. In many cases, it has given more serious attention to other approaches to solving this problem, such as the educational, prevention, and treatment approaches discussed above. One of the most famous of these efforts was the Just Say No program espoused during the administration of President Ronald Reagan by his wife, Nancy Reagan. After her husband's election to the Presidency in 1981, Nancy Reagan announced that her primary field of interest was going to be substance abuse. She began visiting schools around the nation with the goal of educating young people about the risks associated with using illegal drugs. At one of these visits, to the Longfellow Elementary School in Oakland, California, in 1982, she was asked by a student what she should do if she were offered drugs. Mrs. Reagan's reply was that she should "just say no." That brief comment soon became the theme of a nationwide campaign to encourage young people to refuse to become involved in substance abuse. In some ways reflecting the efforts of early temperance workers, Mrs. Reagan and her associates visited dozens of schools across the country, encouraging students to sign agreements not to become involved with drugs. She also appeared on made many television appearances; enlisted the help of the Girl Scouts of America, the Kiwanis Club, and other service organizations; and sponsored an international conference of 30 first ladies from around the world to support her efforts (Women of the GOP 2009). Although for many years the best known educational program on substance abuse, this campaign was hardly the only or even necessarily the most successful of its kind (see above).

The U.S. Congress and many state legislatures also recognized the potential value of educating young people about the dangers of substance abuse and began to commit tax dollars to such programs. In 1998, for example, the U.S. Congress passed and President Bill Clinton signed the National Youth Anti-Drug Media Campaign Act. The purpose of this act was to "conduct a national media campaign in accordance with this subtitle for the purpose of reducing and preventing drug abuse among young people in the United States" ("Public Law 105-277," 1998). The Office of National Drug Control Policy was later to describe this campaign as "the nation's largest anti-drug media campaign ... generally thought to be the single largest source of drug-prevention messaging directed to teens" (Office of National Drug Control Policy 2009a). By 2005, the Congress had appropriated more than $1 billion for this effort.

Given the considerable financial resources devoted to this campaign, legislators have been interested in its effect on the attitudes and practices of its targeted audience, America's teenagers, about substance abuse. Attitudes and reports on this issue have varied considerably. The Office of National Drug Control Policy (ONDCP) has argued that the campaign, known as *Above the Influence*, has been very successful. It reports that the campaign has had:

a significant positive impact on anti-drug beliefs and intentions. As awareness of Above the Influence grows among youth, youth attitudes and beliefs against drug use and the importance of remaining drug-free, including marijuana, have strengthened as well. . . . Further, tracking studies have shown that teens who are more aware of the Above the Influence advertising are more likely to hold stronger anti-drug beliefs compared to those who are unaware of the Media Campaign's advertising. Anti-drug beliefs and intentions are the best available predictor of actual non-drug-using behavior (Office of National Drug Control Policy 2009b).

Independent researchers have sometimes reached somewhat different conclusions, however. For example, in a review of the program's effectiveness published in November 2002, Robert Hornik and his colleagues wrote that:

There is little evidence of direct favorable Campaign effects on youth. There is no statistically significant decline in marijuana use to date, and some evidence for an increase in use from 2000 to 2001. Nor are there improvements in beliefs and attitudes about marijuana use between 2000 and the first half of 2002. Contrarily, there are some unfavorable trends in youth anti-marijuana beliefs. Also there is no tendency for those reporting more exposure to Campaign messages to hold more desirable beliefs (Hornik 2002, xi; Also see "Common Sense on Drug Policy," 2009).

By 2009, Congress had apparently begun to have second thoughts about the massive anti-drug campaign effort. A report from the Senate Committee on Appropriations outlining its recommendations for the 2010 federal budget observed that:

If the best that can be said about the youth media campaign is that there is evidence that it has a "weak" association with anti-drug attitudes, while a comprehensive multi-year evaluation with more extensive data found no evidence of any positive effect at all, consideration must be given to shifting the substantial resources used for the advertising campaign to other uses. That is what the Committee recommendation seeks to do ("Other Federal Drug Control Programs," 2009).

In conclusion, the federal government and individual states have for nearly a century employed a combination of methods to deal with the ongoing problem of substance abuse, including educational, prevention, and treatment programs, along with increasingly severe legal remedies for those convicted of possessing, producing, transporting, and/or selling illegal drugs. In addition, extensive efforts to control the production of illegal drugs in a number of countries around the world have been employed, a topic of greater scope than can be included in this book.

Should Illegal Substances Be Legalized?

The premise underlying most of this chapter has been that the consumption of certain substances is potentially harmful and dangerous for the individuals who use them. Certainly the federal government and both state and local governments appear to have taken this stance over most of the last century. And yet, a number of individuals and organizations have long taken the position that governments should not be involved in legislating the psychoactive substances individuals choose to consume for recreational purposes. Since the 1960s, there has been an ongoing debate as to whether these substances should be made legal or not. The debate has been a somewhat unusual one, with liberal Democrats and conservative Republicans—and individuals at every point between these extremes—agreeing with each other on either one or the other position.

Those in favor of decriminalizing substances currently listed as illegal in the United States make one or more of the following arguments:

The decision as to whether or not to use a particular psychoactive substance is a personal decision in which the state should have no role. One of the fundamental principles of a democratic state is that people should be allowed to do with their own bodies whatever they want, provided they do no harm to other individuals. Having a marijuana cigarette or a Quaalude pill on a Saturday night may provide pleasure to the person who uses these substances without harming anyone else. As one blogger puts this argument:

Someone walking through the park smoking a joint or someone walking around their basement tripping on LSD doesn't affect me at all, so I don't see why I should be compelled to prevent someone from doing something they want to do. That's what personal freedom is ("Legalizing Drugs to Benefit the Economy?" 2009).

The cost of the war on drugs is much too expensive, especially in terms of the benefits received. In the year that President Richard M. Nixon first declared a "war on drugs," the federal budget to carry on that war was about $350 million annually ($1.8 billion in 2008 dollars). Since the mid-1990s, that cost has climbed to about $13–$19 billion, where it has remained ever since (Manski and Petrie 2001, 1; Office of National Drug Control Policy 2008; DrugWarFacts 2009a). When non-direct costs, such as the cost of keeping and caring for prisoners convicted of drug offenses, is taken into account, the cost of the drug war may be nearly twice as much, closer to about $30 billion annually (DrugWarFacts 2009a; DrugSense 2009). Some observers feel this cost is much too high, especially in terms of the progress made in the war on drugs (see next point).

The vast efforts by state, local, and federal governments to reduce substance abuse in the United States have been largely unsuccessful. A number of studies conducted over the past 30 years suggest that many (but certainly not all) efforts to reduce substance abuse by legal means have been a failure. Some examples of those findings have been cited earlier in this chapter. In 1996, a committee of the New York Country Lawyers Association, the oldest bar association in New York City, issued a report on state and federal drug policy. It concluded that "[n]otwithstanding the vast public resources expended on the enforcement of penal statutes against users and distributors of controlled substances, contemporary drug policy appears to have failed, even on its own terms, in a number of notable respects." It went on to suggest that that drug policy may actually have had more damaging effects on society as a whole than have the harmful effects of psychoactive substances and their abusers (Fischler et al. 1996).

A number of other individuals and organizations have come to a similar conclusion. Jack Cole, one of the cofounders of Law Enforcement Against Prohibition (LEAP) has written that "[d]espite all the lives we have destroyed and all the money so ill spent, today illicit drugs are cheaper, more potent, and far easier to get than they were 35 years ago at the beginning of the war on drugs" ("Cops Say Legalize Drugs!" 2009).

Legal prohibitions on drugs have spawned the growth of a huge crime network and provide a significant financial asset for terrorist groups. Since cocaine, heroin, marijuana, and other recreational drugs are illegal, they can be obtained only through black markets. These black markets have become an important element of organized crime in almost every country of the world. Drug organizations maintain control over their operations by means of well-organized and efficient crime groups that involve distributors and enforcers. In addition, substance abusers themselves often turn to crime to earn the dollars they need to maintain their illegal habit. If the government controlled the distribution of substances that are now illegal, the primary motivation for drug cartels would disappear, and drug-related crime rates would decrease dramatically.

In addition, profits made from the sale of illegal substances such as cocaine, heroin, and marijuana is a major source of income for terrorist groups, many of whom control the source of production for such drugs. One report on this issue concluded that "[r]efusing to address the role of prohibition [of drugs] in financing terrorism will enable terrorist groups to continue to build the resources they need to engage in even more extensive acts of terrorism than we have witnessed to date" (Oscapella 2001, 2).

Proponents of the decriminalization of illegal substances also raise a number of other points in defending their position, such as the fact that many legal substances, such as alcohol and tobacco, are far more destructive than most illegal drugs; that some illegal substances have important practical applications in research, medicine, religion, and other fields; that some substance abusers become involved with drugs simply *because* they are illegal and they are attracted by the adventure of becoming involved in an illegal activity; that U.S. policies on illegal substances have proved to be disastrous for domestic policies in nations where these drugs are produced (such as Afghanistan, Colombia, Bolivia, and Mexico); and governments should treat psychoactive substances consistently, not granting approval to some (such as tobacco and alcohol) and heavily penalizing others (such as marijuana and cocaine). (For an excellent overall review of the pro-legalization argument, see Cussen and Block 2000.)

The possibility of legalizing at least some currently illegal substances appears to be gaining some traction among the American public. In a Zogby Inter-American Dialogue Survey conducted in September 2008, 76 percent of respondents indicated that they thought the U.S. war on drugs was failing, and about a quarter of all respondents (27%) agreed with the statement that legalizing at least some currently illegal substances would be the best approach to dealing with this problem ("Zogby/Inter-American Dialogue Survey: Public Views Clash with U.S. Policy on Cuba, Immigration, and Drugs," 2008). The substance that currently receives the greatest support for legalization is marijuana. In a survey completed in October 2009 by the Gallup organization, 44 percent of Americans favored legalizing the substance, while 54 percent opposed. These numbers represented a significant shift in opinion, however, over earlier polls. In 1970, the ratio was 12 percent in favor of legalization and 84 percent opposed. Those numbers gradually changed to 23–25 percent in favor and 73 percent opposed from 1978 to 1994, after which they slowly moved to their present values (Saad 2009).

In spite of these shifts in public opinion, the thought of decriminalizing drugs is still anathema to many people. Some of the arguments for maintaining current prohibitions on illegal substances are the following:

Illegal substances have been so classified at least partly because they are harmful to human health. Hardly anyone who has studied the health effects of drugs like cocaine, heroin, LSD, and MDMA would argue with the contention that the use of such drugs can have devastating short- and long-term effects on a person's health. The argument is less clear for other drugs, marijuana perhaps being the best example. In any case, the proponents of retaining prohibitions on Schedule I and Schedule II drugs often point to mortality statistics for these drugs. The U.S. Drug Enforcement Administration, for example, says on its Web site that "during 2000, there were 15,852 drug-induced deaths; only slightly less than the 18,539 alcohol-induced deaths," this in spite of the fact that seven times as many people use alcohol as use illegal substances (U.S. Drug Enforcement Administration 2003, 16). These data are a bit difficult to interpret, however, since a different and independent report on the same set of data quoted by the DEA claimed that 85,000 deaths could be attributed to alcohol consumption in one form or another, while 17,000 deaths were associated with illegal substance use (Mokdad, Marks, Stroup, and Gerberding 2004, 1238, 1241).

Substance abuse is closely linked to crime and violence, so laws against the illegal use of drugs are needed to reduce crime and violence. This argument is similar to the one presented above in support of decriminalization of drugs in that it recognizes the close relationship between substance abuse and many kinds of crimes. Instead of arguing that legalizing drugs will reduce this problem, however, proponents of drug prohibition say that strong penalties are needed to keep a rein on crime arising out of drug abuse. The DEA claims that legalizing drugs would *not* eliminate the crimes associated with substance abuse because individuals under some age, such as 18 or 21, would still not be allowed to purchase or use certain substances, and that portion of the population is currently and has long been a major consumer of illegal substances. Therefore, a black market for the drugs would still exist, retaining most of the violent crime now associated with illegal drug use.

Drug prohibition programs have worked. Those in favor of retaining strict penalties for the use of marijuana, cocaine, heroin, and other drugs argue that illegal drug use has decreased substantially as a result of stiff drug laws. The DEA reports that illegal drug use has dropped by a third in the last 20 years, and the use of cocaine by 70 percent during that time. The agency claims that "[n]inety five percent of Americans do not use drugs. This is success by any standards" (U.S. Drug Enforcement Administration 2003, 2).

Legalization of drugs will not achieve the objectives that proponents claim for it. Individuals who have argued against the decriminalization of drugs frequently point to previous efforts in this direction, which, they say, have always failed. These commentators tend to use a common set of facts to support their view, such as the claim that decriminalization of marijuana in California in 1976 led to an increase in arrests for driving under the influence of drugs in the state by 46 percent for adults and 71 percent for juveniles. They also point to decriminalization of marijuana by the states of Alaska and Oregon in the 1970s that resulted in a doubling of the use of the substance (see, for example, Maginnis 2009).

Opponents of decriminalization resort to a number of other arguments to support their position. Perhaps the best single source for these arguments is a booklet published by the Drug Enforcement Administration in May 2003, *Speaking Out against Drug Legalization*. In addition to the points made above, this booklet suggests that the war against drugs requires a balanced approach that includes both prevention and treatment, but also requires laws prohibiting their use; that the drug war, although expensive, is only a minor part of the overall federal budget, which represents an important element in dealing with an important national social issue; that alcohol abuse has already caused the nation severe social and health problems, and that the legalization of drugs will only make that situation worse; and that, in any case, most people convicted of substance abuse do not go to prison but, instead, are referred to treatment programs (U.S. Drug Enforcement Administration 2003).

Marijuana and Tobacco

Within the general realm of substance abuse issues, two topics are of special interest at the end of the first decade of the twenty-first century: marijuana and tobacco. In one case, there is an increased emphasis on legalizing the use of a currently illegal substance (marijuana), while in the second case, the stress is on increasing the prohibition of a currently legal drug, tobacco.

Marijuana and Medical Marijuana

Arguments over the legalization or prohibition of marijuana use are generally similar to those for other drugs, outlined in the preceding section. But proponents of legalization also point out that marijuana is probably the least dangerous of all substances listed under Schedule I of the Controlled Substances Act. If used in moderation, it almost certainly has fewer health effects than alcohol and tobacco, both of which are legal in the United States. It is also the least likely of all major drugs (tobacco, alcohol, cocaine, and opiates) to lead to addiction. In its 1999 exhaustive study, *Marijuana and Medicine: The Scientific Base*, the last major study on the subject, the Institute of Medicine found that about 9 percent of all individuals who had tried marijuana eventually became dependent on the drug, compared to 32 percent who became addicted to tobacco, 23 percent to heroin, 17 percent to cocaine, 15 percent to alcohol, and 9 percent to hypnotics and sedatives (Joy, Watson, and Benson 1999, 95).

Opponents of the decriminalization of marijuana point most frequently to the possible role of the substance as a "gateway" drug. A gateway drug is a substance that, when used, leads to an increased risk of the use of other illegal substances. That is, some individuals say that a person who uses marijuana is more likely then to move on to cocaine, heroin, or other more serious drugs. In a publication on the risks of smoked marijuana, for example, the Drug Enforcement Administration argues that "[a]mong marijuana's most harmful consequences is its role in leading to the use of other illegal drugs like heroin and cocaine. . . . The risk of using cocaine has been estimated to be more than 104 times greater for those who have tried marijuana than for those who have never tried it" (U.S. Drug Enforcement Administration 2009).

Other authorities hold different views about the role of marijuana as a gateway drug. In its 1999 study cited above, the Institute of Medicine concluded on this subject that "marijuana is not the most common, and is rarely the first, 'gateway' to illicit drug use. There is no conclusive evidence that the drug effects of marijuana are causally linked to the subsequent abuse of other illicit drugs" (Joy, Watson, and Benson 1999, 6; for further research on this question, also see DrugWarFacts.org 2009b).

Arguably the issue of greatest concern about marijuana at the beginning of the 2010s is its use for medical purposes. Evidence suggests that marijuana; its primary component, cannabis; or related compounds, the cannabinoids have been used for medicinal purposes for over two thousand years. Some of the earliest mentions of these substances for medical uses occur in Chinese herbal and medical works dating to the first century CE, if not earlier (Abel 1980). In recent years, a number of medical benefits have been claimed for these substances. In a review of the literature on medical marijuana, German physician and researcher Franjo Grotenhermen has classified these claims into four major categories, as follows:

Established Effects: Control of nausea and vomiting; treatment of anorexia and weight loss.

Relatively Well-confirmed Effects: Treatment for spasticity, pain, movement disorders, asthma, glaucoma.

Less-confirmed Effects: Treatment for allergies, inflammation, infections, epilepsy, depression, bipolar disorder, anxiety disorders, dependency, and withdrawal symptoms.

Still at the Research Stage: Treatment of autoimmune diseases, cancers, fevers, blood pressure disorders, and protection of the nervous system (Grotenhermen and Russo 2002, 124–125).

These claims have been sufficiently convincing that, as of 2010, 13 states have passed laws permitting the growing and sale of marijuana for medicinal purposes. The first state to pass such a law was California in 1996, later followed by Alaska (1998), Oregon (1998), Washington (1998), Maine (1999), Colorado (2000), Hawaii (2000), Nevada (2000), Montana (2004), Vermont (2004), New Mexico (2007), Rhode Island (2006), and Michigan (2008). Legislation to permit the use of marijuana for medical purposes is also under consideration in a number of other states, including Illinois, Minnesota, New Hampshire, New Jersey, New York, North Carolina, and Pennsylvania. In all cases where marijuana has been approved for medical purposes, prospective users require a physician's prescription, which can be filled for some minimum fee at a state-registered facility.

There remains strong opposition to the use of marijuana, even for medical purposes. Probably the most common objection is that the substance is still listed as a Schedule I drug by the U.S. government under the provisions of the Controlled Substances Act of 1970. That means that a person in California or Maine or New Mexico (or any other state that has approved use of medical marijuana), may be able to purchase and use the drug in his or her own state, but will still be breaking federal law in doing so.

The U.S. Drug Enforcement Administration, for example, says flat out that "[m]arijuana has no medical value that can't be met more effectively by legal drugs." Instead, the agency says, people who promote the use of marijuana for medical purposes really have another goal in mind. "Drug legalizers use 'medical marijuana'," it says, "as red herring in effort to advocate broader legalization of drug use" (U.S. Drug Enforcement Administration 2009).

Federal law enforcement officials have, of course, carried out DEA policy on the use of medical marijuana. During the administration of George W. Bush, for example, law enforcement officials have raided marijuana dispensaries licensed to sell marijuana to individuals with a prescription and have arrested individuals who grow marijuana for such dispensaries (see, for example, Americans for Safe Access 2009). Bush's first "drug czar," John Walters, frequently made clear his views on medical marijuana. Not only was marijuana an invalid tool for treating *any* medical condition, according to Walters, but, in fact, the push for marijuana dispensaries was really a tool for obtaining complete legalization for the substance. During one television interview, for example, he said that:

> In California, where medical marijuana has been used as a kind of a wedge issue, or kind of phony effort to try to say, "It's only going to go to people who are sick." It's not going to people who are sick. In fact, in San Francisco it has been reported in the news there are now more marijuana dispensaries than there are Starbucks in downtown San Francisco ("De-Filtering: Jeffrey Miron vs. John Walters on CNN" 2009).

The administration of President Barack Obama, who took office in January 2009, has had a somewhat different view of this controversy. In October 2009, Attorney General Eric H. Holder, Jr. announced that the federal government would initiate a more lenient view with regard to individuals who distribute or use marijuana for medical purposes. "It will not be a priority to use federal resources to prosecute patients with serious illnesses or their caregivers who are complying with state laws on medical marijuana," Holder said, in a policy statement that represented a 180-degree change from that of the administrations of Presidents Bill Clinton and George W. Bush (Stout and Moore 2009).

Smoking Bans

For much of the twentieth century, the American public has had a love affair with tobacco, especially with cigarettes. At the peak of their popularity, in 1981, 736.5 billion cigarettes were produced in the United States (Capehart 2006, 19, Table 1). Still, concerns about the possible health effects of smoke have long lingered in the public mind, and that of health and public officials. Even at the time when cigarette companies were advertising that doctors themselves recommended smoking, professional health organizations were warning about the possible dangers of smoking.

Some of the earliest legislation restricting smoking dates to the early twentieth century. That legislation was prompted not by health concerns, as it is today, but about the morality of smoking. Indeed, the earliest campaigns against smoking were included in the first temperance movements of the early 1830s that dealt with a host of "sinful" behaviors, that included alcohol and drug abuse, as well as the use of tobacco products, which were regarded by reformers as a type of narcotic. Failed minister and social reformer Sylvester Graham, for example, wrote that the use of tobacco, coffee, alcohol, and other stimulants which "only cause a bothersome and excessive sexual appetite that distracted otherwise decent people from 'civilized endeavors'" (Meredith 2008, 154).

At the time, cigarette smoking was hardly an issue of serious concern in the United States. The per capita consumption of cigarettes was only 0.4 pieces in 1870 and had risen to only 35 pieces by 1890. At the time, health concerns were also insignificant, as only 140 cases of lung cancer had been documented worldwide by 1889 (Borio 2009). At this point, 43 of the 45 states had passed laws banning smoking in public areas.

The popularity of cigarette smoking during the nineteenth century has by now been well documented, with per capita consumption rising from 54 pieces per capita in 1900 to 151 pieces per capita in 1910 to 665 in 1920, and then to 1,485 in 1930, 1,976 in 1940, 3,552 in 1950, 4,171 in 1960, to its peak of 4,345 in 1963. It has since gradually fallen off to a level of 1,814 per capita annually in 2004, the last year for which data are available (Centers for Disease Control and Prevention 2009). This decline is almost certainly due to growing concerns about the health effects of cigarette smoking and the laws that have been passed to deal with this issue.

Local communities and states began passing laws prohibiting smoking in the 1970s. These laws varied considerably with regard to the spaces they covered. One of the earliest comprehensive bans was passed by the state of Arizona in 1973, a ban that applied to public spaces such as libraries, theaters, and concert halls, but not to restaurants or bars. Over the next decade, about two dozen more states adopted smoking bans that covered similar and sometimes expanded areas. As of October 2009, 26 states have comprehensive smoking bans that apply to virtually all private and public enclosed areas; 29 states have laws that include restaurants specifically, and 25 have bans on smoking in bars, often the last refuge for smoking in a nonsmoking state. (Wisconsin was scheduled to join these lists in early 2010.) In addition, several hundred local communities have adopted bans on smoking in all public and at least some private spaces (American Nonsmokers' Rights Foundation 2009). In some of the most extreme cases, smoking has also been banned in outside areas, such as public parks (including eight cities in California, among them Los Angeles, San Diego, and San Jose; Hawaii, Iowa, Louisiana, and Minnesota) and all of the outdoor and indoor areas within health service areas or educational institutions.

There are indications that the most severe restrictions on the use of tobacco are yet to come. In June 2009, the U.S. Congress passed and President Barack Obama signed the Family Smoking Prevention and Tobacco Control Act, giving the Food and Drug Administration the right to regulate tobacco products. With this legislation, the agency has the authority to treat tobacco and its components as drugs for the first time in history.

References

Abel, Ernest L. (1980). "Marijuana—The First Twelve Thousand Years." http://www.druglibrary.org/schaffer/hemp/history/first12000/1.htm. Accessed on October 22, 2009.

American Management Association (2001). "2001 AMA Survey on Workplace Testing: Medical Testing—Summary of Findings." http:// docs.google.com/gview?a=v&q=cache:c8mvYePZoYkJ:www.amanet .org/research/pdfs/mt_2001.pdf+2000+AMA+Survey:+Workplace +Testing:+Medical+Testing&hl=en&gl=us&sig=AFQjCNHZp56z NzyW45F7BPXpLtZQOxAj8A. Accessed on September 24, 2009.

American Management Association (2004). "2004 AMA Survey on Workplace Testing: Medical Testing." http://docs.google.com/gview? a=v&q=cache:bN67xw3yL9cJ:www.amanet.org/research/pdfs/

Medical_testing_04.pdf%3Fref%3Ddizinler.com+2004+%22workplace
+testing+survey%22&hl=en&gl=us&sig=AFQjCNFdM0xGMqxk4O7
XW9dive1V5i8WnA. Accessed on September 24, 2009.

Americans for Safe Access (2009). "Federal Cases." http://www
.safeaccessnow.org/article.php?list=type&type=184. Accessed on
October 22, 2009.

Americans for Nonsmokers' Rights Foundation (2009). http://www
.no-smoke.org/pdf/100ordlist.pdf. Accessed on October 26, 2009.

BLTC Research (2009). "Vintage Wine." http://www.cocaine.org/
cocawine.htm. Accessed on October 2, 2009.

Bonnie, Richard J., and Charles H. Whitebread (1974). *The Marihuana
Conviction*. Charlottesville, VA: University of Virginia Press.

Borio, Gene (2009). "Tobacco Timeline: The Nineteenth Century—The
Age of the Cigar." http://www.tobacco.org/resources/history/Tobacco
_History19.html. Accessed on October 26, 2009.

Brecher, Edward M., and the editors of *Consumer Reports* Magazine
(1972). *The Consumers Union Report on Licit and Illicit Drugs*. Boston: Little,
Brown and Company. Available online at http://www.druglibrary.org/
Schaffer/LIBRARY/studies/cu/cumenu.htm.

Bureau of Narcotics and Dangerous Drugs (1971). "Title 21—Food and
Drugs." *Rules and Regulations*, in *Federal Register* 36 (80; April 24): 7776–7826.

Buxton, Julia (2006). *The Political Economy of Narcotics: Production,
Consumption and Global Markets*. London: Zed Books.

Capehart, Thomas C. (2006). *Tobacco Situation and Outlook Yearbook*.
Washington, D.C.: U.S. Department of Agriculture. Economic Research
Service.

Capital Sports Injury Center (2009). "Anabolic Steroids: The Road to the
Gold or the Road to the Grave." http://www.youcanbefit.com/ster.html.
Accessed on September 25, 2009.

Carpenter, Christopher S. (2007). "Workplace Drug Testing and Worker
Drug Use." *Health Services Research* 42 (2; April): 795–810.

Centers for Disease Control and Prevention (2009). "Smoking & Tobacco
Use: Consumption Data." http://www.cdc.gov/tobacco/data_statistics/
tables/economics/consumption/. Accessed on October 26, 2009.

Common Sense for Drug Policy (2009). "The Persistence Of Folly:
ONDCP's Anti Drug Media Campaign." http://www.csdp.org/news/
news/ondcpads.htm. Accessed on October 19, 2009.

Courtwright, David T. (1995). "The Rise and Fall of Cocaine in the United
States." In Jordan Goodman, Paul E. Lovejoy, and Andrew Sherratt, eds.
Consuming Habits: Drugs in History and Anthropology. London: Routledge.

Cussen, Meaghan, and Walter Block (2000). "Legalize Drugs Now! An Analysis of the Benefits of Legalized Drugs." *American Journal of Economics and Sociology* 59 (3; July): 525–536.

Donohoe, Martin (2005). "Urine Trouble: Practical, Legal, and Ethical Issues Surrounding Mandated Drug Testing of Physicians." *Journal of Clinical Ethics* 16 (1; Spring): 69–81.

Drug Abuse Resistance Council (2009). "About D.A.R.E." http://www.dare.com/home/about_dare.asp. Accessed on September 23, 2009.

Drug Enforcement Administration, Office of Diversion Control (2009). "Controlled Substances Schedule." http://www.deadiversion.usdoj.gov/schedules/schedules.htm. Accessed on October 16, 2009.

Drug Policy Alliance (2001). "The Racial History of U.S. Drug Prohibition." http://www.drugpolicy.org/about/position/race_paper_history.cfm. Accessed on October 2, 2009.

DrugSense.org (2009). "Drug War Clock." http://www.drugsense.org/wodclock.htm. Accessed on October 19, 2009.

DrugWarFacts.org (2009a). "Economics." http://www.drugwarfacts.org/cms/node/38. Accessed on October 19, 2009.

DrugWarFacts.org (2009b). "Gateway Theory." http://www.drugwarfacts.org/cms/node/43. Accessed on October 22, 2009.

Fischler, Alan B., et al. (1996). *Report and Recommendations of the Drug Policy Task Force.* New York: New York Lawyers' Association. Available online at http://www.drcnet.org/nycla.html. Accessed on October 20, 2009.

Forbes, David W., ed. (1998–2003). *Hawaiian National Bibliography, 1780-1900.* Honolulu: University of Hawaii Press.

Frontline (2008). "Busted: America's War on Marijuana." http://www.pbs.org/wgbh/pages/frontline/shows/dope/etc/cron.html. Accessed on October 2, 2009.

Gahlinger, Paul (2004). *Illegal Drugs: A Complete Guide to Their History, Chemistry, Use, and Abuse.* New York: Plume.

Gieringer, Dale (2000). "125th Anniversary of the First U.S. Anti-Drug Law: San Francisco's Opium Den Ordinance (Nov. 15, 1875)." http://www.drugsense.org/dpfca/opiumlaw.html. Accessed on October 4, 2009.

Grotenhermen, Franjo, and Ethan Russo, eds. (2002). *Cannabis and Cannabinoids: Pharmacology, Toxicology, and Therapeutic Potential.* Binghamton, NY: Haworth Press.

Guard, David (2009). "Press Release: Oregon Hemp Farming Bill Becomes Law." http://stopthedrugwar.org/in_the_trenches/2009/aug/05/press_release_oregon_hemp_farmin. Accessed on October 2, 2009.

Hamilton, Alexander (1787). Chapter: "From the New York Packet, Tuesday, November 27, 1787. *The Federalist*, no. 12. Found in *The Works of Alexander Hamilton Vol. 11* (Federal Edition). Henry Cabot Lodge, ed. New York: G. P. Putnam's Sons, 1904.. Accessed from http://oll.libertyfund.org/title/1388/93583/2090825 on October 1, 2009.

Hanson, David J. (2009). "National Prohibition of Alcohol in the U.S." http://www2.potsdam.edu/hansondj/Controversies/1091124904_3.html. Accessed on October 1, 2009.

Hartwell, Tyler D., Paul D. Steele, Michael T. French, and Nathaniel F. Rodman (1996). "Prevalence of Drug Testing in the Workplace." *Monthly Labor Review* 119 (11; November): 35–42.

High Times Magazine (2009). "A Timeline of Drug Testing in the United States." http://hightimes.com/legal/ht_admin/538. Accessed on September 24, 2009.

Hornik, Robert, et al. (2002). "Evaluation of the National Youth Anti-Drug Media Campaign: Fifth Semi-Annual Report of Findings." Rockville, MD: Westat.

House Committee on Appropriations (2009). "Other Federal Drug Control Programs." *Financial Services and General Government Appropriations Bill, 2010*. http://thomas.loc.gov/cgi-bin/cpquery/T?&report=hr202&dbname=111&. Accessed on October 19, 2009.

International Opium Convention Signed at the Hague January 23, 1912. 1912. http://www.tc.edu/centers/cifas/drugsandsociety/background/OpiumConvention.html. Accessed on October 2, 2009.

Johnson, Robert A., and Dean R. Gerstein (1998). "Initiation of Use of Alcohol, Cigarettes, Marijuana, Cocaine, and Other Substances in US Birth Cohorts Since 1919." *American Journal of Public Health* 88 (1; January): 27–33.

Jones, Eliot (2009). "Drug-Testing in Schools." International Debate Education Association. http://www.idebate.org/debatabase/topic_details.php?topicID=95. Accessed on September 25, 2009.

Joy, Janet E., Stanley J. Watson, Jr., and John A. Benson, Jr., eds. (1999). *Marijuana and Medicine: Assessing the Science Base*. Washington, D.C.: National Academies Press.

Judge, J. W. (2007). "Workplace Drug Testing's Mixed Success." *Behavioral Healthcare* 27 (4; April): 14, 16.

Law Enforcement Against Prohibition (2009). "Cops Say Legalize Drugs!" http://www.leap.cc/cms/index.php?name=Content&pid=2. Accessed on October 20, 2009.

Maginnis, Robert L. (2009). "Legalization of Drugs: The Myths and the Facts." http://www.sarnia.com/GROUPS/ANTIDRUG/argument/myths.html. Accessed on October 22, 2009.

Manski, Charles F., John V. Pepper, and Carol V. Petrie, eds. (2001). *Informing America's Policy on Illegal Drugs: What We Don't Know Keeps Hurting Us.* Washington, D.C.: National Academy Press.

MasterYourCard.com (2009). "Legalizing Drugs to Benefit the Economy?" http://masteryourcard.com/blog/2008/09/08/legalizing-drugs-to-benefit-the-economy/. Accessed on October 19, 2009.

Members of the National Academy of Science's Committee on Drug Use in the Workplace (1991). "Focus on Federal Drug Testing: Individual Employment Rights." *Bulletin of the National Academy.*

Meredith, Austin (2008). *Drug Involvement in Previous Centuries.* http://www.kouroo.info/kouroo/trends/dope.pdf. Accessed on October 26, 2009.

Mokdad, Ali H., James S. Marks, Donna F. Stroup, and Julie L. Gerberding (2004). "Actual Causes of Death in the United States, 2000." *Journal of the American Medical Association* 291 (10; March 10): 1238–1245.

Musto, David E. (1987). *The American Disease: Origins of Narcotic Control,* revised ed. New York: Oxford University Press.

National Collegiate Athletic Association (2009). "2009–10 NCAA Banned Drugs." http://www.ncaa.org/wps/wcm/connect/53e6f4804e0b8a129949f91ad6fc8b25/2009-10+Banned+Drug+Classes.pdf?MOD=AJPERES&CACHEID=53e6f4804e0b8a129949f91ad6fc8b25. Accessed on September 25, 2009.

National Commission on Marihuana and Drug Abuse (1971). *Marihuana: A Signal of Misunderstanding.* http://www.druglibrary.org/Schaffer/Library/studies/nc/ncrec1_9.htm. Accessed on September 22, 2009.

National Institute on Drug Abuse (2009). "Treatment Approaches for Drug Addiction." *INDA Info Facts.* Washington, D.C.: U.S. Department of Health and Human Services, National Institutes of Health.

Nephew, Thomas M., et al. (2002). *Surveillance Report #55: Apparent Per Capita Consumption: National, State, and Regional Trends, 1977–98.* Rockville, MD: National Institute on Alcohol Abuse and Alcoholism, Division of Biometry and Epidemiology: Alcohol Epidemiologic Data System, September 2002.

New York Times (2009). "Steroids." *New York Times.* http://topics.nytimes.com/top/news/health/diseasesconditionsandhealthtopics/steroids/index.html. Accessed on September 25, 2009.

Newton, David E. (1999). *Drug Testing: An Issue for School, Sports, and Work.* Springfield, NJ: Enslow Publishers.

Normand, Jacques, Richard O. Lempert, and Charles P. O'Brien, eds. (1994). *Under the Influence: Drugs and the American Workforce.* Washington, D.C.: National Academies Press.

North American Industrial Hemp Council, Inc. (1997). "Hemp Facts." http://www.naihc.org/hemp_information/hemp_facts.html. Accessed on October 2, 2009.

Office of Applied Studies, Substance Abuse and Mental Health Services Administration (2008). "Trends in Marijuana Incidence." http://www.oas .samhsa.gov/MJinitiation/chapter3.htm#top. Accessed on October 2, 2009.

Office of National Drug Control Policy (2008). "National Drug Control Strategy: FY 2009 Budget Summary." http://www.whitehousedrugpolicy .gov/publications/policy/09budget/index.html. Accessed on October 19, 2009.

Office of National Drug Control Policy (2009a). "National Youth Anti-Drug Media Campaign." http://www.mediacampaign.org/. Accessed on October 19, 2009.

Office of National Drug Control Policy (2009b). "National Youth Anti-Drug Media Campaign." http://www.mediacampaign.org/about.html #ir. Accessed on October 19, 2009.

Olson, Dave (2004a). "Advantages and Disadvantages of Workplace Drug Testing." http://www.uncleweed.com/words/essays/ drugtesting-matrix.pdf. Accessed on September 25, 2009.

Olson, Dave (2004b). "Privacy Issues in Workplace Drug Testing." http:// uncleweed.net/words/essays/Workplace-Drug-Testing.pdf. Accessed on September 25, 2009.

Oscapella, Eugene (2001). "How Drug Prohibition Finances and Otherwise Enables Terrorism." Report to the Senate of Canada Special Committee on Illegal Drugs. Available online at http://www.ukcia.org/ research/ProhibitionFinancesTerrorism.pdf. Accessed on October 20, 2009.

"Public Law 105–277." 1998. http://frwebgate.access.gpo.gov/cgi-bin/ getdoc.cgi?dbname=105_cong_public_laws&docid=f:publ277.pdf. Accessed on October 19, 2009.

Robertson, Elizabeth B., Susan L. David, and Suman A. Rao (2003). *Preventing Drug Use Among Children and Adolescents: A Research-Based Guide for Parents, Educators, and Community Leaders*. Bethesda, MD: U.S. Department of Health and Human Services, National Institutes of Health: National Institute of Drug Abuse.

Robins, Lee N. (1973). *The Vietnam Drug User Returns*. Washington, D.C.: U.S. Government Printing Office. Also available online at http://www .eric.ed.gov/ERICDocs/data/ericdocs2sql/content_storage_01/0000019b/ 80/35/72/be.pdf.

Saad, Lydia (2009). "U.S. Support for Legalizing Marijuana Reaches New High." http://www.gallup.com/poll/123728/U.S.-Support-Legalizing -Marijuana-Reaches-New-High.aspx#1. Accessed on October 20, 2009.

Schaffer Library of Drug Policy (2009). "Did Alcohol Prohibition Reduce Alcohol Consumption and Crime?" http://www.druglibrary.org/ Prohibitionresults.htm. Accessed on October 1, 2009.

Schaffer Library of Drug Policy (2009). "The Marihuana Tax Act of 1937." http://www.druglibrary.org/schaffer/hemp/taxact/mjtaxact.htm. Accessed on October 2, 2009.

ShowMeTheFacts.org (2009). "De-Filtering: Jeffrey Miron vs. John Walters on CNN." http://www.showmethefacts.org/2009/05/07/ defiltering-jeffrey-miron-john-walters-cnn/. Accessed on October 22, 2009.

Stepper, Jeff (2009). "The Pros and Cons of Drug Testing." http:// www.helium.com/items/178231-the-pros-and-cons-of-drug-testing. Accessed on September 25, 2009.

Stout, David, and Solomon Moore (2009). "U.S. Won't Prosecute in States That Allow Medical Marijuana." *New York Times*. http://www.nytimes .com/2009/10/20/us/20cannabis.html. Accessed on October 22, 2009.

Uncle Mike [pseud.] (2008). "U.S. District Court, Denver, Colorado Imposes First Federal Marihuana Law Penalties." http://www .unclemikesresearch.com/u-s-district-court-denver-colorado-imposes -first-federal-marihuana-law-penalties/. Accessed on October 2, 2009.

U.S. Code (2009a). Title 21, Chapter 13, Subchapter I, Part A: Definitions. http://frwebgate.access.gpo.gov/cgi-bin/usc.cgi?ACTION=RETRIEVE &FILE=$$xa$$busc21.wais&start=2634952&SIZE=56838&TYPE=PDF. Accessed on October 17, 2009.

U.S. Code (2009b). Title 21, Chapter 13, Subchapter I, Part B: "Treatment of Controlled Substances Analogues." http://frwebgate.access.gpo.gov/ cgibin/usc.cgi?ACTION=RETRIEVE&FILE=$$xa$$busc21.wais&start =2743382&SIZE=1094&TYPE=PDF. Accessed on October 17, 2009.

U.S. Code (2009c). Title 21, Chapter 13, Subchapter I, Part D: "Offenses and Penalties." http://frwebgate.access.gpo.gov/cgi-bin/usc.cgi? ACTION=RETRIEVE&FILE=$$xa$$busc21.wais&start=2940795&SIZE =9867&TYPE=PDF. Accessed on October 17, 2009.

U.S. Department of Health and Human Services, Substance Abuse and Mental Health Services Administration (2009). "SAMHSA's Center for Substance Abuse Prevention." http://prevention.samhsa.gov/. Accessed on September 22, 2009.

U.S. Drug Enforcement Administration (2003). *Speaking Out against Drug Legalization*. Washington, D.C.: U.S. Department of Justice.

U.S. Drug Enforcement Administration (2009). "Exposing the Myth of Smoked Medical Marijuana—Marijuana: The Facts." http://www.justice .gov/dea/ongoing/marijuana.html. Accessed on October 22, 2009.

U.S. House of Representatives (1937). Committee on Ways and Means, Hearings, May 4. "Taxation of Marihuana." As cited in "The Marihuana Tax Act of 1937." http://www.druglibrary.org/schaffer/hemp/taxact/t10a.htm. Accessed on October 2, 2009.

U.S. Public Health Service (2001). *Youth Violence: A Report of the Surgeon General*. Washington, D.C.: Department of Health and Human Services.

U.S. Senate Committee on the Judiciary (1969). "Controlled Dangerous Substances Act of 1969." Senate Report No. 613, 91st Congress, 1st Session.

U.S. Supreme Court (2002). *Board of Education of Independent School District No. 92 of Pottawatomie Cty v. Earls* (536 U.S. 822). Available online at http://supreme.justia.com/us/536/822/case.html. Accessed on September 25, 2009.

Whitebread, Charles. 1995a. "The History of The Non-medical Use of Drugs In the United States: A Speech to the California Judges Association 1995 Annual Conference." http://www.druglibrary.org/olsen/DPF/whitebread08.html. Accessed on October 14, 2009.

Whitebread, Charles (1995b). "The History of The Non-medical Use of Drugs In the United States: A Speech to the California Judges Association 1995 Annual Conference." http://www.druglibrary.org/olsen/DPF/whitebread.html#TOC. Accessed on October 4, 2009.

Women of the GOP Blog (2009). "The Life of Nancy Reagan." http://gopwomen.blogspot.com/2009/09/life-of-nancy-reagan.html. Accessed on October 19, 2009.

Women's Christian Temperance Union (2009). "Early History." http://www.wctu.org/earlyhistory.html. Accessed on October 1, 2009.

Yamaguchi, Ryoko, Lloyd D. Johnston, and Patrick M. O'Malley (2003). *Drug Testing in Schools: Policies, Practices, and Association With Student Drug Use*. Occasional Paper No. 2. Ann Arbor, MI: Institute for Social Research. University of Michigan.

Zimmer, Lynn (1999). *Drug Testing: A Bad Investment*. New York: American Civil Liberties Union.

Zogby (2008). "Zogby/Inter-American Dialogue Survey: Public Views Clash with U.S. Policy on Cuba, Immigration, and Drugs." http://www.zogby.com/NEWS/ReadNews.cfm?ID=1568. Accessed on October 20, 2009.

3

Worldwide Perspective

Introduction

Psychoactive substances have played an important role in the culture of most countries around the world throughout human history. Typically, people discover that a particular plant, plant product, mineral, or other substance has useful biological effects, such as relieving pain or helping a person adjust to environmental conditions. Then, in many instances, that substance is put to other uses, such as playing a role in religious ceremonies or serving as a recreational drug, simply helping people to relax and escape the difficulties of everyday life.

The evolution of cocaine as a popular drug is an example of this pattern. Cocaine is obtained from the coca bush, a plant native to the Andes Mountains of South America. Four varieties of the plant are generally available, *Erythroxylum coca*, *E. ipadu*, *E. novogratense*, and *E. truxillense*. By far the most common and popular of these species is *E. coca*, which accounts for about 95 percent of the modern production of cocaine (Gahlinger 2004, 241). Residents of the Andes region apparently discovered the value of coca as a dietary supplement early in their history. When chewed, dried and smoked, or made into a tea infusion, coca leaves helped suppress hunger pangs and reduced fatigue, making it easier for people to work under the harsh environmental conditions of the high mountains. (Modern travelers from sea-level countries still rely on drafts of coca tea or chewed coca leaves to adjust to high altitudes during their brief visits to Peru, Bolivia, Colombia, Ecuador, and other regions of the

Andes Mountains.) Coca products were also widely used for a variety of medical purposes, such as the treatment of asthma and malaria, as a blood coagulant, as an aphrodisiac, to treat infections, and to extend one's longevity.

The many benefits provided by the coca plant earned it a special place in the cultural traditions and religious pantheon of Andean peoples. Imbibing "Mama Coca" by chewing, drinking, or smoking became a standard part of many Incan ceremonies, a fact that led the Spanish conquistadores to ban the practice as being a heathen custom unworthy of a newly converted (to Roman Catholicism) subject population.

Although half a world apart geographically and in terms of psychoactive properties, the early history of coffee is similar to that of coca. The first recorded use of coffee as a drink among humans dates to the ninth century in a region that is part of modern Ethiopia. According to one account, residents of the area noticed that goats that fed on a particular native plant appeared to have significantly more energy than those that fed elsewhere; they became known as "the dancing goats" (Weinberg and Bealer 2002, 3–4). Upon trying a concoction of the beans of that plant, a member of the genus Coffea, people experienced the same feeling of exhilaration and soon became addicted to the drinking of coffee. As in South America, coffee drinking was also thought to have medicinal benefits and it soon became associated with cultural and religious ceremonies and traditions. Especially in regions where Islam took root, and alcoholic beverages were prohibited, coffee became an essential part of many religious events ("Coffee in Religions," 2009).

News about the potential uses of psychoactive substances eventually spread far beyond the regions in which they originate. As explorers, traders, and conquering armies travel from one region to another, they often carry with them word of these substances, introducing their use to their home countries. The cannabis species from which hemp, hashish, and marijuana are derived is native to China and India, where reports of its use date to at least 6000 BCE. However, travelers carried information about the commercial, medical, and recreational uses of the plant to other countries on a number of occasions. By 500 BCE, for example, Scythian travelers from the region of modern day Iran apparently had introduced cannabis products to northern Europe. An urn containing leaves and seeds of the plant dating to this period has been found in the region of Berlin (Concept 420 2009). By some accounts, one of the most important factors in the spread of hashish use in Europe in the early nineteenth century was introduction of the practice by soldiers from Napoleon's army returning from their battles in Egypt, where the drug was regularly used by a large segment of the local population. By the 1840s, the drug had become one of the most popular of all recreational drugs in coffee houses throughout Europe (Gahlinger 2004, 31).

The spread of tobacco use is similar to that of other psychoactive substances. The tobacco plant is native to North and South America, where it was used for medicinal, religious, and recreational purposes at least as early as the first century BCE. Word about the many uses of the tobacco plant began to spread in the 1490s as a result of the first visits to the New World by Christopher Columbus. Members of Columbus' crew and of other exploratory voyages found pleasure in smoking of tobacco, and soon became addicted (at least in an informal sense) to the practice. Historians point out that Portugese sailors, in particular, began to establish small tobacco farms at their trading posts so that they would always have a guaranteed supply of the product (Brooks 1952, 33–34). Smoking also spread to continental Europe as sailors and explorers returned from their visits to the New World, bringing the Native American custom with them. The practice was apparently introduced to France in 1556, Portugal in 1558, Spain in 1559, England in 1564 or 1565, and Turkey and Poland in 1580 (Borio 2009b).

Legal or Illegal?

As mentioned in Chapter 1, the use of psychoactive substances has often been surrounded by medical, moral, social, and legal controversy. Typically, coca, tobacco, cannabis, coffee, and other psychoactive substances have been accepted by cultures where they have very long histories for their medical, religious, cultural, or recreational uses. But their use has just as often been questioned by cultures into which they are introduced. Early users of tobacco in Europe, for example, often touted the substance's many medical benefits. For example, the first scholarly book on tobacco, *De Hierba Panacea*, by Spanish physician and botanist Nicolás Bautista Monardes, listed 36 medical problems for which tobacco served as a cure (Frampton 1577). At almost the same time, however, other writers were warning about the health hazards posed by smoking. In 1602, for example, a prescient anonymous physician wrote a pamphlet, *Chimny-Sweepers or A Warning for Tabacconists*, cautioning about the potential health effects of exposure to tobacco smoke. He had learned from treating chimney sweeps, he said, that prolonged exposure to smoke could result in "rendering him incapable of propagation" and leaving a man "in a state of depression, 'mopishness and sottishness,' which in the long run must damage memory, imagination and understanding" (Borio 2009a).

Similar tales can be told of other psychoactive substances. For at least two thousand years, marijuana was widely used by Far Eastern and Near Eastern civilizations for medical, religious, ceremonial, and recreational purposes. The drug was commonly used in the form of a purified resinous extract of the plant known as hashish. The first efforts to control its use are perhaps dated to about 1378 when the Ottoman emperor Soudoun Scheikhouni banned the eating of hashish, apparently because it had become so popular among his subjects (Concept 420 2009). Such efforts, repeated a number of times in a number of cultures, were seldom effective in discouraging the use of hashish or other forms of marijuana. In fact, it was not until the early twentieth century that most modern nations began active campaigns against the drug, either attempting to tax it out of use or outrightly banning the use of cannabis products for recreational purposes (Concept 420 2009).

Drug Laws Today

A review of the prohibitions against psychoactive substances worldwide would seem to be a daunting task. Given the variety of histories, moral systems, beliefs, and other characteristics of various cultures, one might expect there to be a bewildering variety of national positions about the recreational use of opiates, cocaine, marijuana, tobacco, alcohol, and other psychoactive substances. And in some respects, that view is correct. Well over a sixth of the world's population, adherents of the Muslim faith, for example, are forbidden by their faith from consuming any type of psychoactive substance other than coffee and tea. As a contemporary writer on the subject has explained,

> The use of alcohol and other drugs is considered a "major sin." Muslims are required to stay away from

khamr [an intoxicant] as it is considered the mother of all evils (Muhammed 2009).

Such a position is clearly at odds with national policies in other countries, such as the United States, where alcoholic products are generally available to any man or woman of legal age, or the Netherlands, where marijuana is freely available for sale and consumption at public establishments. Perhaps more to the point, a cultural or religious ban on the use of psychoactive substances does not necessarily mean that substance abuse does not exist in nations where such prohibitions are in place, as will be noted in greater detail below.

Yet, in another sense, there is a certain continuity in drug prohibition philosophies that extends across the globe. In his paper, "The Secret of World-wide Drug Prohibition," Harry G. Levine, professor of sociology at Queens College of the City University of New York, argues that:

> Every country in the world has drug prohibition. Every country in the world criminalizes the production and sale of cannabis, cocaine and opiates. In addition, most countries criminalize the production and sale of some other psychoactive substances (Levine 2001).

In this paper, Levine outlines the history of the development of drug prohibition policies around the world during the twentieth century, largely as a result of the efforts by the United States government.

The most important element in this worldwide effort to control the recreational use of psychoactive drugs was the Single Convention on Narcotic Drugs of 1961. By the end of World War II, nations around the world had adopted a crazy patchwork of laws restricting the use of psychoactive drugs for recreational purposes. (Such drugs are almost universally permitted for medical and research purposes, such as the control of pain by opiates.) The League of Nations had also made a number of efforts to establish international standards for the control of psychoactive substances. But changes in the types of drugs available and their availability required constant amendments to and revisions of these treaties, a process that was always many years behind the rapid development of new drug technology. Finally, in 1948, the United Nations initiated an effort to write a new treaty that would provide a single standard for the control of psychoactive substances throughout the world. That treaty did not come to fruition for 13 years. It was finally signed in New York City in 1961 and took effect three years later.

The primary provision of the treaty was that all signatories agreed to prohibit the production, export, and consumption of certain specified substances, including opiates and coca products (usually covered by all preceding treaties), as well as marijuana (usually not covered by earlier treaties), and a host of new psychoactive substances as they became generally available, such as methadone, pethidine, morphinan, dextromoramide, fentanyl, piritramide, and their analogs. Currently, 184 nations have signed the Single Convention (*Single Convention on Narcotic Drugs* 1961; United Nations Treaty Collection 2009). One of the main features of the treaty was the establishment of four "schedules" of drugs, very similar to the schedule system developed by the U.S. Controlled Substances Act of 1970.

In his article, Professor Levine argues that drug prohibition serves some very useful purposes that go far beyond simply depriving individuals of the ability to use psychoactive substances for recreational purposes. He claims that drug abuse laws vastly increase the police and military powers of a government, allow governments to demonize the use of drugs and blame them for all manner of social failures, contribute to the belief that strong national governments can act on behalf of the general welfare of people, and provide a single theme on which politicians and legislators of all stripes can agree (Levine 2001). Because of these powerful elements, Levine suggests that revoking or amending national drug laws will never be as simple as it might seem, since such actions violate international treatment agreements that have now been in place for almost half a century.

Whether Professor Levine's argument is correct or not, the fact remains that prohibitions against drug abuse vary widely throughout the world. The following review illustrates the types of laws that exist in a variety of nations around the world.

Canada. The controlling law for substance abuse in Canada is the Controlled Drugs and Substances Act of 1996, which is the nation's implementing legislation for the Single Convention on Narcotics Drugs. The act is similar in many ways to the U.S. Controlled Substances Act of 1970 which, in fact, has served as the model for drug legislation in many countries around the world. One major difference between the Canadian and U.S. laws is that the former has eight schedules of drugs, rather than the five listed in the U.S. act. Without definition, the first five schedules under Canadian laws contain essentially the same substances listed under comparable U.S. laws. Schedule I, for example, includes opiates, coca products, fentanyls, ketamine, methamphetamine, and PCP. Schedule VI includes precursors of illegal drugs and substances, such as 1,4-butanediol, ephedrine, lysergic acid, potassium permanganate, red and white phosphorus, acetone diethyl ether, and hydrochloric and sulfuric acid. Schedules VII and VIII contain two substances each, hashish and cannabis (drugs that are listed under Schedule I in U.S. law). Schedule VII is designed for large quantities of these two drugs, three kilograms or more of either, while Schedule VIII lists much smaller amounts of the two drugs, 1 gram of hashish or 30 grams of cannabis. The distinctions made in Schedules VII and VIII were established because penalties for the two categories are very different. While possession or tracking in large quantities of a cannabis product (Schedule VII) is punished with a prison term of up to seven years, a Schedule VIII offense is punished by no more than a $1,000 fine and/or six months in prison.

Southeast Asia. Most countries in Southeast Asia have among the most severe penalties for substance and drug abuse of any region in the world. Some commentators suggest that the reason for these penalties is the proximity of the countries to regions in which illegal drugs are produced, such as Afghanistan and the so-called Golden Triangle at the intersection of Myanmar, Laos, and Thailand. As an example, Indonesian law calls for the death sentence, life imprisonment, and/or a fine of one billion rupiahs (about $100,000) for conviction of the most serious drug crimes. Even for less offenses, penalties can be severe. A person who uses illegal substances, for example, and does not report himself or herself to authorities may be imprisoned for six months, and the family of such an individual is subject to three months imprisonment for failing to report the relative (National Narcotics Board, Republic of Indonesia 1997). These penalties are not theoretical warnings to drug users and dealers. In June 2008, for example, the Indonesian government executed two Nigerians convicted of drug trafficking. General Sutanto (who, like many Indonesians, uses only one name) argued that "[t]o give them a lesson, drug traffickers must be executed immediately" (Asia Death Penalty 2008). That philosophy did not bode well for at least 57 additional individuals currently in prison because of drug trafficking. Those inmates will be executed, an assistant attorney general announced, "according to the law, after their appeals are exhausted" (Gelling 2008).

Singapore's drug laws may be even more draconian than those of Indonesia. As with many nations, Singapore law presumes that anyone who is carrying more than some stated amount of a drug is not just a user of that drug, but also a trafficker in the drug, a category that almost universally brings a more severe penalty. According to Section 17 of Chapter 185 of the Misuse of Drugs Act the amount of a substance that qualifies a person as a trafficker (rather than simply a user) is 100 grams (3.5 ounces) of opium, 3 grams (0.1 ounces) of morphine, 15 grams (0.5 ounces) of cannabis, 3 grams (0.1 ounces) of cocaine, and 25 grams (0.9 ounces) of methamphetamine ("Misuse of Drugs Act," 2009). For anyone convicted of having more than the stated amount of anyone of these substances, the penalty is death by hanging, a sentence that was carried out more than 400 times between 1991 and 2004 (Aquino 2009).

The death penalty for drug trafficking also remains on the books in the Philippines and Thailand, although it is less commonly imposed than in Indonesia and Singapore. For the Philippines, the penalty (death or life imprisonment) applies to anyone convicted of possession of at least 10 grams (0.3 ounces) of cocaine, heroin, marijuana resin, or morphine, or at least 500 grams (17 ounces) of marijuana. For smaller quantities, such as 5 grams (0.17 ounces) of an illegal drug, the penalty is a sentence of at least 12 years in prison ("Philippine Laws, Statutes & Codes. Republic Act No. 9165," 2009). Harsh penalties for possession of specified amounts of illegal substances also remain in other parts of Southeast Asia. Vietnam legislation describes in detail the amounts of illegal substances for which a person may be prosecuted and punished, and the penalty for each category of drugs, with the maximum penalty being death (The [Vietnam] National Legal Database 2009). In 2007, 85 people were put to death for drug-related crimes (Aquino 2009).

China. Official publications of the Chinese government reinforce the general concern among most Asian countries about the hazards posed by the production, trafficking, sale, and use of illegal substances. A document released by the Embassy of the People's Republic of China in the United States in June 2000, for example, expressed concern about China's exposure to drugs because of its location near the Golden Triangle. It pointed out that China had a long history of struggling against drug abuse dating back hundreds of years and, in particular, to the revolution of 1949 when the new Communist government "wiped out the scourge of opium" (Embassy of the People's Republic of China in the United States 2000). The Chinese government has continued an aggressive stance against the use of illegal substances, according to the embassy statement, because "[l]aunching an anti-drug struggle to eliminate the drug scourge is the historical responsibility of the Chinese government" (Embassy of the People's Republic of China in the United States 2000).

As of the date of the embassy document, the war against illegal substances was being conducted by police anti-drug squads in 24 (out of 31) provinces, autonomous regions, and municipalities, 204 cities and prefectures, and 735 cities and districts as well as agencies of the Chinese People's Armed Police, the frontier defense force, various judicial departments, the customs service, and agencies of the pharmaceutical and other industrial and commercial entities. These groups are guided by a governmental policy that has identified 12 types of crimes involving the use of 118 narcotic drugs and 119 psychoactive substances for which penalties up to and including death have been established.

Near East. Some countries in the Near East have drug laws at least as severe as those of Southeast Asia. In the United Arab Emirates (UAE), for example, penalties for drug trafficking may range from a few years in prison to death. The UAE laws are especially harsh, however, since the possession of even trace amounts of an illegal substance are taken as proof of one's intent to sell drugs, such that trafficking penalties apply for essentially any conviction for the possession of any illegal substance. UAE laws cover a wide array of substances that includes some prescription and over-the-counter drugs, as well as substances that might not be considered as drugs in other cultures. Possession of culinary poppy seeds, for example, falls within the range of the UAE laws (U.S. Department of State 2009d). Similar penalties exist for drug use in other Muslim countries. In Saudi Arabia, for example, penalties for conviction of drug trafficking include heavy fines, imprisonment, public flogging, and death (U.S. Department of State 2009c). As with Southeast Asia, harsh penalties for illegal drug use are not just symbolic representations of a nation's moral codes; they are guides to action. A recent report on the use of death penalties for drug-related crimes indicated that the death penalty had been carried out in at least four Near Eastern nations— Egypt, Iran, Kuwait, and Saudi Arabia—in the period between 2002 and 2006 (Lines 2007, 8).

Africa. Drug policies in Africa appear to be undergoing a significant change. For most of their modern history, African nations were confronted with a number of crucial practical issues—such as internal and cross-border warfare, food shortages, and rampant disease—that left them little time, energy, or resources to deal with a "marginal" issue such as illegal substance abuse. In addition, the use of illegal substances was not a significant part in nations on the continent, except among expatriates, who could often bribe themselves out of legal problems involving drugs in which they became involved (Drug Policy Alliance Network 2009).

That situation appears to have changed with the turn of the new century, at least partly because of more severe laws and more aggressive law enforcement in other parts of the world. The 2000s have seen drug cartels from South America and Southeast Asia increasing their shipments of opiates, cocaine, marijuana, and other illegal substances to the African continent. According to one report, at least 9 drug cartels from Colombia and Mexico have established bases of operation in 11 West African nations alone (Brice 2009).

In response to this new trend, a number of African nations have begun to adopt laws considerably more aggressive than had been in place in the past. In October 2009, for example, Liberia adopted a new drug law that quintupled the penalty for drug possession, from a previous 5-to-10 year prison term to a 25-to-60-year term. In addition, suspects of drug crimes are no longer eligible for bail while awaiting trial, and they are subject to much more severe forfeiture penalties (StoptheDrugWar.org 2009a). Another West African nation, Namibia, has followed Liberia's lead. In 2007, the government proposed a new policy on the use of illegal substances calling for a minimum 20-year sentence for a first-time conviction, and a 30-year sentence for a second conviction. These penalties are to be assessed for use of any quantity of an illegal substance, no matter how small (StoptheDrugWar.org 2009b). Other West Africa countries have adopted similar policies, with Senegal doubling its penalty for drug convictions to hard labor for 10 to 20 years (IRIN 2009).

The growing threat of the drug problem on the African continent has begun to concern regional, continental, and international agencies. For example, at the Third Session of the African Union Conference of Ministers on substance abuse issues, held in Addis Ababa, Ethiopia, on December 3–7, 2007, there was an acknowledgment that the continent's growing drug problem would require a more aggressive and extensive involvement of law enforcement officials, rather than remaining strictly the purview of drug control agencies, as it had in the past. The Revised Plan of Action on Drug Control And Crime Prevention for the period of 2007–2012 adopted by the African Union places a very strong emphasis on the widespread and intensive use of law enforcement resources to deal with the continent's substance abuse problems. Little or nothing is said in the plan about methods for dealing with the problem at the level of individual consumption (African Union 2007).

Latin America. The survey of drug policies in Asia and Africa illustrated thus far presents an almost universal collection of laws that deal harshly with the production, sale, trafficking, and consumption of illegal substances. Sentences ranging from a few years to life imprisonment, and including death penalties, are not uncommon in most nations across these two continents. Yet, a significantly different trend can be detected in some other parts of the world, especially South America, Europe, and North America. In South America, for example, the most recent trend is toward a liberalization of drug policies, with laws emphasizing prevention and treatment of users rather than harsher prison sentences. Within an eight-day period in August 2009, for example, both Mexico and Argentina decriminalized the consumption of small amounts of most drugs. In the former case, the action came about as the result of legislative procedures, while in the latter case, decriminalization came about when the Argentine supreme court ruled that the nation's drug laws against the use of marijuana were unconstitutional. Experts believe that the court's ruling will soon extend to all other Argentine national drug laws.

The actions in Mexico and Argentina were only the most recent steps in a movement taking place throughout Latin America. Colombia's supreme court had announced a ruling similar to that of its Argentine colleagues as early as 1994. Brazil had decriminalized the consumption of small amounts of drugs in 2006, replacing prison sentences with mandatory educational, treatment, or public service sentences. The Uruguayan legislature has given judges the authority to decide whether drug possession falls into the category of trafficking or personal consumption, with the possibility of treatment instead of imprisonment as an appropriate sentence for conviction in the latter instance. And the Ecuadorean legislature was considering (as of early 2010) the decriminalization of the consumption of small amounts of drugs (StoptheDrugWar.org 2009c).

One of the most important factors in the changing attitudes about the decriminalization of drug consumption in South America appears to be a philosophy expressed by the Latin American Commission on Drugs and Democracy, a group of 17 individuals from 10 Latin American countries. The group was formed through the efforts of three political leaders: César Gaviria, former president of Colombia; Ernesto Zedillo, former president of Mexico; and Fernando Henrique Cardoso, former president of Brazil. The commission held its first meeting on April 30, 2008, and issued its final report a year later, in March 2009. The commission came to the conclusion that drug policies pursued in their nations for many years had been a failure, and a new approach to the problem of substance abuse was needed. They formulated five general principles on which they thought future efforts should be based:

- Changing the fundamental assumption that users of illegal substances are criminals with the assumption that they are patients who need to be treated by the public health system.
- Examining the medical evidence about marijuana with a view toward decriminalizing the use of this substance for valid health purposes.
- Reducing the consumption of illegal substances with programs of education for young people.
- Redirecting national policies toward an aggressive campaign against organized crime for which the distribution of drugs is an essential element.
- Reframing national policies on the prohibition of the cultivation of illegal drugs by providing farmers with reasonable alternatives to the growth of these products (*Drugs and Democracy*, 2009, 8–10).

Europe. Arguably the most permissive drug laws in the world can be found in Europe. A number of studies have found that drug policies in this region have been changing to a significant degree to focus on the difference between personal use of small amounts of illegal substances for recreational purposes and large-scale trafficking in drugs such as opiates, cocaine, and analog designer drugs. Authorities now tend to regard the former as a matter of public health concern that should be dealt with through prevention and treatment programs, while the latter remains the concern of law enforcement agencies. Penalties for personal use of small amounts of illegal substances are now likely to consist of required participation in treatment programs, community service, or modest fines, while penalties for the latter continue to involve long-term prison sentences, loss of property, and significant monetary fines. The European Monitoring Centre for Drugs and Drug Addiction summarized this trend in its 2006 report *The State of the Drugs Problem in Europe* (an annual publication of the organization). It noted that:

> A continuing trend . . . is for changes to national drug laws to emphasise more strongly a distinction between offences of drug possession for personal use and those involving trafficking and supply. Generally, there is a shift towards increased penalties for the latter and a reduced emphasis on custodial sentences for the former. This development is in line with a greater emphasis overall across Europe on widening the opportunities for drug treatment and on giving more attention to interventions that divert those with drug problems away from the criminal justice system towards treatment and rehabilitation options (European Monitoring Centre for Drugs and Drug Addiction 2006, 11).

The report provided a number of examples that illustrate this trend. During the year covered by the 2006 report, for example, Romania adopted a new penal code that distinguishes between casual users of illegal substances and drug addicts. Penalties for the former were significantly reduced, restricted to a certain number of hours of community service and/or a day fine (a fine based on a person's income). Penalties can also be adjusted based on an individual's personal circumstances. On the other hand, penalties for more serious drug-related crimes were increased under the new legislation. New legislation in Italy was similar to that in Romania, with the former six-schedule system reduced to just two schedules: drugs with some therapeutic value and those without such value. Penalties for personal use of small amounts of less dangerous drugs were reduced to community service and/or house arrest and the possibility of an alternative to prison sentence was expanded (European Monitoring Centre for Drugs and Drug Addiction, 21). Perhaps the most dramatic example of the trend toward decriminalization in Europe is the reversal of course in Portugal.

At one time, the nation had some of the most severe drug laws in Europe. First instituted in the mid-twentieth century under long-term dictator Antonio Salazar, these laws punished drug possession by harsh prison sentences and/or heavy fines. These laws did little to solve the nation's drug problems, however, and by the 1990s, Portugal was widely acknowledged as having the worst drug problems in Western Europe (Portugal's Drug Laws 2009). At that point, the federal government decided to take a totally different approach to controlling the nation's drug problems. It decided to decriminalize the use of small amounts of all drugs, ranging from marijuana to heroin and cocaine. The new laws did not change penalties for trafficking or dealing drugs, but eliminated prison sentences for users of small amounts of illegal substances and individuals addicted to drugs. Now, anyone convicted of substance abuse is referred to a treatment center, where he or she is helped to understand and control his or her substance abuse problems (Vastag 2009).

A recent study conducted by the Cato Institute in Washington, D.C., has found that the new drug policy appears to be extraordinarily successful. The number of drug overdoses in Portugal dropped from an annual rate of about 400 in 2001 to 290 five years later. During the same period, the number of new cases of HIV infection resulting from the sharing of dirty needles dropped from 1,400 in 2001 to 400 in 2006 (Vastag 2009). By 2006, Portugal, alone in Europe except for Italy, was the only nation to report a decrease in the number of drug law offences (European Monitoring Centre for Drugs and Drug Addiction 2006, 23).

A complete and up-to-date summary of drug laws and policies in all member states of the European Union is available online at http://eldd.emcdda.europa.eu/html.cfm/index5174EN.html?nNodeID=5174&sLanguageISO=EN#c2.

Marijuana: A Special Case?

The one psychoactive substance that continues to pose an issue in many nations around the world is marijuana (and, in some cases, other products of the cannabis plant, such as hashish). An important part of the difficulty is that marijuana, hashish, and related cannabis products have long been an essential part of many religious and cultural ceremonies. As noted above, the product called *bhang* (a dried product made from the leaves and flowers of the female cannabis plant), has been consumed as part of religious ceremonies in India since at least the first millennium BCE. At least as old as bhang may be another cannabis product called *charas*, made by hand-processing resin from the cannabis plant. The earliest use of charas seems to date to the so-called *booz rooz* religious ceremony of ancient Persia (International Cannagraphic 2009). Cannabis products have also been very popular in most of West Africa for centuries. In Swaziland, Lesotho, and South Africa, for example, the consumption of marijuana—known in the region as *dagga* or *insangu*—is a centuries-old custom. Efforts to criminalize the use of cannabis products in these regions fly in the face, then, of long-held cultural traditions (Hall 2009). Even some virulently anti-drug parts of the world maintain traditional practices of using otherwise illegal marijuana-like substances for religious, ceremonial, or recreational purposes. For example, the Muslim population of East Africa and Yemen, who otherwise are prohibited by their religion from using psychoactive substances, have long chewed the leaves of the qat plant (*Catha edulis*, also known as kat, qat, qaat, quat, gat, jaad, chat, chad, chaad and miraa) to obtain a mild psychoactive "buzz." In fact, use of the plant is so popular in some regions that its cultivation is currently threatening the scarce water supplies in the region (Worth 2009, 9).

Probably for more than any other drugs, therefore, the laws dealing with marijuana vary widely throughout the world. Table 3.1 summarizes the legal status of cannabis products in a sample of nations around the world.

As in the United States, there is a vigorous debate in some countries about the decriminalization of marijuana use for medical purposes. The guiding principle on which almost all national laws are based, the Single Convention on Narcotic Drugs of 1961, as amended by the 1972 Protocol, is virtually silent on the subject. It says only in Article 2 that:

> A Party shall, if in its opinion the prevailing conditions in its country render it the most appropriate means of protecting the public health and welfare, prohibit the production, manufacture, export and import of, trade in, possession or use of any such drug except for amounts which may be necessary for medical and scientific research only, including clinical trials therewith to be conducted under or subject to the direct supervision and control of the Party (Single Convention on Narcotic Drugs 1961, 3, Article 2).

TABLE 3.1
Some Marijuana Laws around the World

Country	Law
Australia	Varies by state, but usually possession is illegal but punished by modest fines or warning (The Age 2009).
Brazil	Possession of small amounts punished by a warning, required community service, or drug education classes (Organization of American States 2006).
Canada	In dispute. Still illegal, although a number of court decisions have declared marijuana laws unconstitutional (Munroe 2009).
Comoros	Legalized by president Ali Soilih in 1975 (Rushby 2001).
Cyprus	Punishable for imprisonment for up to eight years for use and up to life for possession (European Monitoring Centre for Drugs and Drug Addiction 2007, Cyprus).
Czech Republic	1998 law makes "possession of more than a small amount of drugs" illegal, currently viewed as decriminalizing the consumption of small amounts of marijuana (Fleishman 2006).
France	Possession and use are illegal, punished by imprisonment of up to 10 years for the former, and up to one year for the latter (European Legal Database on Drugs 2007, "France").
Germany	De facto decriminalization of "small amounts" of marijuana by virtue of a decision of the Federal Constitutional Court in 2003 (Everything2 2003).
India	"Production, manufacture, possession, sale, purchase, transport, import, export inter-state or use" of "small amounts" of drugs, including cannabis: up to six months of "rigorous imprisonment." For more than a small quantity, but less than a commercial quantity: rigorous imprisonment for up to 10 years. However, government of India operates shops for the sale of bhang (cannabis) to the general public (Centre for Narcotics Training, National Academy of Customs, Excise and Narcotics 2009; Sharma 2007).
Ireland	Punishment by a fine for first or second conviction for use of marijuana and by a prison term for later convictions (European Legal Database on Drugs 2007, "Ireland").
Japan	Anyone who "unlawfully possesses, receives, or transfers cannabis" is subject to imprisonment for up to five years (a law passed during the U.S. occupation in 1948; "Cannabis Control Act," 1948).
Malaysia	Mandatory death sentence for anyone convicted of drug trafficking. Possession of more than 15 grams (0.5 ounce) is presumptive evidence of one's intention to traffic in a drug (U.S. Department of State 2009a).
Mexico	Small amounts of marijuana and other drugs are legal for personal use (Grillo 2009).
Peru	Possession of less than eight grams of marijuana intended for personal use is legal. Possession of larger amounts is severely punished as an indication of intent to traffic in the drug (Codigo Penal. Decreto Legislativo Nº 635, "Articulo 299—Posesión no punible").
Saudi Arabia	Possession of any quantity of marijuana (or any other drug) is punishable by death (U.S. Department of State 2009b).
Switzerland	Laws and policies differ in each canton in the country, but penalties for small amounts of marijuana intended for personal use tend to be light, consisting of small fines, usually adjusted for a person's income, that increase with repeat convictions (Verband Bernischer Richter und Richterinnen 2006, 27).
United Arab Emirates	Severe penalties for even vanishingly small quantities of marijuana and other drugs ("Travelers Warned of UAE Drug Laws," 2008).
United Kingdom	Possession of marijuana is punishable by imprisonment for up to five years. This policy has changed twice in the last decade ("UK Marijuana Policy Sees Two More Resign," 2009).

Sources: All sources listed in References at end of chapter.

TABLE 3.2
Legal Status of Medical Marijuana Worldwide

Country	Legal Status of Medical Marijuana
Australia	Laws vary from state to state, and the issue is being debated in a number of states. All uses of cannabis products have been decriminalized in Northern Territory, and growing cannabis for one's person use is currently legal there and in Western Australia, South Australia, and Australian Capital Territory (StoptheDrugWar 2004).
Austria	A 2008 law allows the cultivation of marijuana for scientific and medical purposes, but only by state agencies. Those agencies may then distribute the substance for therapeutic uses (NORML 2008).
Cameroon	Cannabis products may be used to treat the symptoms of HIV/AIDS infection (Songwe 2001). Controversy surrounds the importation of the substance from Canada when cannabis is widely grown in the country.
Canada	Following a series of court decisions, the federal government decriminalized the use of cannabis products by individuals "suffering from grave or debilitating illnesses, where conventional treatments are inappropriate or are not providing adequate relief." For details of the program, see Health Canada 2009.
Israel	Originally approved for use in the treatment of the most extreme symptoms of terminal cancer and HIV/AIDS, marijuana is now used widely for a broader range of disorders and milder symptoms. Research is also being conducted on the use of marijuana for the treatment of post-traumatic stress disorder among soldiers who have been stressed after return from battle (Shadmi 2009; "Israel to Soothe Trauma with Marijuana" 2004).
Netherlands	Pharmacies are allowed to stock and sell marijuana to individuals who have a physician's prescription for the product. Growers of the plant must have a license from the federal government to supply marijuana for medical uses (NORML 2003).

Sources: All sources listed in References at end of chapter.

Thus far, only a handful of countries have approved the use of cannabis products for medical purposes, almost all of them in Europe. A handful of other nations have debated or are currently debating changing their laws to allow this option. Table 3.2 summarizes the current status of this issue as of early 2010.

Alcohol and Tobacco

As noted previously in this book, alcohol and tobacco remain the two psychoactive substances most widely approved for general use in most nations of the world. One major exception to that statement is the religious prohibition against the use of alcohol within the Islamic faith. Because of this prohibition, 10 countries with large Muslim populations prohibit the sale or consumption of alcohol, either just to citizens of that nation or to anyone living or traveling in the country. For example, the drinking of alcoholic beverages is not permitted in Brunei, although foreigners can obtain a temporary license for the purchase and consumption of small amounts of alcohol (U.S. Department of State 2009b). By contrast, the drinking of alcohol is forbidden to anyone in Saudi Arabia, whether citizen or foreigner (U.S. Department of State 2009a).

Very few countries around the world have attempted to institute an outright ban on cigarette smoking. One exception is Bhutan, which attempted to institute such a ban in 2004. That ban prohibited both the sale and consumption of tobacco products, with a fine equivalent to about $230, equivalent to a two-months salary for the average citizen of the country (Weiner 2005). The effort survived only five years, however. In 2009, the National Council decided to revoke the ban on smoking because it had been largely ineffective. The smuggling of cigarettes allowed smokers to continue pursuing their habit, but at a much greater expense than before the ban had been instituted. The council's new approach is to place very high taxes on the sale of cigarettes, hoping that this plan will reduce the use of tobacco in the nation (National Portal of Bhutan 2009).

By far, the more common approach among governments has been to place prohibitions on the places and circumstances under which a person may smoke. These bans are similar to the range of prohibitions adopted by the various states in the United States. The World Health Organization (WHO) has classified these bans according to the spaces to which they apply, such as:

- The outright ban of smoking in all public places. Belgium has probably come as close to such a law as any nation. In 2009, the national legislature adopted a law banning smoking in all public places with a small number of exceptions, such as hotels and restaurants where alcoholic beverages and simple snacks are served. Before the law even went into effect, however, a ruling by the Antwerp Court of Appeals on an earlier law made it seem likely that even the exception would have to be dropped and that all facilities of all kind would have to be covered by the law ("New Smoking Ban Will Not Be Long-Lived" 2009).

- The prohibition of smoking in all public places except for areas that are specifically exempted and the designation of specific locations in which smoking is banned. WHO gives the smoking laws in Finland as an example of this approach.
- Combining a prohibition of smoking in all public places with additional bans on specific locations, such as the places at which children are likely to congregate. A ban of this kind went into effect in Iceland in 2007 (Icelandguest.com 2007).
- Specifying specific spaces where smoking is allowed and prohibited, and making it the responsibility of facility owners to ensure that patrons abide by those regulations. Israeli statutes, for example, require owners to set aside at least 75 percent of the space in their establishment for nonsmokers, to ensure that nonsmoking areas are well ventilated, that smoking paraphernalia are not present in nonsmoking areas, and that proper signage designates smoking and nonsmoking areas. Fines for ignoring these regulations are substantial, amounting to 10,000 shekels (about US$3,000; Khazzoom 2004).

The prohibition of tobacco smoking appears to be an idea whose time has come in many parts of the world. Whether based on concerns about the possibility of fires started by smokers, the health effects of tobacco, children's welfare, or other issues, governments appear to be gradually ratcheting up their efforts to reduce the use of tobacco. Where bans have been put into place, smokers appear to adjust to the new limitations placed upon them, and agencies forced to take new actions to comply with those bans appear not to be unreasonably inconvenienced (World Health Organization 2009). Any review of the changes in smoking legislation around the world suggests rather strongly that more and more nations are adopting increasingly severe restrictions on the use of tobacco products (TimelinesDB 2009).

Still, smoking bans are absent from very large parts of the world, especially in eastern Europe, central and eastern Asia, and most parts of Africa. A partial list of the countries that have yet to institute national laws on smoking includes Poland, Russia, Hungary, Belarus, Ukraine, China, Mongolia, Japan, South Korea,

Sudan, Mauritania, Senegal, Congo, Angola, Namibia, Honduras, Costa Rica, Nicaragua, Chile, and Paraguay (World Lung Foundation 2009). This list is somewhat misleading, however, since some countries included have already begun a discussion of legislation limiting or prohibiting smoking in various types of facilities, while other countries have a patchwork of laws and regulations established by the federal government, state, and/or local governments. In this regard, these nations are taking an approach to the control of smoking similar to that which exists in the United States and Canada.

The future direction of bans on the use of tobacco may be seen in an important document prepared by the World Health Organization in 2003. That document, the *Draft WHO Framework on Tobacco Control*, was prepared for submission to the 56th World Health Assembly held in Geneva on May 19–28, 2003. It clarified its goal as finding a way

> to protect present and future generations from the devastating health, social, environmental and economic consequences of tobacco consumption and exposure to tobacco smoke by providing a framework for tobacco control measures to be implemented by the Parties at the national, regional and international levels in order to reduce continually and substantially the prevalence of tobacco use and exposure to tobacco smoke (World Health Organization 2003, 5, Article 3).

Adoption of the document at the Geneva Conference resulted in the creation of an ambitious WHO program, the Tobacco Free Initiative, which continues to direct and guide WHO's efforts to reduce smoking around the world today. Perhaps the most important guiding principle for the program (among seven stated in the draft framework) was that:

> Every person should be informed of the health consequences, addictive nature and mortal threat posed by tobacco consumption and exposure to tobacco smoke and effective legislative, executive, administrative or other measures should be contemplated at the appropriate governmental level to protect all persons from exposure to tobacco smoke (World Health Organization 2003, 5, Article 4).

The draft framework also laid out a number of strategies by which a smoke-free world could be achieved. These strategies include the following:

- The adoption of pricing and tax policies sufficiently formidable to reduce the demand for tobacco products.
- Provision of enough smoke-free areas of sufficient size to permit citizens to escape from exposure to tobacco smoke.
- Regulation of the contents of tobacco products.
- Regulation of the advertising of tobacco products.
- Regulation of the labeling of tobacco products.
- Aggressive public education programs about the health and other risks associated with smoking.
- Aggressive programs to reduce and eventually eliminate the smuggling of tobacco products between countries.
- Legislative actions to prohibit the sale of tobacco products to minors.
- Provision of support programs for the development of alternatives to cigarette smoking (World Health Organization 2003).

Substance Abuse Worldwide

Perhaps the best way to conclude a review of the worldwide status of substance abuse is simply to ask how extensive that problem currently is in various nations of the world. Probably the best source of information on that question is an annual report of the United Nations Office on Drugs and Crime (UNODC), *World Drug Report*. That publication, running in 2009 to more than 300 pages, covers many aspects of the production, trafficking, and consumption of illegal substances in most countries around the world. The report's value is somewhat limited for a number of reasons, primarily because some countries do not respond to UNODC surveys, some countries are more thorough in their research on substance abuse than others, and countries use a variety of methods for collecting data. For example, relatively few nations outside Europe, North America, and Australasia collect and provide detailed information on long-term or current trends in the consumption of illegal substances. It is difficult, therefore, to make generalizations about worldwide trends in substance abuse issues, especially with regard to consumption.

Nonetheless, *World Drug Report* almost certainly provides the best overview of trends in drug use among people of all ages in nations in all parts of the world. For example, it provides information on long-term trends of the use of opiates, cocaine, marijuana, methamphetamine, and ecstasy, even though those data are not precisely comparable. As an example, Table 3.3 summarizes some trends in the use of cocaine and marijuana in selected nations where those records have been kept for more than a decade.

Determining the consumption of illegal substances other than cocaine and marijuana is even more difficult than it is for these two drugs. In its 2009 *World Drug Report*, UNODC estimated that there were between 16 and 51 million people aged 15–64 who used amphetamine-like substances (ATS) and 12 to 24 million worldwide who used an ecstasy-like drug. The annual prevalence rate for these two groups of drugs were 0.4–1.2 percent and 0.3–0.5 percent respectively. About half of these users are thought to live in North America (United Nations Office on Drugs and Crime 2009, 144). In terms of prevalence, the largest group of ATS users are found in Oceania (rate = 2.6), followed by Asia (0.2–1.4), North and South America (0.9–1.0), Africa (0.3–0.8), and Europe (0.4–0.6) (United Nations Office on Drugs and Crime 2009, 146, Table 23). The increase in drug use of ATS substances is considerably greater across the world than it is for any other drug or group of drugs.

Because of the difficulties in collecting consistent and reliable statistics across many nations about some forms of substance abuse, UNODC officials also use a second means of assessing drug abuse trends. They ask experts in the field of substance abuse to provide their best expert opinions as to the trends they see in their nation or region. In the 2009 *World Report on Drugs*, UNODC reported on expert perspectives on trends for three groups of drugs: opiates, amphetamine-type substances (ATS), and ecstasy-type substances (ETS). In the first of these categories, UNODC received responses from 87 experts in Africa, Asia, North and South America, and Europe. They received no responses from experts in Oceania. Just over 40 percent of these experts (38 respondents) felt that the situation for opiates in their region had become more serious with an average increase in the

TABLE 3.3
Prevalence[‡] in Consumption of Cocaine and Marijuana in Selected Nations

						Cocaine					
Country	*	2000	2001	2002	2003	2004	2005	2006	2007	2008
England	1.2	2.0				2.4		2.6	2.3	
Germany	0.6	0.9			1.0			0.6		
Hungary		0.7			0.4				0.2	
Ireland	1.3				1.1				1.7	
Italy			1.1		1.2		2.2			2.2
Poland				0.5				0.2		
Spain	1.6				2.5		3.0		3.0	
Uruguay	0.2/0.4		0.2						1.4	
United States[†]		1.5	1.9	2.5	2.5	2.4	2.3	2.5	2.3	2.1

[*]England: 1998; Germany: 1997; Ireland: 1998; Spain: 1999; Uruguay: 1994/1998.
[†]For comparison.
Sources: United Nations Office on Drugs and Crime. *World Drug Report*. Geneva, Switzerland: 2008, 82–84, Figures 45, 46, 47, 49; Substance Abuse and Mental Health Services Administration. *National Survey on Drug Use and Health*. Washington, D.C., 2001, Table 1.1B; 2008, Table 1.1B.

						Marijuana					
Country	*	2000	2001	2002	2003	2004	2005	2006	2007	2008
Australia	17.9		12.9			11.3			9.1	
Austria	3.5			5.6		7.5				3.5
Denmark	5.0	6.2					5.2			
England	9.5	10.5			10.9					7.4
France	4.7	8.4		9.8			8.6			
Germany	4.4	6.0			6.9			4.7		
Hungary			2.4		3.9				2.3	
Ireland					5.0			6.3		
Italy			6.2		7.1		11.2		14.6	
Spain	7.0		9.2		11.3		11.2			10.1
Sweden		0.7				2.2		2.0		
Uruguay	0.7/1.2		1.3						5.3	
United States[†]		8.3	9.3	11.0	10.6	10.6	10.4	10.3	10.1	10.3

[*]Australia: 1998; Austria: 1984; Denmark: 1990; England: 1996; France: 1995; Germany: 1995; Spain: 1999; Uruguay: 1994/1998.
[†]For comparison.
[‡]Ratio of individuals who used the substance in the past year in the general population.
Sources: United Nations Office on Drugs and Crime. *World Drug Report*, 108–111, Figures 62, 64, 65, 66,67; Substance Abuse and Mental Health Services Administration. *National Survey on Drug Use and Health*. Washington, D.C.: 2001, Table 1.1B; 2008, Table G.4.

extent of their problem of 44 percent. The problem was thought to be most serious in Asia, the Americas, and Africa (worsening by more than 50%), and less serious in Europe (worsening by 26%). Another 32 percent of respondents (28 experts) said the drug situation was about the same in their regions, and about a quarter of respondents (21 experts) felt that the drug problem was improving in their region (United Nations Office on Drugs and Crime 2009, 54, Table 4).

Expert opinions on the abuse of amphetamine-like substances and ecstasy-like substances were similar to those for opiates. In the former case, 40 of 86 experts (47%) thought that the ATS problem was becoming worse in their region of the world, with the average increase in severity being 47 percent. Little difference among regions was observed, with Asian experts reporting somewhat more of a problem and European experts somewhat less of a problem than experts from Africa and the Americas. 34 experts (40%) reported little change in ATS problems in their regions and 12 experts (14%) thought those problems were improving (United Nations Office on Drugs and Crime 2009, 147, Table 24).

In the matter of ecstasy-like drugs, about a third of experts who provided an opinion (22 of 63) felt the problem was becoming worse in their part of the world, 32 of 63 (51%) saw no change, and 9 of 63 (14%) saw their situation improving. Perhaps the most troubling trend for both ATS and ETS drugs was a slow, but steady, increase in the seriousness of substance abuse for these two groups of drugs in every region of the world (United Nations Office on Drugs and Crime 2009, 157, Figure 113 and Table 26).

One might expect the authors of *World Drug Report* to wade through the volume of statistics and data presented in this document and provide the reader with an overview of the current status of substance abuse issues around the world. And they have done so. In the preface to this report, those authors express the view that "[d]rug statistics keep speaking loud and clear. Past runaway growth has flattened out and the drug crisis of the 1990s seems under control (United Nations Office on Drugs and Crime 2009, 1). (A somewhat more disinterested observer might be forgiven for taking a somewhat less optimistic view of the situation, however.) The authors then devote the majority of their overview of the report discussing current efforts to decriminalize or legalize substances that have long been illegal. They argue that this approach is wrong, that current drug policies have essentially the right objective in mind, although the methods for achieving those objectives may need to be reassessed and modified. What nations need to do, they say, is to find *"different means* to protect society against drugs, rather than by pursuing the *different goal* of abandoning such protection (United Nations Office on Drugs and Crime 2009, 1)."

Such may very well be the case. Certainly, few people in the world know more about the misuse of illegal substances than members of UNODC. However, as the authors of this report themselves indicate, in the opening sentence of this report, the war on drugs has now been going on for a hundred years, beginning with the International Opium Commission conference held in Shanghai, China, in February 1909. The world has been looking for ways of dealing with substance abuse problems ever since, often driven by promises that the world has finally turned the corner, the drug problem is finally being solved, and we need only to tweak our present system of criminalizing drug production, trafficking, and consumption to reach a drug-free world. We will see.

References

African Union (2007). "3rd Session of the AU Conference Of Ministers for Drug Control And Crime Prevention." Addis Ababa, Ethiopia. http://www .africa-union.org/root/AU/Conferences/2007/December/sa/ACMDCC PIII/docs/en/Plan%20of%20Action%20FINAL%20-%2008-11-07.doc. Accessed on November 11, 2009.

Age (2009). "Australia's Cannabis Laws." http://www.theage.com.au/articles/ 2003/05/22/1053585645363.html. Accessed on November 10, 2009.

Aquino, Michael (2009). "Harsh Punishments for Drug Use in Southeast Asia." http://goseasia.about.com/od/travelplanning/a/seasia_drugs.htm. Accessed on November 8, 2009.

Asia Death Penalty Blog (2008). "Indonesia: Drug Offenders Executed, More to Come." http://asiadeathpenalty.blogspot.com/2008/06/ indonesia-drug-offenders-executed-more.html. Accessed on November 8, 2009.

BBC News (2008). "Travelers Warned of UAE Drug Laws." http:// news.bbc.co.uk/2/hi/uk_news/7234786.stm. Accessed on November 11, 2009.

Borio, Gene (2009a). "Tobacco Timeline: The Seventeenth Century—The Great Age of the Pipe." http://www.tobacco.org/resources/history/ Tobacco_History17.html. Accessed on October 30, 2009.

Borio, Gene (2009b). "Tobacco Timeline: The Sixteenth Century—Sailors Spread the Seeds." http://www.tobacco.org/resources/history/Tobacco _History16.html. Accessed on October 30, 2009.

Brice, Arthur (2009). "Latin American Drug Cartels Find Home in Africa." http://www.cnn.com/2009/WORLD/africa/09/21/africa.drug .cartels/index.html. Accessed on November 9, 2009.

Brooks, Jerome E. (1952). *The Mighty Leaf: Tobacco through the Centuries.* Boston: Little, Brown and Company.

"Cannabis Control Law" (1948). Law No. 124 of July 10, 1948, as amended. http://www.japanhemp.org/en/taimalaw.htm#f05. Accessed on November 11, 2009.

Centre for Narcotics Training, National Academy of Customs, Excise and Narcotics (2009). "Drug Laws in India." http://www.antidrugs.gov .il/download/files/indian_drug-laws.pdf. Accessed on November 11, 2009.

Codigo Penal (1991). Decreto Legislativo No. 635. Penal Code of Peru (in Spanish), as amended. http://www.devida.gob.pe/documentacion/ Decreto%20Legislativo%20635-CODIGO%20PENAL.doc. Accessed on November 11, 2009.

Coffee Information Portal (2009). "Coffee in Religions." http://coffee -bean-java.com/Coffee_in_religions.html. Accessed on October 28, 2009.

Concept 420 (2009). "Marijuana History and Timeline." http://www .concept420.com/marijuana_cannabis_history_timeline.htm. Accessed on October 30, 2009.

Drug Policy Alliance Network (2009). "Drug Policy around the World: Africa." http://www.drugpolicy.org/global/drugpolicyby/africa/. Accessed on November 9, 2009.

Embassy of the People's Republic of China in the United States (2000). http://www.china-embassy.org/eng/zt/mzpkz/t36387.htm. Accessed on November 8, 2009.

European Legal Database on Drugs (2007). http://eldd.emcdda.europa.eu/ html.cfm/index5769EN.html. Accessed on November 11, 2009.

European Monitoring Centre for Drugs and Drug Addiction (2006). *The State of the Drugs Problem in Europe.* Luxembourg: Monitoring Centre for Drugs and Drug Addiction. Available online at http://ar2006.emcdda .europa.eu/download/ar2006-en.pdf.

European Monitoring Centre for Drugs and Drug Addiction (2007). "Country Overviews." http://www.emcdda.europa.eu/publications/ country-overviews. Accessed on November 11, 2009.

Everything2 (2003). "The German Federal Constitutional Court's Cannabis Decision." http://everything2.com/title/The+Cannabis

+Decision+%2528German+Federal+Constitutional+Court%2529. Accessed on November 11, 2009.

Flanders Today (2009). "New Smoking Ban Will Not Be Long-Lived." *Flanders Today.* http://www.mediargus.be/flanderstoday.admin.en/rss/22365789.html?via=rss&language=en. Accessed on November 12, 2009.

Fleishman, Jeffrey (2006). "A Czech Toke on Freedom." *Los Angeles Times,* January 24. http://74.125.155.132/search?q=cache:92idsHx3OnoJ: articles.latimes.com/2006/jan/24/world/fgweed24+czech+republic +marijuana+los+angeles+times&cd=1&hl=en&ct=clnk&gl=us. Accessed on November 11, 2009.

Frampton, John (trans.) (1577). "Of the Tabaco and of His Greate Vertues." http://www.tobacco.org/resources/history/monardes.html. Accessed on October 30, 2009.

Gahlinger, Paul (2004). *Illegal Drugs: A Complete Guide to Their History, Chemistry, Use, and Abuse.* New York: Plume.

Gelling, Peter (2008). "Executions for Drug Crimes Are Resumed in Indonesia." *New York Times.* http://www.nytimes.com/2008/07/13/world/asia/13indo.html. Accessed on November 8, 2009.

Grillo, Ioan (2009). "Mexico's New Drug Law May Set an Example." *Time.* http://www.time.com/time/world/article/0,8599,1918725,00 .html. Accessed on November 11, 2009.

Hall, James (2004). "Cultural Practices Hamper Anti-drug Campaigns." http://www.newsfromafrica.org/newsfromafrica/articles/art_6082 .html. Accessed on November 10, 2009.

Health Canada (2009). "Fact Sheet—Medical Access to Marijuana." http://www.hc-sc.gc.ca/dhp-mps/marihuana/law-loi/fact_sheet -infofiche-eng.php#a4. Accessed on November 12, 2009.

Icelandguest.com (2007). "Smoking Ban Takes Effect in Iceland." http://www.icelandguest.com/in-focus/nr/945/. Accessed on November 12, 2009.

International Cannagraphic (2009). "Cannabis." http://www.icmag.com/ic/showthread.php?t=32703. Accessed on November 10, 2009.

IRIN (2009). "Senegal: Stiffer Penalties for Drug Traffickers." http://www.irinnews.org/Report.aspx?ReportId=75953. Accessed on November 9, 2009.

Israel Is Real Blog (2004). "Israel to Soothe Trauma with Marijuana." 2004. http://israel_is_real.blogspot.com/2004/10/israel-to-soothe -trauma-with-marijuana.html. Accessed on November 12, 2009.

Khazzoom, Loolwa (2004). "Israel Struggles with No-smoking Laws." *Jewish News of Greater Phoenix.* 56(19), January 30. http://www.jewishaz.com/jewishnews/040130/struggles.shtml. Accessed on November 12, 2009.

Latin American Commission on Drugs and Democracy (2009). *Drugs and Democracy: Toward a Paradigm Shift* (2009). [n.p.]

Levine, Harry G. (2001). "The Secret of World-wide Drug Prohibition: the Varieties and Uses of Drug Prohibition." Hereinstead.com. http://www.cedro-uva.org/lib/levine.secret.html. Accessed on November 2, 2009.

Lines, Rick (2007). *The Death Penalty for Drug Offences: A Violation of International Human Rights Law.* London: International Harm Reduction Association. Also available online at http://www.scribd.com/doc/7979638/Death-Penalty-for-Drug-Offences-A-Violation-of-International-Human-Rights-Law.

Muhammad, Judith K. (2009). "Islam and Addiction." IslamOnline.net. http://www.islamonline.net/servlet/Satellite?c=Article_C&pagename=Zone-English-Family/FYELayout&cid=1157365822643. Accessed on November 2, 2009.

Munroe, Susan (2009). "Marijuana Reform Bill." http://canadaonline.about.com/od/bills/p/mjreform.htm. Accessed on November 10, 2009.

National Legal Database [Vietnam] (2009). http://vbqppl3.moj.gov.vn/law/en/1991_to_2000/1996/199610/199610100001_en/lawdocument_view. Accessed on November 8, 2009.

National Narcotics Board, Republic of Indonesia (1997). "Law of the Republic of Indonesia. Number 22, Year 1997. On Narcotics." http://74.125.155.132/search?q=cache:Gqa4VecjDYJ:www.aseansec.org/Law%2520of%2520the%2520Republic%2520of%2520Indonesia%2520Number%252022,%2520Year%25201997%2520on%2520Narcotics.doc+%22Law+of+the+Republic+of+Indonesia+on+Narcotics%22+ASEANSEC.org&cd=1&hl=en&ct=clnk&gl=us. Accessed on November 8, 2009.

National Portal of Bhutan (2009). "NC Decides to Revoke Tobacco Ban." http://www.bhutan.gov.bt/government/newsDetail.php?id=1331%20&%20cat=5. Accessed on November 12, 2009.

New Zealand Herald (2009). "UK Marijuana Policy Sees Two More Resign." http://www.nzherald.co.nz/united-kingdom/news/article.cfm?l_id=428&objectid=10606766. Accessed on November 11, 2009.

NORML (2008). "Austrian Parliament Approves Medical Marijuana Use." http://norml.org/index.cfm?Group_ID=7654. Accessed on November 12, 2009.

NORML (2003). "Dutch Government Legalizes Prescription Pot Pharmacies Allowed To Distribute Medical Cannabis; Government To License Prescription Pot Growers." http://norml.org/index.cfm?Group_ID=5581. Accessed on November 12, 2009.

Organization of American States (2006). "New Drug Legislation in Brazil." http://www.cicad.oas.org/APPS/Document.aspx?Id=440. Accessed on November 10, 2009.

Philippine Laws, Statutes & Codes (2009). "Republic Act No. 9165." http://74.125.155.132/search?q=cache:7D347Zpuy0UJ:www.aseansec.org/Comprehensive%2520Dangerous%2520Drugs%2520Act%2520of %25202002,%2520Republic%2520Act%2520No.%25209165%2520%2520 Philippines.doc+%22Dangerous+Drugs+Act+of+2002%22+Philippines +aseansec.org&cd=1&hl=en&ct=clnk&gl=us. Accessed on November 8, 2009.

Rushby, Kevin (2001). "Another Day, Another Coup." *Guardian*. http://www.guardian.co.uk/theguardian/2001/oct/01/features11.g2. Accessed on November 11, 2009.

Shadmi, Haim (2009). "Medical Marijuana Transforms into Big Business in Israel." *Haaretz*. http://www.haaretz.com/hasen/spages/1094284 .html. Accessed on November 12, 2009.

Sharma, Anil (2007). "Starting the Day with the Cup That Kicks." *Hindustan Times*. http://www.hindustantimes.com/News-Feed/ rajasthan/Starting-the-day-with-the-cup-that-kicks/Article1-255630 .aspx. Accessed on November 11, 2009.

Singapore Attorney General's Chambers (2009). "Misuse of Drugs Act." http://statutes.agc.gov.sg/non_version/cgi-bin/cgi_retrieve.pl?actno =REVED-185. Accessed on November 9, 2009.

Songwe, Omer (2001). "Cameroon to Import Cannabis." BBC News. http://news.bbc.co.uk/2/hi/africa/1106510.stm. Accessed on November 12, 2009.

StoptheDrugWar.org (2009a). "Africa: Liberia Institutes Draconian New Drug Sentences." http://stopthedrugwar.org/chronicle/604/liberia_harsh _new_drug_law. Accessed on November 9, 2009.

StoptheDrugWar.org (2009b). "Africa: Proposed Draconian Drug Law in Namibia Runs Into Intense Opposition." http://stopthedrugwar.org/ chronicle/472/proposed_namibia_drug_law_runs_into_opposition. Accessed on November 9, 2009.

StoptheDrugWar.org (2009c). "Feature: Mexico and Argentina Enact Drug Decriminalization." http://stopthedrugwar.org/chronicle/599/mexico _argentina_drug_decriminalization. Accessed on November 9, 2009.

StoptheDrugWar.org (2004). "Western Australia Marijuana Moves: Possession Now a Ticketable Offense, Hemp Bill Passes." http:// stopthedrugwar.org/chronicle-old/330/westernau.shtml. Accessed on November 12, 2009.

The Health Report (2009). "Portugal's Drug Laws." http://www.abc.net .au/rn/healthreport/stories/2009/2661510.htm. Accessed on November 10, 2009.

Timelines DB (2009). "Smoking." http://timelinesdb.com/listevents.php ?subjid=398&title=Smoking. Accessed on November 12, 2009.

United Nations (1961). *Single Convention on Narcotic Drugs*. http://www
.incb.org/pdf/e/conv/convention_1961_en.pdf. Accessed on
November 2, 2009.

UN Office on Drugs and Crime (2009). *World Drug Report*. Vienna: United
Nations Office on Drugs and Crime. Also available on the Internet at
http://www.unodc.org/documents/wdr/WDR_2009/WDR2009_eng
_web.pdf.

UN Treaty Collection (2009). "Single Convention on Narcotic Drugs,
1961, as Amended by the Protocol Amending the Single Convention on
Narcotic Drugs, 1961." http://www.unodc.org/unodc/en/treaties/
single-convention.html. Accessed on November 2, 2009.

U.S. Department of State (2009a). "Brunei." http://travel.state.gov/
travel/cis_pa_tw/cis/cis_1073.html. Accessed on November 12, 2009.

U.S. Department of State (2009b). "Malayasia." http://travel.state.gov/
travel/cis_pa_tw/cis/cis_960.html. Accessed on November 11, 2009.

U.S. Department of State (2009c). "Saudi Arabia." http://travel.state.gov/
travel/cis_pa_tw/cis/cis_1012.html. Accessed on November 8, 2009.

U.S. Department of State (2009d). "United Arab Emirates." http://
travel.state.gov/travel/cis_pa_tw/cis/cis_1050.html. Accessed on
November 8, 2009.

Vastag, Brian (2009). "5 Years After: Portugal's Drug Decriminalization
Policy Shows Positive Results." *Scientific American*. http://www
.scientificamerican.com/article.cfm?id=portugal-drug-decriminalization.
Accessed on November 10, 2009.

Verband Bernischer Richter und Richterinnen (Bernese Judge and Judges
Association) (2006). *Richtlinien für die Strafzumessung* (*Guidelines for
Sentencing*), Version 2. Available online (in German) at http://www
.bav-aab.ch/art/pdf/regelemente_richtlinien/VBR-Richtlinien_01-01
-07.pdf. Accessed on November 11, 2009.

Weinberg, Bennett Alan, and Bonnie K. Bealer (2002). *The World of
Caffeine: The Science and Culture of the World's Most Popular Drug*. London:
Routledge.

Weiner, Eric (2005). "The First Nonsmoking Nation?" *Slate*. http://
www.slate.com/id/2112449/. Accessed on November 12, 2009.

World Health Organization (2003). *Draft WHO Framework Convention on
Tobacco Control*. March 3. [no location: no publisher]. Available online at
http://apps.who.int/gb/fctc/PDF/inb6/einb65.pdf. Accessed on
November 12, 2009.

World Health Organization (2009). "Tobacco Free Initiative." http://
www.emro.who.int/tfi/Giant-TobaccoFreePublic.htm. Accessed on
November 12, 2009.

World Lung Foundation (2009). "Smoke-Free Areas." *Tobacco Atlas.* http://www.cancer.org/downloads/AA/TobaccoAtlas3Revised/TA3 _Chapter_23.pdf. Accessed on November 13, 2009.

Worth, Robert F. (2009). "Thirsty Plant Steals Water in Dry Yemen." *New York Times*, November 1.

4

Chronology

The use of natural plant products to produce altered states of consciousness dates to the earliest years of human history. There has hardly been a period since then when substances such as cocaine, opiates, marijuana and other cannabis products, and a host of other natural and synthetic materials have not been used for such effects. This chapter lists a number of important events in the history of the use of psychoactive substances in human cultures, along with a number of efforts to control the use of such products.

ca. 50,000 BCE	Archaeologists discover remains of the herbal stimulant ephedra at a burial site in Iraq dated to about 50,000 years ago.
ca. 10,000 BCE	Among products discovered at the earliest agricultural sites, dating to about 10,000 years ago, are cannabis, tobacco, and mandrake, which contains hallucinogenic alkaloids.
ca. 7000– 9000 BCE	Prehistoric rock art suggests the use of psychedelic mushrooms by early humans.
ca. 7000 BCE	Seeds of the betel nut, still chewed today for their stimulant effects in many parts of the world, are found at sites dating to 7,000 years ago.

ca. 7000 BCE	Clay vessels containing remnants of wine dating to about 7000 BCE are found at the site of a Neolithic village in Iran.
ca. 6000 BCE	The first cultivation of tobacco in the New World (South America) dates to about 6000 BCE.
ca. 4300 BCE	The first recipes for making beer, recorded on clay tablets from Babylonia, date to about 4300 BCE.
3300 BCE	The earliest written records of the use of opium date to about 3300 BCE, although evidence for its cultivation dates to about 1,000 years earlier.
3000 BCE	Charred seeds of the cannabis plant found in a ritual brazier at a burial site in modern-day Romania, suggesting that they were used in a religious ceremony, are found in modern day Romania at a location that dates to about 3000 BCE.
2500– 1800 BCE	The earliest evidence for the cultivation of the coca plant in northern Peru dates to 2500–1800 BCE.
5th century CE	Greek historian Herodotus records the use of cannabis as a recreational drug by the Scythians in his *Persian Wars*.
620 CE	In one of the earliest (perhaps the earliest) attempts at regulating drinking, the prophet Muhammed prohibits the consumption of alcohol by Muslims (Qur'an 2:219 and 5:91).
1484	Pope Innocent VIII bans the use of cannabis. His action was part of the Church's program against heretics because common belief at the time was that witches used cannabis as an "antisacrament" in place of wine at their "black masses."
1493	Christopher Columbus and his crew, returning from America, introduce the use of tobacco products to Europe.

ca. 1525   The Swiss-Austrian physician and alchemist Phillip
            von Hohenheim (better known as Paracelsus) introdu-
            ces the use of a tincture of opium called *laudanum* to
            medical practice in Europe. He has learned about the
            beneficial effects of the substance during his visits to
            the Middle East.

1590   A Japanese law makes possession of tobacco illegal.
            Anyone found with the substance is subject to impris-
            onment and/or loss of property.

1613–1614   John Rolfe, husband of the Indian princess Pocahontas,
            sends the first shipment of tobacco from the New
            World to Europe.

1619   The Jamestown Colony adopts the first so-called
            "must grow" law for hemp, noting that the product
            has many useful applications. Other colonies soon
            adopt similar laws as a way of improving the supply
            of an essential raw material in difficult economic
            times.

1633   The Sultan Murad IV of Turkey declares the use of
            tobacco a capital offense, punished by hanging,
            beheading, or starvation.

1638   A Chinese law declares use of tobacco a capital
            offense, to be punished by beheading.

1690   The British Parliament passes an Act for the Encour-
            aging of the Distillation of Brandy and Spirits from
            Corn, which results in the production of about a mil-
            lion gallons of alcoholic beverages, primarily gin,
            only four years later.

1736   Concerned about the widespread popularity of gin
            among all classes, the British Parliament passes the
            Gin Act, which raises taxes on the drink to 20 shil-
            lings per gallon, a point at which only members of
            the upper classes can afford the substance.

1751   The British Parliament passes a new Gin Act. After the Gin Act of 1736 resulted in riots in the streets, it was revoked for a few years, before being reimposed by this act, which imposes a tax of five shillings per gallon on gin.

1785   In his book *An Inquiry into the Effects of Ardent Spirits Upon the Human Body and Mind*, physician Benjamin Rush calls the intemperate use of alcohol a disease and lists a number of symptoms, such as unusual garrulity, unusual silence, profane swearing and cursing, a clipping of words, fighting, and certain extravagant acts which indicate a temporary fit of madness, such as singing, roaring, and imitating the noises of brute animals. He estimates the annual death rate from alcoholism at about 4,000 in a population of about six million.

1789   An estimated 200 farmers living in the vicinity of Litchfield, Connecticut, meet to form the nation's first temperance society.

1791   The U.S. Congress enacts the nation's first tax on whiskey, the so-called "whiskey tax."

1793–1797   Opposition to the whiskey tax of 1791 leads to outbreaks of violence in various parts of Pennsylvania, all of which are eventually put down by federal forces.

ca. 1800   Members of Napoleon's army, returning from the war in Egypt, bring with them information about the use of cannabis (in the form of hashish and marijuana) to France. Medical personnel are impressed by the pain-killing properties of the drug, and some members of the general public are more interested in its use as a recreational drug.

1802   The whiskey tax of 1791 is repealed.

1805   German chemist Friedrich Sertürner extracts morphine from opium. He names the substance after Morpheus, the Greek god of dreams.

1819   German chemist Friedrich Ferdinand Runge isolates caffeine from coffee.

1848   President James Polk signs the Drug Importation Act, which establishes standards for the purity of drugs imported to the United States. The act is necessitated primarily by the fact that the United States is the last major nation in the world without legislation of this kind. The act does not, however, establish standards for drugs manufactured domestically.

1859   As a doctoral student, German chemist Albert Niemann obtains pure cocaine from coca leaves.

1868   In one of the first efforts to regulate the sale and use of drugs, the British Parliament passes the Pharmacy Act, which makes it illegal to sell opium and other drugs without a license.

1870   In New York City, a group of "scientific and medical gentlemen" found the American Association for the Cure of Inebriates, with the goals of studying the condition of "inebriety," discussing its proper treatment, and bringing about a "co-operative public sentiment and jurisprudence." The action was significant because it was one of the first times that the medical profession acknowledged that alcoholism might be a hereditary disease that could be treated like other medical conditions.

1875   The city of San Francisco adopts an ordinance prohibiting the smoking of opium, apparently the first law in the United States to deal with the practice.

1884   Largely through the influence of the Women's Christian Temperance Union, the New York state legislature passes a bill requiring the inclusion of an anti-alcohol curriculum in all schools in the state. Pennsylvania follows suit the next year, as do many other states in succeeding years.

1887   Romanian chemist Lazar Edeleanu first synthesizes amphetamine in an effort to make ephedrine synthetically. With no known use, the compound is essentially forgotten for about 40 years.

1893   Japanese chemist Nagayoshi Nagai synthesizes methamphetamine.

1902   Physician C. B. Burr writes in the *Journal of the American Medical Association* about the problems of morphine addiction and its treatment. This article is one of the earliest commentaries on the addictive properties of morphine and heroin and their potential medical implications.

1906   The U.S. Congress passes the Pure Food and Drug Law, among whose provision is a requirement that all products containing alcohol be labeled to indicate that fact.

1909   The U.S. Congress passes the Smoking Opium Exclusion Act, the first federal regulation of the nonmedical use of a substance. The law bans the importation, possession, and smoking of opium.

1910   New York becomes the first state to adopt a drunk driving law.

1912   The International Opium Convention is signed at The Hague, the Netherlands, signed by China, France, Germany, Italy, Japan, the Netherlands, Persia, Portugal, Russia, Siam, the United States, and the United Kingdom. The convention called on all signatories to make every effort to control "all persons manufacturing, importing, selling, distributing, and exporting morphine, cocaine, and their respective salts, as well as the buildings in which these persons carry such an industry or trade." The convention is the first effort at reaching an international agreement on the control of illicit drugs.

The first opium clinic in the United States is opened by Dr. Charles Terry, public health officer in

Jacksonville, Florida. The purpose of this and similar clinics is to provide support for drug addicts who, because of new laws and regulations (primarily at the state level), are unable to obtain the drugs to which they are addicted from physicians or other sources.

1913   New York State passes a strict law prohibiting the use of cocaine for other than specific medical, dental, and veterinary purposes.

1914   The Harrison Act requires importers, exporters, manufacturers, and distributors of all opiate products to register with the U.S. government and pay taxes on their sales. The act does not make the use of opiates illegal.

1916   In the case of *United States v. Jin Fuey Moy* (241 U.S. 394 [1916]), the U.S. Supreme Court severely restricts implementation of the Harrison Act, passed two years earlier.

1919   Secretary of State Francis Polk certifies the ratification of the Eighteenth Amendment to the U.S. Constitution, placing severe restrictions on the manufacture, sale, and transportation of "intoxicating liquors" within the United States. The amendment was eventually ratified by every state in the union except for Connecticut and Rhode Island.

The International Opium Convention is incorporated into the conditions of the Versailles Peace Treaty signed at the end of World War I. This action obligated all signatories to the peace treaty to become signatories to the opium treaty also.

1922   The Narcotic Import and Export Act restricts the importation of crude opium except for medical use.

1924   The Heroin Act makes the manufacture and possession of heroin illegal.

1925   The last narcotics clinic in the United States (see 1912) in Knoxville, Tennessee, is closed by the U.S. Treasury Department.

1927   The Bureau of Prohibition in the Bureau of Internal Revenue is established as the enforcement arm of the Eighteenth Amendment to the Constitution, which had been adopted in 1919.

1928   Great Britain bans the use of cannabis for non-medical purposes.

1930   The Federal Bureau of Narcotics is established to enforce provisions of the Harrison Narcotic Act of 1914 and the Narcotic Drugs Import and Export Act of 1922.

1931   At a meeting held in Geneva, a group of nations adopt the Convention for Limiting the Manufacture and Regulating the Distribution of Narcotic Drugs in an effort to bring under control the manufacture, distribution, and use of a number of narcotic drugs. The convention establishes two groups of drugs, one consisting of morphine, cocaine, heroin, and dihydrohydrooxycodeinone and related compounds, and one consisting of codeine, ethylmorphine, and related compounds. The convention enters into force in 1933.

1932   The U.S. Congress passes the Uniform State Narcotics Act, which encourages all states to adopt model legislation described in the act so that the same penalties for drug use will be applied throughout the nation. By the mid-1930s, all states have adopted the model legislation, essentially establishing a national drug policy.

                The pharmaceutical firm of Smith, Kline, and French markets amphetamine as benzedrine, an over-the-counter inhalant for respiratory congestion.

1933   Secretary of State Cordell Hull certifies the ratification of the Twenty First Amendment to the United States, nullifying the Eighteenth Amendment and ending national laws against the manufacture, sale, and transportation of alcohol beverages in the United States.

1935   Two American alcoholics, William Griffith ("Bill") Wilson and Robert Holbrook ("Bob") Smith, found Alcoholics Anonymous.

1936   A film entitled *Reefer Madness* about the dangers of smoking marijuana is released to the general public. The film is reputedly produced originally by a small church group aimed at frightening their youth members about the risks of substance abuse. Although produced at little cost with a cast of essentially unknown actors, the film has come to be a cult classic and, in 2001, premiers as an off-Broadway musical show.

Representatives of a number of nations meet in Geneva to adopt the Convention for the Suppression of the Illicit Traffic in Dangerous Drugs, an effort to criminalize trafficking in illegal drugs. When the United States finds itself unable to support the final document, it loses any chance of being a strong step in preventing the worldwide distribution of illegal drugs.

1937   The American Medical Association endorses the sale of amphetamine tablets for the treatment of narcolepsy and attention deficit hyperactivity disorder (ADHD).

The Marijuana Tax Act imposes a tax on anyone who deals in any form of cannabis, hemp, or marijuana. The act does not criminalize the use of marijuana, but it does provide for severe penalties for anyone who fails to pay the tax associated with cannabis use.

1941–1945 The U.S. government distributes both amphetamine and methamphetamine to military personnel to improve their performance in battle.

1942   The Opium Poppy Control Act prohibits the growing of opium poppies (*Papaver somniferum*) in the United States.

1948   The United Nations sponsors an international conference to update a treaty for the control of narcotic drugs signed in 1931. The document signed at the meeting is called the Protocol Bringing under International Control Drugs outside the Scope of the Convention of 13 July 1931 for Limiting the Manufacture and Regulating the Distribution of Narcotic Drugs. It takes an important step in recognizing that a number of substances not previously defined formally as illegal substances—including a number of synthetic products—have effects similar to those of marijuana, cocaine, heroin, morphine, and other "traditional" drugs.

1951   The Boggs Act increases federal penalties for violations of federal drug laws. The act is the first piece of legislation in which marijuana and other illegal drugs are given equal treatment.

In Executive Order 10302, President Harry S Truman creates the Interdepartmental Committee on Narcotics, consisting of one representative each from the departments of Treasury, State, Defense, Justice, and Agriculture, and of the Federal Security Agency to maintain information about illegal drugs, to study problems of prevention and treatment, and to advise the President on national drug policy. The committee is the first such body to be established within the federal government.

Lois W., wife of Bill W., cofounder of Alcoholics Anonymous, and Anne B. found Al-Anon, a support group for family members of alcoholics.

1956   The Narcotics Control Act further increases federal penalties for violations of federal drug laws.

1957   The teenage son of alcoholic parents and members of Alcoholics Anonymous in California form Alateen, an organization designed to provide support for the children of one or more alcoholic parents. A year later, the organization is adopted by Al-Anon as a special committee of the organization.

1961   A conference sponsored by the United Nations adopts the Single Convention on Narcotic Drugs, an effort to update and consolidate a number of previously adopted conventions, protocols, and agreements on the manufacture, distribution, and sale of illegal drugs, including the International Opium Convention of 1912; the Agreement Concerning the Manufacture of, Internal Trade in and Use of Prepared Opium of 1925; the International Opium Convention of 1925; the Convention for Limiting the Manufacture and Regulating the Distribution of Narcotic Drugs of 1931; the Agreement for the Control of Opium Smoking in the Far East of 1931; the Protocol Amending the Agreements, Conventions and Protocols on Narcotic Drugs of 1912; 1925, 1931, 1936, and 1946; the Protocol Bringing under International Control Drugs Outside the Scope of the Convention of 1931; and the Protocol for Limiting and Regulating the Cultivation of the Poppy Plant, the Production of, International and Wholesale Trade in, and Use of Opium of 1953.

1964   In the largest and most definitive study of its kind, the so-called "Grand Rapids Study" finds that the risk of a driver's being involved in an accident rises sharply with his or her blood alcohol concentration. These findings are replicated a number of times in the future with a variety of modifications in variables studied.

1965   The Drug Abuse Control Amendments Act is passed for the purpose of dealing with problems caused by the use of stimulants, depressants, and hallucinogens. It authorizes the Food and Drug Administration to designate such drugs as controlled substances and to require that a federal license be obtained for their distribution and sale. The possession of small amounts of such drugs for personal use is allowed.

1965
(*cont.*)
An advisory committee to the Surgeon General issues a report, *Smoking and Health*, that represents the first significant review of the health effects of smoking. The report is instrumental in the passage in the same year of the Federal Cigarette Labeling and Advertising Act, which, among other provisions, requires that all cigarette packages carry the warning label: "Caution: Cigarette Smoking May Be Hazardous to Your Health."

1968
The Bureau of Narcotics and Dangerous Drugs is formed as an agency within the U.S. Department of Justice. It combines the preexisting Bureau of Narcotics and Bureau of Drug Abuse Control.

1969
The Public Health Cigarette Smoking Act of 1969 amends the 1965 Federal Cigarette Labeling and Advertising Act to require the following warning on all cigarette packages: "The Surgeon General Has Determined That Cigarette Smoking is Dangerous to Your Health."

1970
The U.S. Congress passes the Comprehensive Drug Abuse Prevention and Control Act in an effort to consolidate a number of earlier laws regulating the manufacture and distribution of narcotics, stimulants, depressants, hallucinogens, anabolic steroids, and chemicals used in the production of controlled substances. Title II of the act is called the Controlled Substances Act, which establishes a five-tier system of categorizing drugs that is still used today.

The U.S. Congress passes legislation banning cigarette advertising on television and radio. The ban takes effect in 1971.

The cigarette industry voluntarily agrees to list tar and nicotine content on all cigarette packages.

The U.S. Congress passes the Comprehensive Alcohol Abuse and Alcoholism Prevention, Treatment, and Rehabilitation Act of 1970. One provision of the act establishes the National Institute on Alcoholism and Alcohol Abuse (NIAAA), with the responsibility of conducting intramural research and supporting extramural research on issues of alcoholism and alcohol abuse.

1971   President Richard M. Nixon declares a "war on drugs," calling for an aggressive anti-drug policy at both federal and state level. He calls drug abuse "Public Enemy #1" in the United States.

The United Nations Protocol on Psychotropic Substances is adopted in Vienna. The purpose of the protocol is to expand coverage of the 1961 Single Convention on Narcotic Drugs (which covered natural substances and their derivatives exclusively) to a host of synthetic psychotropic substances, such as ketamine, ephedrine, 3,4-methylenedioxymethamphetamine (MDMA), and tetrahydrocannabinol not covered by the 1931 agreement.

1972   The National Commission on Marijuana and Drug Abuse (also known as the Shafer Commission, after its chairman) issues its report, recommending, among other things, that simple possession of marijuana be decriminalized and that all distinctions between legal and illegal drugs be dropped. The commission has been created by the U.S. Congress by Public Law 91–513 to study the problem of substance abuse in the United States. President Richard M. Nixon declines to implement any of the commission's recommendations.

1973   As part of the Reorganization Plan No. 2 of 1973, President Richard M. Nixon establishes the Drug Enforcement Agency to replace the Bureau of Narcotics and Dangerous Drugs, the Office of Drug Abuse Law Enforcement, and a handful of other federal agencies with drug control responsibilities.

The Methadone Control Act provides funding for the establishment of clinics through which recovering

1973
(*cont.*)

heroin addicts can receive methadone therapy. Doctors at this point are no longer allowed to write prescriptions for methadone for the same purpose.

1974

The National Institute on Drug Abuse is created to conduct research on drug abuse and drug addiction.

1976

The Democratic Party national platform calls for decriminalization of marijuana, with the abolishment of all penalties for possession of one ounce or less of the drug.

1978

The U.S. Food and Drug Administration introduces the Compassionate Investigational New Drug program, allowing a small number of patients to use marijuana grown at a federal facility at the University of Mississippi to relieve symptoms of medical conditions. Currently seven individuals remain in that program.

The U.S. Congress passes the American Indian Religious Freedom Act that acknowledges the elements of traditional Native American religious ceremonies and the conflicts that may arise between those ceremonies and some U.S. laws. It declares that Native Americans do have the right to practice their traditional religious customs. The use of peyote is implicitly, but not explicitly, guaranteed by this act.

1984

The 1965 Federal Cigarette Labeling and Advertising Act is amended to require that one of four warning labels appear in a specific format on cigarette packages and in most related advertising: "SURGEON GENERAL'S WARNING: Smoking Causes Lung Cancer, Heart Disease, Emphysema, and May Complicate Pregnancy," "SURGEON GENERAL'S WARNING: Quitting Smoking Now Greatly Reduces Serious Risks to Your Health," "SURGEON GENERAL'S WARNING: Smoking By Pregnant Women May Result in Fetal Injury, Premature Birth, and Low Birth Weight," or "SURGEON GENERAL'S WARNING: Cigarette Smoke Contains Carbon Monoxide."

The U.S. Congress passes the National Minimum Drinking Age Act (also known as the Uniform Drinking Age Act) requiring all states to raise the minimum age for drinking to 21. Any state that refuses to adopt this standard is subject to loss of 10 percent of the funds due it annually under the Federal Aid Highway Act.

First Lady Nancy Reagan launches her "Just Say No" campaign against drug use.

The U.S. Congress passes the Comprehensive Crime Control Act as an amendment to the Controlled Substance Act of 1970, allowing the administrator of the Drug Enforcement Administration to classify a substance as a Schedule I drug on a temporary (up to one year) basis without the normal legislative action needed for such a decision.

1985   Minnesota becomes the first state to enact legislation setting aside a portion of the state tobacco tax for smoking prevention programs.

1986   The U.S. Congress passes the Anti-Drug Abuse Act of 1986. The act consists of two major titles, one dealing with Anti-Drug Enforcement, and the other with International Narcotics Control. The first title is divided into 21 subtitles dealing with a host of issues, perhaps the most important of which is Subtitle E: Controlled Substances Analogue Enforcement Act of 1986, which states that substances that are chemically and pharmacologically similar to substances listed in Schedule I or Schedule II of the Controlled Substances Act of 1970 (known as analogues of the listed drugs) are also classified as Schedule I drugs. Perhaps the most controversial section is Subtitle B: Drug Possession Penalty Act of 1986, which establishes the so-called 100-to-1 rule, in which possession of 100 grams of powder cocaine (the drug of choice among wealthy white Americans) is considered to be legally equivalent to 1 gram of crack cocaine (used most commonly by Blacks).

1986
(*cont.*)

President Ronald Reagan signs Executive Order 12564 requiring all federal agencies to establish drug-free workplace programs.

1988

The Anti-Drug Abuse Act of 1988 for the first time imposes penalties on the users of illegal drugs. Prior to this time, penalties for illegal drug use were limited to the producers and distributors of such substances. One provision of the act establishes the Office of National Drug Control Policy, with responsibility for developing policies for control of the nation's drug abuse problems. First director of the office is William Bennett.

Francis L. Young, administrative law judge at the Drug Enforcement Agency (DEA), issues an opinion that marijuana has clear and unquestionable medical uses and should be reclassified as a Schedule II drug from its current status as a Schedule I drug. The DEA declines to act on that recommendation.

The U.S. Congress passes the Chemical Diversion and Trafficking Act, whose purpose it is to reduce the supply of precursor chemicals and manufacturing devices (such as pill machines) used in the manufacture of drugs. Prior to the law, the United States was the major supplier of these materials to (primarily) South America companies, where raw materials were converted to commercial-grade drugs.

The U.S. Congress passes the Drug Free Workplace Act, which extends President Ronald Reagan's 1986 executive order to require all contractors and grantees of the federal government to develop programs for a drug-free workplace.

1990

The U.S. Congress passes legislation banning smoking on all U.S. commercial airline flights.

1992

President George H. W. Bush discontinues the Food and Drug Administration's Compassionate Investigational

New Drug program because it conflicts with his administration's drug use policies.

1993   The U.S. Congress passes the Native American Free Exercise of Religion Act, which confirms, clarifies, and expands the American Indian Religious Freedom Act of 1978. In particular, it specifically allows the use of peyote, a drug banned by the Controlled Substance Act of 1970.

1994   China passes the nation's first laws requiring health warnings on cigarette packages, limiting tobacco advertising, and initiating anti-smoking programs.

China passes the nation's first laws requiring health warnings on cigarette packages, limiting tobacco advertising, and initiating anti-smoking programs.

Mississippi becomes the first state to sue the tobacco industry to recover costs for tobacco-related illnesses.

The Omnibus Crime Bill, introduced by then-Senator Joseph Biden (D–DE) introduces the death penalty for anyone convicted to operating large-scale drug distribution programs, one of the first times the death penalty is permitted for crimes in which a death is not involved.

1995   The U.S. Sentencing Commission issues a report to the U.S. Congress confirming that serious racial imbalances exist in sentencing for powder cocaine and "crack" cocaine and recommending the Congress act to ameliorate these disparities. Congress declines to do so, one of the very few times in history it refuses to follow the commission's recommendations.

In the case of *Vernonia School District 47J, Petitioner V. Wayne Acton, et ux.*, the U.S. Supreme Court rules, in a vote of 6 to 3, that a school district may impose suspicionless drug tests on students who wish to engage in extracurricular activities.

1996   Arizona voters pass Proposition 200, otherwise known as the Drug, Medicalization, Prevention and Punishment Act, which requires that a person convicted of

1996
(*cont.*)

possession or use of an illegal drug receive drug treatment for the first and second offense, and a prison term only after the third such conviction. Physicians in the state are also authorized to write prescriptions for Schedule I drugs when federal law permits such actions.

The U.S. Congress passes the Drug-Induced Rape Prevention and Punishment Act, which provides for penalties of up to 20 years in prison for supplying a drug to another person with the intent of committing a crime, such as rape, against that person. The primary motivation for the act is the spread of so-called "date rape," in which one person provides a second person with a psychoactive drug—most commonly ketamine, gamma hydroxybutyrate (GHB), gamma butyrolactone (GBL), or Rohypnol—without that second person's knowledge or approval.

California voters pass Proposition 215, the Compassionate Use Act of 1996, which allows individuals with a doctor's prescription to grow small amounts of marijuana for their own personal medical use.

The U.S. Congress passes the Comprehensive Methamphetamine Control Act, which further restricts the sale of precursors used in the production of methamphetamine, such as pseudoephedrine, iodine, red phosphorus, and hydrochloric acid.

1997

The tobacco industry reaches a settlement with 46 state attorneys general to pay $360 billion over a period of 25 years to fund anti-smoking campaigns, to add health warnings to cigarette packages, and to pay substantial fines if the number of teenage smokers is not reduced.

For the first time in history, a major tobacco executive, Bennett LeBow, CEO of Liggett, admits during public testimony that cigarette smoking causes cancer.

1998   The U.S. Congress passes the Controlled Substances
          Trafficking Prohibition Act, which limits the amount
          of certain controlled substances that a person can bring
          into the United States for personal use to 50 pills or
          less or a two-week supply. The law is designed to
          remove a loophole which previously allowed individ-
          uals to bring back unlimited quantities of Schedule II
          drugs, supposedly for their own personal medical
          needs but, in reality, for resale in the United States.

2000   The U.S. Supreme Court rules that the Food and Drug
          Administration does not have the authority to regu-
          late tobacco products.

          The Drug Addiction Treatment Act of 2000 allows
          certain qualifying physicians to treat patients with
          opioid addictions using substances on Schedules III,
          IV, and V of the Controlled Substances Act. The only
          drug that meets this specification is buprenorphine.

          President Bill Clinton signs a new federal law requir-
          ing all states to pass a law setting a blood alcohol con-
          centration (BAC) of 0.08 percent as the legal limit.
          States that do not adopt this standard are to be denied
          a portion of the federal highway funding normally
          due them. Eventually 49 states do adopt such laws,
          the only exception being Massachusetts, where a
          BAC of 0.08 percent is consider legal proof of impair-
          ment, but is not illegal in and out itself.

          The U.S. government gives $1.3 billion to Colombia
          for the purpose of improving its anti-drug campaign.
          The money is designated to be used for aerial spray-
          ing of coca and other drug crops, for training of
          Colombian troops in anti-drug programs, and for
          the purchase of equipment, such as helicopters, to be
          used against drug manufacturers and distributors.

2001   In the case of *United States v. Oakland Cannabis Buyers'
          Cooperative* 532 U.S. 483 (2001), the U.S. Supreme Court
          unanimously rules that marijuana has no medical

2001 (*cont.*)	value and that its sale by the Oakland Cannabis Buyers' Cooperative (and similar organizations) is illegal.
2002	The British government changes its policies on the use of cannabis products, downgrading the drug from Class B to Class C. That change leaves the drug as an illegal substance, although an arrest for possession is likely to result in confiscation of the drug and a warning, but no prosecution, prison time, or fine.
2003	All forms of advertising for tobacco products in the United Kingdom is banned. A ban by the European Union on the use of the terms "light" or "mild" on cigarette packages takes effect. The same regulations require that health warnings cover at least 30 percent of the front and 40 percent of the back of all cigarette packages. Concerned about the estimated 30,000 deaths annually caused by smoking, French president Jacques Chirac announces a "war on smoking" that includes an investment of more than $500 million for anti-smoking campaigns, a near doubling of cigarette taxes, and greater limitations on places that people may smoke.
2004	All forms of advertising and promotions for tobacco products are banned in India.
2005	The U.S. Congress passes and President George W. Bush signs the USA PATRIOT Improvement and Reauthorization Act which includes, as an unrelated amendment, a version of the Combat Meth Act, originally proposed by Senator James Talent (R-MO). One of the primary features of the act is the imposition of severe restrictions on the sale of cough and cold products whose ingredients can be used in the manufacture of methamphetamine.

In the case of *Gonzalez v. Raich* 545 U.S. 1 (2005), the U.S. Supreme Court rules, by a vote of 6 to 3, that it is illegal for medical doctors to write prescriptions for their patients to use marijuana for medical purposes.

2006   In the case of *United States of America v. Philip Morris, USA, Inc., et al.*, Civil Action No. 99-CV-02496 (GK) (2006), Judge Gladys Kessler finds that U.S. tobacco companies have engaged in a "massive 50-year scheme to defraud the public, including consumers of cigarettes, in violation of RICO [Racketeer Influenced and Corrupt Organizations Act of 1970]." She imposes a fine of $280 billion on the tobacco companies.

2009   Congress approves the largest ever increase in the federal cigarette tax, boosting it 62 cents, to $1.01 a pack.

The U.S. Congress passes and President Barack Obama signs the Family Smoking Prevention and Tobacco Control and Federal Retirement Reform act, which authorizes the Food and Drug Administration to regulate cigarettes and other tobacco products.

5

Biographical Sketches

Any history of drugs, substance abuse, alcoholism, smoking, and the political, legal, and social issues surrounding these topics must include a long list of women and men who have had a significant impact on that history. Some individuals have conducted research on these substances; others have advocated for or against their use; still others have devoted their lives to developing prevention programs or methods of treatment; and many have been involved in the development of local, state, national, or international policy with respect to substance use and abuse. This chapter provides biographies of a number of individuals, with a review of their contribution to the history of substance abuse, as well as a brief biographical sketch of each person.

Richard Alpert (Ram Dass; 1931–)

During the 1960s, Alpert was involved in research on psychoactive substances at Harvard University, along with his good friend and colleague Timothy Leary. He later spent time studying spiritualism in India and devoted the greatest part of his life to studying and teaching about this subject in the United States.

Richard Alpert was born on April 6, 1931, in Newton, Massachusetts. His father was a prominent attorney, president of the New York, New Haven, and Hartford railroad, and a founder of Brandeis University and the Albert Einstein College of Medicine in New York City. Alpert received his B.A. from Tufts University, his M.A. in motivation psychology from Wesleyan University, and his Ph.D. in human development from Stanford

University. He then accepted a teaching and research post in the Department of Social Relations and the Graduate School of Education at Harvard University. While at Harvard, he met Timothy Leary, from whom he learned about the psychoactive effects of a number of substances. Between 1960 and 1961, Alpert and Leary began a series of experiments on psilocybin, using graduate students at their subjects. The direction of these experiments was sufficiently troubling to Harvard administrators that both men were dismissed from their academic positions. That move was of little concern to Alpert, who later said that he had already become disillusioned with academics as a "meaningless pursuit."

In 1967, Alpert traveled to India, where he met his spiritual teacher, Neem Karoli Baba, and received his new name, Ram Dass, or "servant of God." He has spent the rest of his life studying a variety of spiritualistic philosophies, including Hinduism, karma, yoga, and Sufism. He is probably best known today not for his early studies of psychoactive substances, but for his 1971 book, *Be Here Now*. His other publications include *The Psychedelic Experience: A Manual Based on the Tibetan Book of the Dead* (with Leary and Ralph Metzner); *Doing Your Own Being* (1973); *The Only Dance There Is* (1974); *Journey of Awakening: A Meditator's Guidebook* (1978); *Compassion in Action: Setting Out on the Path of Service* (with Mirabai Bush; 1991); *Still Here: Embracing Aging, Changing and Dying* (2000); and *Paths to God: Living The Bhagavad Gita* (2004). In 1997, Alpert suffered a stroke that paralyzed the right side of his body and left him with Broca's aphasia, a brain condition that makes speech difficult. Nonetheless, he continues to write, teach, and lecture, as his condition permits.

Harry J. Anslinger (1892–1975)

Anslinger was appointed the first commissioner of the Federal Bureau of Narcotics when it was established in 1930. He held that office for 32 years, one of the longest tenures of any federal official in modern history. He was consistently a strong advocate for severe penalties against the manufacture, distribution, sale, and use of certain drugs, especially marijuana.

Harry Jacob Anslinger was born in Altoona, Pennsylvania, on May 20, 1892, to Robert J. and Rosa Christiana Fladt Anslinger, immigrants from Switzerland and Germany, respectively. Upon completing high school, Anslinger attended the Altoona Business College before taking a job with the Pennsylvania Railroad.

He received a leave of absence from the railway that allowed him to matriculate at Pennsylvania State College (now Pennsylvania State University), where he received his two-year associate degree in engineering and business management. From 1917 to 1928, Anslinger worked for a number of private and governmental agencies on problems of illegal drug use, a job that took him to a number of countries around the world. He has been credited with helping to shape drug policies both in the United States and in a number of foreign countries where he worked or consulted.

In 1929, Anslinger was appointed assistant commissioner in the United States Bureau of Prohibition, a position he held only briefly before being selected as the first commissioner of the newly created Federal Bureau of Narcotics in 1930. He assumed that post at a time when state and federal officials were debating the need (or lack of need) for regulations of hemp and marijuana. Both hemp and marijuana are obtained from plants in the genus Cannabis, the former with many important industrial applications, and the latter used almost exclusively as a recreational drug. Historians have discussed the motivations that may have driven Anslinger's attitudes about the subject, but his actions eventually demonstrated a very strong opposition to the growing, processing, distribution, and use of all products of the Cannabis plant. He was instrumental in formulating federal policies and laws against such use that developed during the 1930s.

Anslinger remained in his post until 1970, staying on even after his seventieth birthday until a replacement was found. He then served two more years as U.S. representative to the United Nations Narcotic Convention. By the end of his tenure with the convention, he was blind and suffered from both angina and an enlarged prostate. He died in Hollidaysburg, Pennsylvania, on November 14, 1975, of heart failure.

Steve Bechler (1979–2003)

Bechler, a pitcher in the Baltimore Orioles professional baseball organization, died on February 17, 2003, after using the herbal supplement ephedra in an ongoing effort to lose weight. He is only one of many professional and amateur athletes who have died or suffered permanent physical or mental injury from using both legal and illegal drugs to achieve an increase in desirable physical traits, such as strength, speed, or endurance.

Steven Scott Bechler was born in Medford, Oregon, on November 18, 1979. He attended South Medford High School, from which he graduated in 1998. He was then selected by the Orioles in the third round of the national baseball draft and assigned to the Gulf Coast Orioles in the Gulf Coast League. The following year he played for the Delmarva Shorebirds in the Class A South Atlantic League, and was then promoted to the Frederick Keys of the Class A+ Carolina League in 2000 and 2001 and to the Bowie Baysox in the Class AA Eastern League and the Rochester Redwings in the Class AAA International League in 2001 and 2002. At the end of 2002, he was called up to the home club and pitched four and one-third innings, ending with an earned run average of 13.52. He was given a better than average chance of making the Orioles for the 2003 season when he died during spring training for that season.

Weight control had long been a problem for Bechler, and he tried a number of methods of reducing his weight. During the 2003 spring training season, he apparently used various legal drug combinations to achieve this goal, one of which contained the drug ephedrine (also known as ephedra). During a workout after having taken the drug, Bechler's temperature rose to 108 degrees, and he collapsed, suffered multi-organ failure, and died the following day at the Orioles' training camp in Fort Lauderdale, Florida. Ephedrine had previously been banned by the International Olympic Committee, the National Football League, and the National Collegiate Athletic Association, but not by Major League Baseball (MLB). It has since been placed on the MLB list of banned substances.

William Bennett (1943–)

Bennett was named the first director of the Office of National Drug Control Policy in 1989 by President George H. W. Bush. That office had been created by the Anti-Drug Abuse Act of 1988.

William John Bennett was born in Brooklyn, New York, on July 31, 1943, but later moved to Washington, D.C. He graduated from Gonzaga High School in Washington and attended Williams College in Williamstown, Massachusetts, from which he earned his B.A. in philosophy in 1965. He then continued his education at the University of Texas, from which he received his Ph.D. in philosophy in 1970, and at Harvard Law School, which granted him a J.D. in 1971. He has held teaching posts at Boston University, the University of North Carolina at Chapel Hill, and North Carolina State University, although he is probably best known as a conservative writer, speaker, commentator, and political theorist.

Bennett's political career began in 1981 when President Ronald Reagan appointed him to the post of president of the National Endowment for the Humanities. He remained there until 1985, when Reagan appointed him Secretary of the Department of Education (DOE), a post he held for three years. After leaving the DOE, Bennett was appointed the first director of the White House Office of National Drug Control Policy, where he remained until the end of President Bush's term in 1991. Throughout his public and private careers, Bennett has taken strong stances against substance abuse, abortion, and other activities to which he is opposed. In an appearance on the Larry King Live radio show on June 15, 1989, for example, he said in response to a caller's suggestion that drug dealers be beheaded that "Morally, I don't have a problem with that at all."

In addition to his many speaking appearances before public audiences and on television and radio, Bennett has been a prolific author with more than a dozen books to his credit, including *The Book of Virtues: A Treasury of Great Moral Stories*, *The Children's Book of Virtues*, *The Death of Outrage: Bill Clinton and the Assault on American Ideals*, *The American Patriot's Almanac: Daily Readings on America* (with John Cribb), *Why We Fight: Moral Clarity and the War on Terrorism*, *The Broken Hearth: Reversing the Moral Collapse of the American Family*, and *Body Count: Moral Poverty . . . and How to Win America's War Against Crime and Drugs*. Bennett has sometimes been criticized for leading a life that is sometimes at odds with the moral principles he espouses in public. In 2003, for example, he was widely criticized when it became public knowledge that he was addicted to gambling and had lost $8 million over the preceding years at the gaming tables in Las Vegas.

Bill W. (1895–1971)

Bill W. was cofounder with Dr. Bob of Alcoholics Anonymous (AA), an organization devoted to helping alcoholics attain sobriety. He had his last alcoholic drink on December 11, 1934, shortly after cofounding AA, and maintained his sobriety ever after that time.

Bill W. is the name much preferred by William Griffith Wilson because it reflects and emphasizes the anonymity that AA asks of and offers to its members as they fight their battle against alcohol addiction. He was born on November 26, 1895, in East Dorset, Vermont, to Gilman Barrows Wilson, a womanizer and heavy drinker, and Emily Griffith Wilson, a strong-willed and abusive mother. His father abandoned the family in 1905, and his mother decided to do the same, choosing to study for a career in osteopathic medicine. Bill W. then became the ward of his maternal grandparents, with whom he spent the rest of his childhood.

After graduating from high school, Bill entered Norwich University, but remained for only a short time, partly because of his shyness and lack of social skills, and partly because of his own misconduct and that of other classmates. It was during these years that he had his first drink, before rapidly becoming an alcoholic with many "lost weekends" in his life. He eventually was readmitted to Norwich, from which he graduated with a degree in electric engineering in 1917. He then served as a second lieutenant in the U.S. Army, a time during which his drinking became even more of a problem. When he returned at the end of the war, he took a job in the insurance department of the New York Central Railroad, while attending the Brooklyn Law School at night. He earned his law degree in 1920, but is said to have been too drunk to pick up his diploma. Over the next decade, Bill worked as a field investigator for a number of financial firms, traveling over most of the United States to complete his assignments. Eventually, his drinking problem became so severe that he was unable to hold a job and he was admitted to the Charles B. Towns Hospital for Drug and Alcohol Addictions in New York City.

Bill experienced his first, short-lived recovery in 1934 when he met an old drinking friend, Ebby Thacher, and learned that he (Thacher) had become sober largely through the efforts of an evangelical Christian organization known as the Oxford Group. Bill's own efforts to achieve a similar result failed, however, and he was returned to the Towns Hospital a second time. Finally, in May 1935, on a business trip to Akron, Ohio, Bill met another alcoholic who was going through struggles similar to his own, Robert Holbrook Smith ("Dr. Bob"), with whom he developed plans for a new group to help themselves and other alcoholics like themselves. That organization eventually grew to become the largest and most successful group for the treatment of alcoholism in the world. Bill spent the rest of his life serving in one role or another in AA. In 2009, *Time* magazine named Bill one of the 100 most important people of the twentieth century.

Thomas de Quincey (1785–1859)

De Quincey was an English author best known for his autobiographical work, *Confessions of an Opium Eater*. He also wrote a number of other works, including novels, essays, critical reviews, and additional autobiographical sketches.

Thomas de Quincey was born on August 15, 1785, in Manchester, England. After his father died in 1796, de Quincy's mother moved the family to Bath, where he was enrolled in King Edward's School. He was an outstanding scholar, able to read Greek and compose poems in the language as a teenager. His home life was difficult, however, and he ran away to Wales at the age of 17, with the blessings and minimal financial support of his mother and uncle. Eventually he found his way to London, where he nearly died of starvation and survived only because of the kindness of a 15-year-old prostitute whom we now know of only as "Anne of Oxford Street."

In 1804, he was found by friends in London and returned to his family, who arranged for him to enroll at Worcester College, Oxford. It was at Oxford that he first took opium, in the form of laudanum, for a painful and persistent toothache. He soon became addicted to the drug, an addiction that persisted to a greater or lesser degree for the rest of his life. He describes his years of addiction in *Confessions*, as well as its effects on his life and writing and his efforts to overcome his addiction. From time to time, he was able to withdraw from use of the drug but, a point noted by some of his biographers, the quantity and quality of his literary work suffered significantly during these periods of abstinence.

In 1816, de Quincey married Margaret Simpson, who was eventually to bear him eight children. She has been described as the "anchor" in his life, and, after her death in 1837, de Quincey's use of opium increased significantly.

De Quincey survived for most of his life after about 1820 partially through the financial support of his family and partially through his own literary efforts. In the early 1820s, he moved to London where he worked as a novelist, essayist, translator, reporter, and critic. Publication of *Confessions* in 1821 essentially made his career as a writer, although he never again produced a work with such wide popularity. In addition to his opium addiction, de Quincey spent most of his life battling financial problems, and he was convicted and imprisoned on five occasions for nonpayment of his debts.

Biographers have noted de Quincey's substantial influence on later writers and artists, including Edgar Allan Poe, Charles Baudelaire, Nikolai Gogol, Aldous Huxley, William Burroughs, and Hector Berlioz, whose *Symphonie Fantastique* is reputedly loosely based on *Confessions*. The most recent collection of de Quincey's works was published in 21 volumes between 2000 and 2003. De Quincey died in Glasgow on December 8, 1859.

Pablo Escobar (1949–1993)

Escobar was a Colombian drug lord who, at the height of his powers, was said to control more than 80 percent of the world's supply of cocaine. He is perhaps the penultimate example of powerful men who have gained almost unbelievable wealth and power by trafficking in illegal substances, moving such substances, in almost all cases, from poor, developing nations to wealthy, developed nations, such as the United States. At one point, *Fortune* magazine listed Escobar as the seventh richest man in the world.

Pablo Emilio Escobar Gaviria was born in the Medellin suburb of Envigado in 1949 (various biographies give different dates in that year). He fell into crime early in his life, stealing gravestones from cemeteries in order to resell them as new stones, according to one report. In the 1970s, he added drug-running to his criminal activities, obtaining coca paste from Bolivia and Peru, having it refined, and then shipping it to the United States. In 1975, he reached the zenith of his power when a rival, Fabio Restrepo, was murdered (perhaps at Escobar's behest), leaving a power vacuum into which Escobar stepped. For the next 15 years, he ruled the trade in cocaine in Colombia virtually without competition. He also became politically active, achieving election to the Colombian Congress in 1982. Although he was very popular with the common people, he stopped at virtually no deed to gain and strengthen his control over the drug trade. He is said to have been responsible for a bomb attack on the Colombian Supreme Court in which 11 of the 25 justices on the court were killed. He was also implicated in the bombing of Avianca airlines flight 203 in 1989, an apparent effort to kill one of his political opponents.

As national and international efforts to bring Escobar under control increased, he withdrew from public attention and retired to his private homes throughout the country. Then, in 1991, Escobar surrendered to the Colombian government, fearing that he would be captured and extradited to the United States. Colombian officials banished Escobar to his own private prison, a palatial home called La Catedral for a period of five years, after which he was to be declared immune from extradition. While ensconced at La Catedral, Escobar apparently continued his ruthless campaign against opponents and is thought to have been responsible for the deaths of a number of "visitors" to his "prison." Finally, the Colombian government decided to move him to other facilities in July 1992. During the moving process, Escobar escaped. After more than a year of intense searching by Colombian and American forces, Escobar was found and killed on December 2, 1993.

Francis B. Harrison (1873–1957)

Harrison is probably best known today as author of the Harrison Narcotics Tax Act of 1914, an act that was passed, somewhat ironically, only after Harrison himself had left office. The act did not specifically prohibit any illegal substance, but it provided for the registration and taxation of "all persons who produce, import, manufacture, compound, deal in, dispense, sell, distribute, or give away opium or coca leaves, their salts, derivatives, or preparations, and for other purposes." Law enforcement officers and the courts immediately began to interpret the law as restricting physicians from writing prescriptions for the nonmedical use of opiates, and they began arresting, prosecuting, and convicting individuals for such activities. To a significant extent, then, the Harrison Act marked the beginning of a national campaign against the use of certain substances for other than medical uses.

Francis Burton Harrison was born in New York City on December 18, 1873, to Burton Harrison, an attorney and private secretary to Jefferson Davis, president of the Confederate States, and Constance Cary Harrison, a novelist and social activist. He attended the Cutler School in New York City, and Yale University, from which he received his B.A. in 1895. He then earned his L.L.B. at New York Law School in 1897. Harrison was elected to the U.S. Congress from New York's 13th District, but resigned after one term to run (unsuccessfully) for lieutenant governor of New York.

After a brief hiatus in the private practice of law, he ran for Congress again in 1907, this time from New York's 20th district, and was elected. He served for three terms in the Congress before accepting an appointment as Governor General of the Philippine Islands, where he remained until 1921. Following his service in the Philippines, Harrison essentially retired from public life, spending extended periods of time in Scotland and Spain. He returned to the Philippines on a number of occasions, however, as consultant and advisor, especially when the islands were granted their independence in 1934. Harrison was married six times, with five of those marriages ending in divorce. He died in Flemington, New Jersey, on November 21, 1957.

Albert Hoffman (1906–2008)

Hoffman discovered the psychedelic compound lysergic acid diethylamide (LSD) and experienced its hallucinogenic effects in 1943. He later studied chemicals present in so-called "magic mushrooms" also responsible for hallucinogenic effects and synthesized the most important of these, psilocybin.

Albert Hoffman was born in Baden, Switzerland, on January 11, 1906, to Adolf Hoffman, a toolmaker, and Elisabeth Schenk Hoffman. He attended Zürich University, from which he received his bachelor's degree in chemistry in 1929 and his doctorate in the same subject in 1930. He then accepted an appointment as research chemist at Sandoz Pharmaceuticals, a company with which he remained for the rest of his professional career.

The event in Hoffman's life for which he is best known and that has now been recounted endlessly occurred on April 16, 1943. At the time, Hoffman was involved in a long-term study of some naturally occurring psychedelic plants, including the fungus ergot and the herb squill. He was working in particular with a chemical found in a number of these plants, known in German as Lysergsäure-diethylamid, and in English as lysergic acid diethylamide (LSD). In particular, he was studying LSD-25, that is, the twenty-fifth preparation of the substance. During his research, Hoffman spilled a small amount of LSD-25 on his hands and, before long, began to feel mentally disoriented. After a period of time, he found he could no longer continue working and jumped on his bicycle to ride home. That bicycle ride, as Hoffman has recounted the event on a number of occasions, was such a bizarre experience that he thought for some time that he had perhaps lost his mind. After about six hours of "extremely stimulated imagination . . . a dreamlike state . . . and an uninterrupted stream of fantastic pictures, extraordinary shapes with intense, kaleidoscopic play of colors" (as he later described the experience), Hoffman returned to normal, but with a desire to learn more about the compound he had discovered.

Much of Hoffman's career was devoted to further studies of LSD and other psychedelic compounds, research that was supported and encouraged by Sandoz because of its potential for application in the treatment of psychological disorders. In 1962, for example, Hoffman and his wife traveled to Mexico to collect the psychoactive herb Ska Maria Pastora (*Salvia divinorum*) for study and analysis. He also identified the most important active agent in another psychedelic plant, the Mexican morning glory (*Rivea corymbosa*), a close relative of LSD, lysergic acid amide. Hoffman retired from Sandoz in 1971 but continued a career of writing, public speaking, and participation in a variety of professional organizations. Perhaps his most popular book is his own account of his research on LSD and its psychedelic effects, *LSD: My Problem Child* (1980). Hoffman died on April 29, 2008, in the village of Burg im Leimental, near Basel, Switzerland, at the age of 102.

Aldous Huxley (1894–1963)

Huxley is probably best known as the author of *Brave New World*, which describes a world in which the state takes control of every aspect of a person's individual life. He is perhaps somewhat less well known among the general public as an enthusiastic advocate of the use of psychedelic drugs, arguing that all of the world's great beliefs arise out of hallucinogenic experiences of their founders and early disciples.

Aldous Leonard Huxley was born in Godalming, Surrey, England, on July 26, 1894. The Huxley family was then one of the most famous in Great Britain. Huxley's brother, Julian, was an eminent biologist, his father was a successful author, and his grandfather, T. H. Huxley, had been a great defender of Charles Darwin's theory of evolution, earning himself the accolade of "Darwin's Bulldog." After an early period of home schooling, Huxley attended the Hillside School before enrolling at Eton College. In 1911, he developed a case of keratitis punctata, an eye condition that left him essentially blind for more than two years and which, incidentally, disqualified him for service in World War I. When he recovered, Huxley enrolled at Balliol College, Oxford, from which he graduated in 1916.

After leaving Oxford, Huxley taught briefly at Eton and worked for a short time at a chemical plant in Billingham, but he was not very successful or happy in either job. It gradually became clear that his real career was in the arts, specifically, as a writer. He produced his first book of poems in 1916 (*Burning Wheels*), his first book of short stories in 1920 (*Limbo*), and his first novel in 1921 (*Chrome Yellow*). He was eventually to produce many more novels, books of poetry, travel writings, essays, short story collections, magazine articles, biographies, and plays.

Huxley may have been introduced to psychedelic drugs as early as 1930, although his first real experimentation dates to the 1950s. He is said to have taken his first dose of mescaline in 1950 and his first dose of LSD in 1953, after which he became a firm advocate of psychedelics as a key to out-of-body experiences that could be of enormous value to a person. He described and discussed these experiences in his collection of essays, *Doors of Perception* (1954), which was named after a book by William Blake and which served as an inspiration for the name of a rock band of the time, The Doors. He is said to have been a favorite writer of many hippies of the 1960s and a spiritual guide for other researchers in psychedelic substances, including Timothy Leary and Richard Alpert. Huxley is said to have requested an intramuscular injection of LSD on his deathbed, a believer in the psychedelic experience to the very end. He died in Los Angeles on November 22, 1963, which was also the date on which John F. Kennedy was assassinated and C. S. Lewis died.

C. Everett Koop (1916–)

Koop served as U.S. Surgeon General under President Ronald Reagan from 1982 to 1989. During his tenure, he was a vigorous advocate for a number of public health programs, perhaps the best known of which was his campaign against smoking.

Charles Everett Koop was born in Brooklyn, New York, on October 14, 1916. He earned his B.A. from Dartmouth College in 1937 and his M.D. from Cornell Medical College in 1941. He then took a position at the University of Pennsylvania, where he held a number of posts over the next 35 years, including surgeon-in-chief at the university's Children's Hospital (1948–1981) and professor of pediatric surgery (1959–1989). In 1981, President Reagan asked Koop to become Deputy Assistant Secretary for Health in the U.S. Public Health Service, with the understanding that he would be eventually be promoted to surgeon general, a promise that was kept in January 1982. Koop remained in that position until almost the end of Reagan's second term of office, leaving his post in October 1989.

Koop's term of service as surgeon general was marked by aggressive campaigns on a number of public health fronts, smoking perhaps being the most notable. His first public action as surgeon general, in fact, was to issue a report, *Report on Smoking and Health*, that summarized the association between smoking and cancer of the lung, oral cavity, larynx, esophagus, stomach, bladder, pancreas, and kidneys. He used that report as the basis for a national program that he called the Campaign for a Smoke-Free America by the Year 2000. As an integral part of the campaign, Koop called for legislation requiring very specific notices about the health effects of smoking on all cigarette packages, legislation that was adopted by the U.S. Congress in 1984. In spite of pressure from tobacco-state legislators, Koop continued his antismoking crusade throughout his term of office. In 1986, he issued an important report on the effects of secondhand smoke, *The Health Consequences of Involuntary Smoking*, which demonstrated that secondhand smoke was not simply an inconvenience, but a quantifiable health risk.

After leaving federal service, Koop became president of the National Safe Kids Campaign, a post he held until 2003. He also accepted an offer to return to Dartmouth College, where he is now Elizabeth DeCamp McInerny Professor of Surgery at Dartmouth Medical School and senior scholar at the C. Everett Koop Institute at Dartmouth College. He continues to write and speak on a variety of medical and health topics and is the author of more than 200 books and articles of such topics.

Timothy Leary (1920–1996)

In his *New York Times* obituary, Leary was remembered as the man who "effectively introduced many Americans to the psychedelic 1960s." He is perhaps best remembered for having coined the phrase "turn on, tune in, drop out."

Timothy Francis Leary was born in Springfield, Massachusetts, on October 22, 1920. After graduating from Springfield Classical High School, he entered the College of the Holy Cross in Worcester, Massachusetts, where he spent two years. He then transferred to the University of Alabama, where he also remained only briefly. He is reputed to have had disciplinary problems at both institutions, and did not receive his bachelor's degree (in psychology) from Alabama until 1943. During World War II he served in the Medical Corps. After completing his studies at Alabama, he studied for his master's degree at Washington State University, which he received in 1946, and then continued with his doctoral studies at the University of California at Berkeley, which awarded him his Ph.D. in psychology in 1950. Over the next decade, Leary followed a somewhat traditional academic pathway, serving as assistant professor at Berkeley from 1950 to 1955, director of psychiatric research at the Kaiser Family Foundation, in Menlo Park, California, from 1955 to 1958, and lecturer in psychology at Harvard University from 1958 to 1963.

The turning point in Leary's life came in August 1960 when he first consumed psilocybin mushrooms on a visit to Cuernavaca, Mexico. He later said that, as a result of this experience, he "learned more about . . . (his) brain and its possibilities . . . (and) more about psychology in the five hours after taking these mushrooms than . . . (he) had in the preceding fifteen years of studying doing research in psychology." For the rest of his life, Leary devoted his energies to learning more about psychedelic substances and spreading the word about his discoveries to the world.

After his return from Mexico in 1960, Leary decided to incorporate his new passion into his research and teaching at Harvard. Along with his colleague Richard Alpert, Leary enlisted prison inmates and graduate students in a series of experiments using psychedelic substances to determine how they might be used in the treatment of psychological and psychiatric disorders. The university was somewhat less than enthusiastic about Leary's research and out-of-classroom activities, and it eventually terminated his contract on May 6, 1963, for failing to show up for his scheduled classes. Harvard also terminated Alpert at about the same time for providing psychedelic substances to an undergraduate in an off-campus setting.

After leaving Harvard, Leary and Alpert moved to an estate furnished them by a wealthy admirer at Millbrook, New York. Although planned as a research institute, the facility soon became better known as a "hippie hangout" where all types of drugs were used. Over the next two decades, Leary fell afoul of the law a number of times, sometimes spending time in prison, and, on occasion, having to flee the country to escape prosecution and further imprisonment. During the last two decades of his life, Leary spent his time writing and lecturing. He was the author of more than a dozen books, including *Interpersonal Diagnosis of Personality; a Functional Theory and Methodology for Personality Evaluation; Design for Dying; Flashbacks: An Autobiography; The Politics of Ecstasy; High Priest; Confessions of a Hope Fiend;* and *Turn On, Tune In, Drop Out.*

Otto Loewi (1873–1961)

Loewi was a German physician and pharmacologist who discovered that nerve messages are transmitted between neurons by means of specific chemicals, now known as neurotransmitters. Loewi gave to the first of the chemicals of this type that he discovered the name *Vagusstoff* ("vagus material"). The substance was later shown to be acetylcholine, one of the most important of all neurotransmitters. An understanding of the function of neurotransmitters is absolutely fundamental to an interpretation of the way drugs work in the human body. For his work on neurotransmitters, Loewi was awarded a share of the 1936 Nobel Prize in Physiology or Medicine.

Otto Loewi was born at Frankfurt-am-Main on June 3, 1873. He attended the University of Strasbourg, from which he received his medical degree in 1896. He then worked for a period of time at University College in London, the University of Vienna, and the University of Graz (Austria), where he remained for nearly three decades. It was at Graz that Loewi conducted the work on neurotransmitters for which he is best known.

Like many prominent Jewish scientists of the time, Loewi was increasingly at professional and personal risk as the Nazi Party came to power in Germany and, later, Austria. In fact, he was the only Jewish professor hired at Graz between 1903 and the end of World War II. On the evening of March 11, 1938, Loewi and two sons were arrested by Nazi authorities and were allowed to leave the country only under the condition that they give up all of their personal property and possessions. Loewi moved to Belgium, where he served as professor of pharmacology for one year at the University of Brussels. He then moved on to the University of

Leeds in England, before accepting an appointment in 1940 as professor of pharmacology at New York University (NYU). He served at NYU until 1955, when he retired. Loewi died in New York City on December 25, 1961.

Albert Niemann (1834–1861)

During his short life, Niemann made two important discoveries. The first was the active ingredient in coca leaves responsible for their psychoactive properties, a compound that he named cocaine. The second was a powerful gas produced by reacting ethylene (C_2H_4) with sulfur dichloride (SCl_2). The product became known as mustard gas, a chemical agent used widely during World War I.

During the late 1850s, Niemann was studying for his doctoral degree in chemistry at the University of Göttingen under the great chemist Friedrich Wöhler. For some years, Wöhler had been interested in the chemical composition of coca leaves brought back to Germany from South America, but had been unable to find the active ingredient for the plant's extraordinary psychoactive properties. When he received a shipment of fresh leaves in 1859, he assigned to Niemann the task of analyzing the natural product. Niemann responded successfully to this assignment, extracting from the leaves a white powder which he described as having a bitter taste (like other alkaloids, of which this compound was an example), promoting the flow of saliva, and having a numbing effect on the tongue. Niemann gave the name of *cocaine* to the new substance, a combination of the plant name from which it came ("coca") and the traditional suffix used by chemists for all alkaloids ("-ine"). Niemann's research on cocaine earned him his Ph.D. from Göttingen in 1860. In the same year, Niemann described his research on mustard gas (chemically, 1,1'-thiobis[2-chloroethane]; also known as sulfur mustard). He said that the gas caused terrible burns that festered for a long period of time and were very painful.

Following his research on mustard gas, Niemann's health deteriorated rapidly, and he returned to his home in Goslar, Germany, where he died on January 19, 1861, at the age of 26. Although some uncertainty surrounds the circumstances of his death, some historians believe that his exposure to mustard gas may have been a contributing factor. Two years after his death, a colleague at Göttingen, Wilhelm Lossen, determined the chemical formula for cocaine.

Quanah Parker (ca. 1845–1911)

Parker was the last chief of the Quahadi Comanche Indian tribe and a leading proponent of the melding of Christian and Native American Church movements, in which peyote is incorporated into traditional forms of worship. His most famous commentary is probably is comment that "The White Man goes into his church and talks about Jesus. The Indian goes into his Tipi and talks with Jesus."

The details of Quanah Parker's birth, as well as some other aspects of his life, are somewhat unclear. He is thought to have been born in the mid-1840s somewhere in the present state of Oklahoma. He himself claimed to have been born on Elk Creek, south of the Wichita Mountains, although other places have also been mentioned as a probable birthplace. His parents were Comanche warrior Noconie, (also known by the Indian name of Tah-con-ne-ah-pe-ah and called Peta Nocona by the whites) and Cynthia Ann Parker (later given the Indian name of Nadua, or "the found"), who had been captured by the Comanche during a raid on Fort Parker in Texas. Parker apparently grew up in a traditional Native American community, replete with tribal customs. After his father was killed in 1860, Parker took shelter with a subgroup of the Comanches, the Quahadi tribe. Over time, he grew in respect and responsibility within the tribe and became its leader. From the mid-1860s to the mid-1870s, Parker fought against surrender to or assimilation by whites who were committed to taking over Native American lands and property. He eventually lost that fight at the battle of Adobe Walls, and was resigned to retiring to the reservation to which his tribe had been assigned.

Parker's connection with peyote is reputed to stem from 1884, when he fell very ill from an infection. Although he had, by then, become thoroughly absorbed by white culture, the medicines available to him from white practitioners were of no use. Only when he was provided with a concoction of peyote did he recover. The experience proved to be life-changing for him, convincing him of the value of native traditions (and native drugs) even in the modern world of the reservation. He spent much of the rest of his life in developing and promoting the National American Indian church movement, which incorporates elements of both white Christianity and traditional Native American beliefs and practices. Largely through his efforts, the modern Native American church still includes the use of peyote in its rituals.

Nancy Reagan (1921–)

Reagan is the widow of former President Ronald Reagan. She was First Lady during the Reagan presidential administration, from 1981 to 1989. Among the accomplishments for which she is most famous is her "Just Say No" anti-drug campaign, initiated in 1982.

Reagan was born in New York City on July 6, 1921, as Anne Francis Robbins. Her father was a car salesman, Kenneth Seymour Robbins, and her mother, Edith Luckett, an actress. After her parents were divorced shortly after her birth, she was raised for six years by an aunt and uncle in Bethesda, Maryland. When her mother remarried in 1929, the family moved to Chicago, where Nancy attended the Girls' Latin School of Chicago. After graduation, she enrolled at Smith College in Northampton, Massachusetts, where she majored in drama and English. She was awarded her bachelor's degree from Smith in 1943 and returned to Chicago, where she held a series of jobs in retail. Partially through her mother's influence, she was able to find work in the entertainment industry, with roles on Broadway, in traveling shows, and, eventually, in Hollywood films. In November 1949, she met Ronald Reagan, then president of the Screen Actors' Guild. They were married in March 1952.

As First Lady, Reagan was the subject of considerable admiration and disdain, both for her political views and her personal beliefs and actions. She was widely criticized in 1988, for example, when President Reagan wrote about his wife's use of astrologers to make public and private decisions. She was also widely applauded and criticized for her "Just Say No" campaign against drug abuse. The campaign had its beginnings when Nancy Reagan visited the Longfellow Elementary School in Oakland, California, in 1982. When a girl in the classroom she was visiting asked what she should do if she were offered drugs, Reagan responded by saying, "Just say no." That phrase soon became a slogan for a national, and eventually, international, campaign to combat drug abuse. Reagan appeared on a number of television programs, spoke widely across the country, worked with a number of national organizations, and visited many drug treatment and prevention programs to spread her message. Experts disagree as to the effectiveness of the campaign. Some point to an apparent decline in drug use during the Reagan administration and suggest that "Just Say No" was an important contributor to that trend. Others believe that sloganeering had only a limited effect on substance abuse patterns.

Since President Reagan's death in 2004, Nancy Reagan has remained visible and active on the national scene. Perhaps her most important efforts have been on behalf of stem-cell research, attempting to convince then-President George W. Bush to change his mind and extend opportunities for research in this field, an effort in which she was not successful.

Friedrich Sertürner (1783–1841)

While still a young pharmacist's apprentice, Sertürner isolated the psychoactive agent morphine from the opium plant. His accomplishment is especially important because it was not only the first such agent extracted from opium, but also the first alkaloid obtained from any plant. Sertürner named his new discovery after the Greek god of dreams, Morpheus, for its powerful analgesic and sedative properties.

Friedrich Wilhelm Adam Ferdinand Sertürner was born in Neuhaus, Prussia, on June 19, 1783. His parents were in service to Prince Friedrich Wilhelm, who was also his godfather. When both his father and the prince died in 1794, he was left without means of support and, therefore, was apprenticed to a court apothecary by the name of Cramer. One of the topics in which he became interested in his new job was the chemical composition of opium, a plant that had long been known for its powerful analgesic and sedative properties. By 1803, he had extracted from opium seeds a white crystalline powder clearly responsible for the pharmacological properties of the plant. He named the new substance morphine and proceeded to test its properties, first on stray animals available at the castle, and later on his friends and himself. His friends soon withdrew from the experiments because, while pleasurable enough in its initial moderate doses, the compound ultimately caused unpleasant physical effects, including nausea and vomiting. Sertürner continued, however, to test the drug on himself, unaware of its ultimate addictive properties.

Sertürner was awarded his apothecary license in 1806 and established his own pharmacy in the Prussian town of Einbeck. In addition to operating his business, he continued to study the chemical and pharmacological properties of morphine for a number of years. His work drew little attention from professional scientists, however, and he eventually turned his attention to other topics, including the development of improved firearms and ammunition. During the last few years of his life, he became increasingly depressed about his failure to interest the scientific community in his research on opium. He withdrew into his own world and turned to morphine for comfort against his disillusionment with what he saw as the failure of his life. He did receive some comfort in 1831 when he was awarded a Montyon Prize by the Académie Française, sometimes described as the forerunner of the Nobel Prizes, with its cash award of 2,000 francs. By the time of his death in Hamelin, Prussia, on February 20, 1841, however, the scientific world in general had still not appreciated the enormous significance of his research on morphine.

Alexander "Sasha" Shulgin (1925–)

Shulgin is arguably the best known and most highly regarded advocate of so-called designer drugs within the scientific community. He is thought to have synthesized and tested more than 200 psychoactive compounds in his life and has written a number of important books and articles on the properties and potential benefits of such substances.

Alexander Shulgin, widely known as "Sasha," was born in Berkeley, California, on June 17, 1925. He graduated from high school at the age of 16 and received a full scholarship to Harvard University. His tenure at Harvard was cut short, however, with the beginning of World War II, during which he served with the U.S. Navy in both the North Atlantic and the Pacific campaigns. After the war, he returned to Berkeley, where he eventually earned his B.A. in chemistry at the University of California in 1949 and his Ph.D. in biochemistry at 1954. He completed his postdoctoral studies at the University of California at San Francisco (UCSF) in pharmacology and psychiatry. After working for a year at the BioRad Laboratories company, he took a position with Dow Chemical, where he was a research scientist from 1955 to 1961 and senior research chemist from 1961 to 1966.

Shulgin's most significant accomplishment at Dow was to develop a pesticide known as physostigmine, a substance that was to become one of Dow's best selling products. In appreciation of Shulgin's work, Dow provided him with a laboratory of his own where he was allowed to work on projects that were of special interest to him. One of those projects turned out to be the synthesis and study of psychedelic compounds. Shulgin later reported that his interest in psychedelics was prompted by his first experience in taking mescaline in 1960. As a result of that experience, he told an interviewer from *Playboy* magazine in 2004, he had found his "learning path," the direction he wanted the rest of his career to go.

In 1965, Shulgin decided to leave Dow in order to enter medical school at UCSF. He left that program after only two years, however, to pursue his interest in psychedelics. That decision posed a problem for both Shulgin and the U.S. Drug Enforcement Administration (DEA), the federal agency responsible for control of illegal drug use in the United States. Although its primary function is to discourage the development and use of illegal drugs, the DEA apparently saw some benefit in Shulgin's work, and they agreed to a special dispensation that allowed him to synthesize and study a number of otherwise illegal substances. That relationship eventually worked out well for both partners, as it permitted Shulgin to pursue the studies in which he was most interested and provided the DEA with invaluable information on substances about which it might otherwise have little or no information. In 1988, for example, he wrote *Controlled Substances: Chemical & Legal Guide to Federal Drug Laws*, a book that has become a standard reference for DEA employees.

Shulgin's special relationship with the DEA ended in 1994 when the agency raided his Berkeley laboratory and withdrew his license to conduct research on illegal substances, claiming that he had failed to keep proper records. Some observers believe, however, that the agency's actions were prompted by a book that Shulgin and his wife Ann had written a few years earlier, *PiHKAL: A Chemical Love Story*. (The PiHKAL of the title stands for "phenylethylamines I have known and loved.") The Shulgins later wrote a second book about another group of psychedelic substances, *TiKHAL: The Continuation*. In this case, the title word TiKHAL stands for "tryptamines I have known and loved." Shulgin's most recent book is somewhat more technically oriented, *The Simple Plant Isoquinolines* (with Wendy E. Perry). In 2008, his first two laboratory books were scanned and placed online.

Luther L. Terry (1911–1985)

Terry was the ninth Surgeon General of the United States. He was appointed to the office by President John F. Kennedy, and he served through Kennedy's incomplete first term in office and the first year of Lyndon B. Johnson's first term. He is probably best known today for the first report issued by the U.S. Public Health Service on the health effects of smoking, *Smoking and Health: Report of the Advisory Committee to the Surgeon General*, released in 1964. Among the many findings in that report, some of the most outstanding were that the mortality rate was 70 percent higher for smokers than for nonsmokers of a comparable age, that moderate smokers were 9 to 10 times more likely (and heavy smokers 20 times more likely) to develop cancer than nonsmokers, and that health risks rose and fell consistently with increases and decreases, respectively, in the amount of smoking.

Luther Leonidas Terry was born in Red Level, Alabama, on September 15, 1911, to James Edward and Lula M. (Durham) Terry. He attended Birmingham Southern College, from which he received his B.A. degree in 1931, and the Tulane Medical School, which awarded his M.D. in 1935. Terry completed his internship at the Hillman Hospital in Birmingham and his residency at City Hospitals in Cleveland. In 1938, he served an additional internship in pathology at Washington University, in St. Louis. In 1940, he accepted an appointment as instructor at the University of Texas, Galveston, where he remained for four years. He then moved to the Johns Hopkins University Medical School in Baltimore, while also holding an appointment at the Public Health Service Hospital in Baltimore. In 1950, he accepted an appointment as Chief of General Medicine and Experimental Therapeutics at the National Heart Institute in Bethesda in 1950. The position was, at first, a part-time appointment, but it became a full time post three years later when his division was transferred to the newly established National Institutes of Health Clinical Center. In 1958, Terry was appointed assistant director of the National Heart Institute, and, three years later, became Surgeon General of the United States.

Shortly after assuming his post as Surgeon General, Terry appointed a committee to study the health effects of smoking. His action was motivated to a large extent by a similar study that had just been completed and announced by the Royal College of Physicians in Great Britain, in which strong evidence for somewhat dramatic health effects as a result of smoking had been reported. Terry decided that a similar report for the United States was needed, although it would almost certainly be controversial and economically risky. The final report, issued on January 11, 1964, summarized the findings of more than 7,000 scientific articles and the expert testimony of more than 130 witnesses before Terry's committee.

After his retirement as Surgeon General in 1965, Terry took a post as vice-president for medical affairs and professor of medicine and community medicine at the University of Pennsylvania. He maintained his affiliation with Pennsylvania until 1982, and then accepted a position as corporate vice president for medical affairs and, later, as consultant to ARA Services, Inc. Terry died in Philadelphia on April 29, 1985.

R. Gordon Wasson (1898–1986)

Wasson was a wealthy New York City banker with a lifelong intense interest in mushrooms. He conducted a number of original studies on all varieties of mushrooms, put forth an attempt to prove that psychedelic mushrooms were integrally involved in the development of many religions, and provided financial assistance to a number of researchers in the field of psychoactive studies, including Timothy Leary and Richard Alpert.

Robert Gordon Wasson was born in Great Falls, Montana, on September 22, 1898. His father was an Episcopalian priest with a strong interest in languages, being fluent in Latin and Greek and conversant in Icelandic, Hebrew, and Sanskrit. His mother has been described as a "vivacious woman," who was also learned and one of six women selected to organize the Columbia University Library. When the senior Wasson accepted an appointment at a small parish in Newark, New Jersey, the family reestablished its home on the East Coast. During his childhood, Gordon was apparently subjected to serious instruction in language, the arts, and theology. Biographers note that he and his brother had each read the Bible completely through three times before the age of 13.

After three years of high school, Gordon joined his older brother Thomas Campbell Wasson, and the two young man spent the early war years traveling through Europe. Gordon then enlisted in the U.S. Army in 1917, serving in France as a radio operator. After the war, he enrolled at Columbia University, from which he received his bachelor's degree in literature in 1920. After working as a reporter and an editor for various newspapers and magazines, including the New Haven *Register*, the *New York Herald Tribune*, and *Current Opinion*, for eight years, he decided to pursue a career in finance. He joined the Guaranty Company of New York in 1928, where he was given a number of international assignments, before moving to the J. P. Morgan Company in 1934.

He remained affiliated with Morgan for the rest of his career, retiring in 1963.

Wasson's interest in mushrooms can be traced to a honeymoon trip to the Catskill Mountains that he and his wife took in 1925. On that trip, the couple found a number of species of mushrooms that Mrs. Wasson (the former Valentina Pavlovna Guercken) recognized from her native Russia. Over the years, the couple continued their research not only on the scientific aspects of mushrooms, but also on their involvement in other fields, including literature, history, theology, mythology, art, and archaeology. In 1953, Wasson visited Mexico, where he was introduced to the so-called magic mushrooms widely used in religious ceremonies there. He is credited with having brought back the first herbarium samples of those mushrooms, and having made his experience famous by means of an article in the May 17, 1957, edition of *Life* magazine, entitled "The Discovery of Mushrooms That Cause Strange Visions." Wasson was the author or coauthor of a number of scholarly articles and 11 books on psychedelic mushrooms, including *Persephone's Quest: Entheogens and the Origins of Religion* (1986), *The Wondrous Mushroom: Mycolatry in Mesoamerica* (1980), *The Road to Eleusis: Unveiling the Secret of the Mysteries* (1978), *Maria Sabina and Her Mazatec Mushroom Velada* (1976), and *Soma: Divine Mushroom of Immortality* (1968). Wasson died in Danbury, Connecticut, on December 23, 1986.

Hamilton Wright (1867–1917)

Wright has been described as the Father of Drug Laws in the United States because of his strong objections to the use of illegal drugs and his vigorous efforts to have laws passed against the manufacture, transport, sale, and consumption of illegal substances. Although he was not a member of Congress at the time, he is generally regarded as the author of the Harrison Narcotics Tax Act of 1914, which instituted taxes on opiates for the first time in U.S. history.

Hamilton Wright was born in Cleveland, Ohio, on August 2, 1867. After graduating from high school in Boston, he enlisted in the U.S. Army, where he served in the 7th Fusiliers in the Reale Rebellion, earning a medal for his valor during the war. He then attended McGill University in Montréal, Canada, from which he received his M.D. in 1895. From 1895 to 1908, he was engaged in a variety of research projects at a number of sites around the world, studying tropical diseases such as beri-beri, plague, and malaria. His work took him to China, Japan, Malaya, Great Britain, Germany, and France. In 1908, President Teddy Roosevelt appointed Wright the nation's first commissioner on international opium, a capacity in which he represented the United States at the International Opium Conference held at The Hague, The Netherlands, in 1911. He spent the rest of his life campaigning against opium use in the United States, which, as he wrote in a 1911 article for the *New York Times*, had the highest proportion of opium users of any country in the world.

Wright is known today for his willingness to use inflammatory, often inaccurate statements about the dangers posed by opium. He was especially critical of Blacks and Chinese Americans for their use of the drug, suggesting at one point that "one of the most unfortunate phases of the habit of smoking opium in this country is the large number of women who have become involved and are living as common-law wives or cohabiting with Chinese in the Chinatowns of our various cities." He also railed against cocaine use, suggesting at one time that "cocaine is often the direct incentive to the crime of rape by the Negroes of the South and other sections of the country."

Wright was very successful in pushing his anti-opium agenda both domestically and internationally. At home, his greatest achievement was the adoption of the Harrison Act in 1914; overseas, it was the adoption of the International Opium Convention in 1912. In both cases, Wright had pushed for even broader, more comprehensive control over drugs other than opium, especially marijuana, but without success. Wright died at his home in Washington, D.C., on January 9, 1917 as the result of complications resulting from an automobile accident in France two years earlier. He was assisting in U.S. relief efforts in that country following the conclusion of World War II.

6

Data and Documents

An overview of the way in which the United States and other nations have tried to deal with substance abuse problems can be found by reviewing important documents related to the issue. This chapter contains examples of laws, treaties, reports, court cases, and other documents associated with one or another aspect of substance abuse. The chapter also provides data and statistics on the extent and effects of substance abuse.

Documents

Laws and Treaties

Harrison Narcotic Act (1914)

Probably the first effort by the U.S. government to exert some control over the production, distribution, and consumption of recreational drugs was the Harrison Narcotic Act of 1914. Although this act did not make the drugs with which it dealt—opiates—illegal, it did place a tax on their production, distribution, and sale. In retrospect, the Harrison Act was a weak effort to control substance abuse, but it is historically significant because of its being the first attempt to interrupt substance abuse in any way whatsoever by the federal government. The core of the act is expressed in its first section, reproduced here.

Be it enacted by the Senate and House of Representatives of the United States of America in Congress assembled, that on and after the first day of March, nineteen hundred and fifteen, every person who produces, imports, manufactures, compounds, deals in, dispenses, distributes, or gives away opium or coca leaves or any compound, manufacture, salt, derivative, or preparation thereof, shall register with the collector of internal revenue of the district, his name or style, place of business, and place or places where such business is to be carried on: Provided, that the office, or if none, then the residence of any person shall be considered for purposes of this Act to be his place of business. At the time of such registry and on or before the first of July annually thereafter, every person who produces, imports, manufactures, compounds, deals in, dispenses, distributes, or gives away any of the aforesaid drugs shall pay to the said collector a special tax at the rate of $1 per annum: Provided, that no employee of any person who produces, imports, manufactures, compounds, deals in, dispenses, distributes, or gives away any of the aforesaid drugs, acting within the scope of his employment, shall be required to register or to pay the special tax provided by this section: Provided further, That officers of the United States Government who are lawfully engaged in making purchases of the above-named drugs for the various departments of the Army and Navy, the Public Health Service, and for Government hospitals and prisons, and officers of State governments or any municipality therein, who are lawfully engaged in making purchases of the above-named drugs for State, county, or municipal hospitals or prisons, and officials of any Territory or insular possession, or the District of Columbia or of the United States who are lawfully engaged in making purchases of the above-named drugs for hospitals or prisons therein shall not be required to register and pay the special tax as herein required.

Source: 63rd Congress. Public Law 223. 38 Stat. 785.

Eighteenth Amendment to the U.S. Constitution (1919)

On December 17, 1917, the U.S. House of Representatives took the first step in amending the U.S. Constitution to prohibit the use of alcoholic beverages in the United States. The U.S. Senate approved the same act the following day. The proposed amendment was then submitted to the separate states, where it was finally approved by the required number of states (36) on January 16, 1919. Ultimately, only two states defeated the proposed amendment, Connecticut and Rhode Island. On January 26, 1919, acting secretary of state Frank L. Polk certified adoption of the amendment. The amendment did not specifically prohibit the use of alcohol beverages in the United States, although it made it very difficult to obtain such beverages legally. The text of the amendment is as follows:

Amendment XVIII

Section 1. After one year from the ratification of this article the manufacture, sale, or transportation of intoxicating liquors within, the importation thereof into, or the exportation thereof from the United States and all territory subject to the jurisdiction thereof for beverage purposes is hereby prohibited.

Section 2. The Congress and the several states shall have concurrent power to enforce this article by appropriate legislation.

Section 3. This article shall be inoperative unless it shall have been ratified as an amendment to the Constitution by the legislatures of the several states, as provided in the Constitution, within seven years from the date of the submission hereof to the states by the Congress.

Source: National Archives. United States Constitution. http://www .archives.gov/exhibits/charters/constitution_amendments_11-27.html. Accessed on August 23, 2009.

Twenty-First Amendment to the U.S. Constitution (1933)

After more than a decade of Prohibition in the United States, many people were convinced that the great experiment to control the use of alcohol in this country was a failure. In response to that feeling, the U.S. Congress on February 20, 1933, adopted an act initiating the repeal of the Eighteenth Amendment by the adoption of a new amendment to the Constitution, the Twenty-First Amendment, which abrogated the earlier amendment. On December 5, 1933, the thirty-sixth state, Utah, ratified the amendment, and it was certified on the same date. Only one state, South Carolina, rejected the proposed amendment, although eight other states never took action on the amendment. The text of the amendment is as follows.

Amendment XXI

Section 1. The eighteenth article of amendment to the Constitution of the United States is hereby repealed.

Section 2. The transportation or importation into any state, territory, or possession of the United States for delivery or use therein of intoxicating liquors, in violation of the laws thereof, is hereby prohibited.

Section 3. This article shall be inoperative unless it shall have been ratified as an amendment to the Constitution by conventions in the several states, as provided in the Constitution, within seven years from the date of the submission hereof to the states by the Congress.

Source: National Archives. United States Constitution. http://www .archives.gov/exhibits/charters/constitution_amendments_11-27.html. Accessed on August 23, 2009.

Federal Cigarette Labeling and Advertising Act (1965)

The first significant government report on the health effects of smoking—
"Smoking and Health: Report of the Advisory Committee to the Surgeon
General of the Public Health Service"—was issued in 1965. The report
had a significant impact on the general public, on advocacy groups
opposed to smoking, and on lawmakers. One direct result of the report
was the Federal Cigarette Labeling and Advertising Act of 1965, which
was later amended a number of times. The provisions of the original law
and later amendments are now part of the U.S. Code, at Title 15, Chapter
36. A note about the 1984 amendment is included in the following excerpt.

§ 1331. Congressional declaration of policy and purpose

It is the policy of the Congress, and the purpose of this chapter, to
establish a comprehensive Federal Program to deal with cigarette
labeling and advertising with respect to any relationship between
smoking and health, whereby—

(1) the public may be adequately informed about any adverse health
effects of cigarette smoking by inclusion of warning notices on each
package of cigarettes and in each advertisement of cigarettes; and

(2) commerce and the national economy may be

(A) protected to the maximum extent consistent with this declared
policy and

(B) not impeded by diverse, nonuniform, and confusing cigarette
labeling and advertising regulations with respect to any relationship
between smoking and health.

Section 1332 provides definitions for a number of terms used in the act.
The core of the bill is found in Section 1333 which provides, in part, that:

§ 1333. Labeling; requirements; conspicuous statement

(a) Required warnings; packages; advertisements; billboards

(1) It shall be unlawful for any person to manufacture, package, or
import for sale or distribution within the United States any cigarettes
the package of which fails to bear, in accordance with the
requirements of this section, one of the following labels:

SURGEON GENERAL'S WARNING: Smoking Causes Lung Cancer,
Heart Disease, Emphysema, And May Complicate Pregnancy.

SURGEON GENERAL'S WARNING: Cigarette Smoke Contains
Carbon Monoxide.

(2) It shall be unlawful for any manufacturer or importer of
cigarettes to advertise or cause to be advertised (other than through

the use of outdoor billboards) within the United States any cigarette unless the advertising bears, in accordance with the requirements of this section, one of the following labels:

SURGEON GENERAL'S WARNING: Smoking Causes Lung Cancer, Heart Disease, Emphysema, And May Complicate Pregnancy.

SURGEON GENERAL'S WARNING: Cigarette Smoke Contains Carbon Monoxide.

(3) It shall be unlawful for any manufacturer or importer of cigarettes to advertise or cause to be advertised within the United States through the use of outdoor billboards any cigarette unless the advertising bears, in accordance with the requirements of this section, one of the following labels:

SURGEON GENERAL'S WARNING: Cigarette Smoke Contains Carbon Monoxide.

SURGEON GENERAL'S WARNING: Smoking Causes Lung Cancer, Heart Disease, And Emphysema.

(b) Conspicuous statement; label statement format; outdoor billboard statement format

(1) Each label statement required by paragraph (1) of subsection (a) of this section shall be located in the place label statements were placed on cigarette packages as of October 12, 1984. The phrase "Surgeon General's Warning" shall appear in capital letters and the size of all other letters in the label shall be the same as the size of such letters as of October 12, 1984. All the letters in the label shall appear in conspicuous and legible type in contrast by typography, layout, or color with all other printed material on the package.

This section continues with more detailed instructions about the precise nature of the labeling to be used.

In 1984, the original act was amended to change the wording required on all cigarette packages. The new ruling required the use of one of the four following statements:

- SURGEON GENERAL'S WARNING: Smoking Causes Lung Cancer, Heart Disease, Emphysema, And May Complicate Pregnancy.
- SURGEON GENERAL'S WARNING: Quitting Smoking Now Greatly Reduces Serious Risks to Your Health.
- SURGEON GENERAL'S WARNING: Smoking By Pregnant Women May Result in Fetal Injury, Premature Birth, and Low Birth Weight.
- SURGEON GENERAL'S WARNING: Cigarette Smoke Contains Carbon Monoxide.

The remaining sections of Title 15, Chapter 36, dealing with cigarette labels deals with issues such as preemption of state law by federal law (§1334), unlawful advertising on electronic communications (§1335), annual required listing of cigarette ingredients to the Secretary and Health and Human Services (§1336), and similar issues.

Source: GPO Access. U.S. Code, Title 15, Chapter 36, Sections 1331 and 1333. Available online at http://frwebgate.access.gpo.gov/cgi-bin/usc.cgi?ACTION=RETRIEVE&FILE=$$xa$$busc15.wais&start=7382061&SIZE=4518&TYPE=PDF and http://frwebgate.access.gpo.gov/cgi-bin/usc.cgi?ACTION=RETRIEVE&FILE=$$xa$$busc15.wais&start=7390608&SIZE=11181&TYPE=PDF. Accessed on August 25, 2009.

Controlled Substances Act (1970)

The cornerstone of the U.S. government's efforts to control substance abuse is the Controlled Substances Act of 1970, now a part of the U.S. Code, Title 21, Chapter 13. That act established the system of "schedules" for various categories of drugs that is still used by agencies of the U.S. government today. It also provides extensive background information about the domestic and international status of drug abuse efforts. Some of the most relevant sections for the domestic portion of the act are reprinted here.

Section 801 of the act presents Congress's findings and declarations about controlled substances, with special mention in Section 801a of psychotropic drugs.

§ 801. Congressional findings and declarations: controlled substances

The Congress makes the following findings and declarations:

(1) Many of the drugs included within this subchapter have a useful and legitimate medical purpose and are necessary to maintain the health and general welfare of the American people.

(2) The illegal importation, manufacture, distribution, and possession and improper use of controlled substances have a substantial and detrimental effect on the health and general welfare of the American people.

. . .

(7) The United States is a party to the Single Convention on Narcotic Drugs, 1961, and other international conventions designed to establish effective control over international and domestic traffic in controlled substances.

§ 801a. Congressional findings and declarations: psychotropic substances

The Congress makes the following findings and declarations:

(1) The Congress has long recognized the danger involved in the manufacture, distribution, and use of certain psychotropic substances for nonscientific and nonmedical purposes, and has provided strong and effective legislation to control illicit trafficking and to regulate legitimate uses of psychotropic substances in this country. Abuse of psychotropic substances has become a phenomenon common to many countries, however, and is not confined to national borders. It is, therefore, essential that the United States cooperate with other nations in establishing effective controls over international traffic in such substances.

(2) The United States has joined with other countries in executing an international treaty, entitled the Convention on Psycho-tropic Substances and signed at Vienna, Austria, on February 21, 1971, which is designed to establish suitable controls over the manufacture, distribution, transfer, and use of certain psychotropic substances. The Convention is not self-executing, and the obligations of the United States thereunder may only be performed pursuant to appropriate legislation. It is the intent of the Congress that the amendments made by this Act, together with existing law, will enable the United States to meet all of its obligations under the Convention and that no further legislation will be necessary for that purpose.

. . .

Section 802 deals with definitions used in the act, and section 803 deals with a minor housekeeping issue of financing for the act. Section 811 deals with the Attorney General's authority for classifying and declassifying drugs and the manner in which these steps are to be taken. In general:

§ 811. Authority and criteria for classification of substances

(a) Rules and regulations of Attorney General; hearing

The Attorney General shall apply the provisions of this subchapter to the controlled substances listed in the schedules established by section 812 of this title and to any other drug or other substance added to such schedules under this subchapter. Except as provided in subsections (d) and (e) of this section, the Attorney General may by rule—

(1) add to such a schedule or transfer between such schedules any drug or other substance if he—

(A) finds that such drug or other substance has a potential for abuse, and

(B) makes with respect to such drug or other substance the findings prescribed by subsection (b) of section 812 of this title for the schedule in which such drug is to be placed; or

(2) remove any drug or other substance from the schedules if he finds that the drug or other substance does not meet the requirements for inclusion in any schedule.

. . .

Section (b) provides guidelines for the evaluation of drugs and other substances. The next section, (c), is a key element of the act.

(c) Factors determinative of control or removal from schedules

In making any finding under subsection (a) of this section or under subsection (b) of section 812 of this title, the Attorney General shall consider the following factors with respect to each drug or other substance proposed to be controlled or removed from the schedules:

(1) Its actual or relative potential for abuse.

(2) Scientific evidence of its pharmacological effect, if known.

(3) The state of current scientific knowledge regarding the drug or other substance.

(4) Its history and current pattern of abuse.

(5) The scope, duration, and significance of abuse.

(6) What, if any, risk there is to the public health.

(7) Its psychic or physiological dependence liability.

(8) Whether the substance is an immediate precursor of a substance already controlled under this subchapter.

Section (d) is a lengthy discussion of international aspects of the nation's efforts to control substance abuse. Sections (e) through (h) deal with related, but less important, issues of the control of substance abuse. Section 812 is perhaps of greatest interest to the general reader in that it establishes the system of classifying drugs still used in the United States, along with the criteria for classification and the original list of drugs to be included in each schedule (since greatly expanded):

§ 812. Schedules of controlled substances

(a) Establishment

There are established five schedules of controlled substances, to be known as schedules I, II, III, IV, and V. Such schedules shall initially consist of the substances listed in this section. The schedules established by this section shall be updated and republished on a semiannual basis during the two-year period beginning one year after October 27, 1970, and shall be updated and republished on an annual basis thereafter.

(b) Placement on schedules; findings required

Except where control is required by United States obligations under an international treaty, convention, or protocol, in effect on October 27, 1970, and except in the case of an immediate precursor, a drug or other substance may not be placed in any schedule unless the findings required for such schedule are made with respect to such drug or other substance. The findings required for each of the schedules are as follows:

(1) Schedule I.—

(A) The drug or other substance has a high potential for abuse.

(B) The drug or other substance has no currently accepted medical use in treatment in the United States.

(C) There is a lack of accepted safety for use of the drug or other substance under medical supervision.

(2) Schedule II.—

(A) The drug or other substance has a high potential for abuse.

(B) The drug or other substance has a currently accepted medical use in treatment in the United States or a currently accepted medical use with severe restrictions.

(C) Abuse of the drug or other substances may lead to severe psychological or physical dependence.

(3) Schedule III.—

(A) The drug or other substance has a potential for abuse less than the drugs or other substances in schedules I and II.

(B) The drug or other substance has a currently accepted medical use in treatment in the United States.

(C) Abuse of the drug or other substance may lead to moderate or low physical dependence or high psychological dependence.

(4) Schedule IV.—

(A) The drug or other substance has a low potential for abuse relative to the drugs or other substances in schedule III.

(B) The drug or other substance has a currently accepted medical use in treatment in the United States.

(C) Abuse of the drug or other substance may lead to limited physical dependence or psychological dependence relative to the drugs or other substances in schedule III.

(5) Schedule V.—

(A) The drug or other substance has a low potential for abuse relative to the drugs or other substances in schedule IV.

(B) The drug or other substance has a currently accepted medical use in treatment in the United States.

(C) Abuse of the drug or other substance may lead to limited physical dependence or psychological dependence relative to the drugs or other substances in schedule IV.

(c) Initial schedules of controlled substances

Schedules I, II, III, IV, and V shall, unless and until amended [1] pursuant to section 811 of this title, consist of the following drugs or other substances, by whatever official name, common or usual name, chemical name, or brand name designated: *The initial list of drugs under each schedule follows.*

Source: GPO Access. U.S. Code, Title 21, Chapter 13. Available online at http://frwebgate.access.gpo.gov/cgi-bin/usc.cgi?ACTION=RETRIEVE &FILE=$$xa$$busc21.wais&start=2565831&SIZE=62758&TYPE=PDF; http://frwebgate.access.gpo.gov/cgi-bin/usc.cgi?ACTION=RETRIEVE &FILE=$$xa$$busc21.wais&start=2628595&SIZE=5461&TYPE=PDF; http://frwebgate.access.gpo.gov/cgi-bin/usc.cgi?ACTION=RETRIEVE &FILE=$$xa$$busc21.wais&start=2691987&SIZE=25833&TYPE=PDF; and http://frwebgate.access.gpo.gov/cgi-bin/usc.cgi?ACTION =RETRIEVE&FILE=$$xa$$busc21.wais&start=2717826&SIZE =24600&TYPE=PDF. Accessed on August 24, 2009.

Combat Meth Act (2005)

By the mid-2000s, one of the most serious substance abuse problems in the United States involved the manufacture, sale, and use of methamphetamine, also known by a number of common names, such as "meth," "ice," "crystal," and "crank." One of the problems in dealing with the methamphetamine epidemic was the ready availability of the raw materials needed to produce the drug in a simple home-based laboratory. In order to deal with this problem, and issues related to the misuse of the drug, Senator James Talent (R-MO) introduced Senate Bill S 103 in the 109th Congress. The bill was referred to committee, but never acted on in its original form. Instead, it was incorporated into the USA PATRIOT Improvement and Reauthorization Act of 2005, which was passed by Congress and signed by President George W. Bush on March 9, 2006. Perhaps the most important part of the methamphetamine control portion of the bill was the limitations it placed on the sale of a number of widely used cough and cold products whose ingredients included raw materials from which meth can be made. The core

*provisions of the act in this respect are to be found in Section (b) of
Section 711 of Title VII of the main act, as follows:*

(b) Restrictions on Sales Quantity; Behind-the-Counter Access; Logbook
Requirement; Training of Sales Personnel; Privacy Protections—

(1) IN GENERAL-Section 310 of the Controlled Substances Act (21
U.S.C. 830) is amended by adding at the end the following subsections:

Section (c) is absent from the final version of the bill.

(d) Scheduled Listed Chemicals; Restrictions on Sales Quantity;
Requirements Regarding Nonliquid Forms—With respect to ephedrine
base, pseudoephedrine base, or phenylpropanolamine base in a
scheduled listed chemical product—

(1) the quantity of such base sold at retail in such a product by a
regulated seller, or a distributor required to submit reports by
subsection (b)(3) may not, for any purchaser, exceed a daily amount
of 3.6 grams, without regard to the number of transactions; and

(2) such a seller or distributor may not sell such a product in
nonliquid form (including gel caps) at retail unless the product is
packaged in blister packs, each blister containing not more than
2 dosage units, or where the use of blister packs is technically
infeasible, the product is packaged in unit dose packets or pouches.

(e) Scheduled Listed Chemicals; Behind-the-Counter Access; Logbook
Requirement; Training of Sales Personnel; Privacy Protections—

(1) REQUIREMENTS REGARDING RETAIL TRANSACTIONS—

(A) IN GENERAL—Each regulated seller shall ensure that, subject to
subparagraph (F), sales by such seller of a scheduled listed chemical
product at retail are made in accordance with the following:

(i) In offering the product for sale, the seller places the
product such that customers do not have direct access to the
product before the sale is made (in this paragraph referred to
as 'behind-the-counter' placement). For purposes of this
paragraph, a behind-the-counter placement of a product
includes circumstances in which the product is stored in a
locked cabinet that is located in an area of the facility involved
to which customers do have direct access.

(ii) The seller delivers the product directly into the custody of
the purchaser.

(iii) The seller maintains, in accordance with criteria issued by
the Attorney General, a written or electronic list of such sales that
identifies the products by name, the quantity sold, the names

and addresses of purchasers, and the dates and times of the sales (which list is referred to in this subsection as the 'logbook'), except that such requirement does not apply to any purchase by an individual of a single sales package if that package contains not more than 60 milligrams of pseudoephedrine.

(iii) applies, the seller does not sell such a product unless

(iv) In the case of a sale to which the requirement of clause

(I) the prospective purchaser—

(aa) presents an identification card that provides a photograph and is issued by a State or the Federal Government, or a document that, with respect to identification, is considered acceptable for purposes of sections 274a.2(b)(1)(v)(A) and 274a.2(b)(1)(v)(B) of title 8, Code of Federal Regulations (as in effect on or after the date of the enactment of the Combat Methamphetamine Epidemic Act of 2005); and

(bb) signs the logbook and enters in the logbook his or her name, address, and the date and time of the sale; and

(II) the seller—

(aa) determines that the name entered in the logbook corresponds to the name provided on such identification and that the date and time entered are correct; and

(bb) enters in the logbook the name of the product and the quantity sold.

(v) The logbook includes, in accordance with criteria of the Attorney General, a notice to purchasers that entering false statements or misrepresentations in the logbook may subject the purchasers to criminal penalties under section 1001 of title 18, United States Code, which notice specifies the maximum fine and term of imprisonment under such section.

(vi) The seller maintains each entry in the logbook for not fewer than two years after the date on which the entry is made.

(vii) In the case of individuals who are responsible for delivering such products into the custody of purchasers or who deal directly with purchasers by obtaining payments for the products, the seller has submitted to the Attorney General a self-certification that all such individuals have, in accordance with criteria under subparagraph (B)(ii), undergone training provided by the seller to ensure that the individuals understand the requirements that apply under this subsection and subsection (d).

(viii) The seller maintains a copy of such certification and records demonstrating that individuals referred to in clause (vii) have undergone the training.

(ix) If the seller is a mobile retail vendor:

(I) The seller complies with clause (i) by placing the product in a locked cabinet.

(II) The seller does not sell more than 7.5 grams of ephedrine base, pseudoephedrine base, or phenylpropanolamine base in such products per customer during a 30-day period.

(B) ADDITIONAL PROVISIONS REGARDING CERTIFICATIONS AND TRAINING—

(i) IN GENERAL-A regulated seller may not sell any scheduled listed chemical product at retail unless the seller has submitted to the Attorney General the self-certification referred to in subparagraph (A)(vii). The certification is not effective for purposes of the preceding sentence unless, in addition to provisions regarding the training of individuals referred to in such subparagraph, the certification includes a statement that the seller understands each of the requirements that apply under this paragraph and under subsection (d) and agrees to comply with the requirements.

The remainder of this long section describes in detail the process by which a retailer obtains a certificate of the kind described above.

Remaining sections of Title 7 deal with topics such as certain types of regulated transactions (§712), authority to sell production quotas (§713), penalties (§714), importation and legal uses of otherwise restricted products (§715), importation and exportation of restricted materials (§716), and a variety of "housekeeping" issues.

Source: USA Patriot Improvement and Reauthorization Act of 2005. Available online at http://thomas.loc.gov/cgi-bin/cpquery/T?&report=hr333&dbname=109&. Accessed on August 24, 2009.

Family Smoking Prevention and Tobacco Control and Federal Retirement Reform (2009)

The question as to whether the federal government should have any control over the use of tobacco has been an issue in the United States for many years. Since tobacco use is not prohibited by any federal law, some people have argued that the federal government has no authority, legal or moral, to control the use of tobacco products. Other observers disagree. They point out that tobacco products contain substances that are harmful to a person's health and that some agency in the U.S. government— presumably the Food and Drug Administration (FDA)—should have some authority to regulate the use of tobacco products. In 2009, that issue was resolved to some extent when the U.S. Congress passed legislation to give the FDA authority to regulate the use of tobacco products. The legislation was originally introduced in the House of

Representatives by Representative Henry Waxman (D–CA) on March 22, 2009, as H.R.1256, while matching legislation was introduced in the U.S. Senate by Senator Edward Kennedy (D–MA) on May 5, 2009. In a somewhat surprising turn of events, the bills moved quickly through the Congress, were approved on June 12, 2009, and signed by President Barack Obama on June 22, 2009. The bill is 84 pages in length in the U.S. Code, but the fundamental rationale of the act is expressed in its first few sections, which are reprinted below.

Public Law 111-31
111th Congress

The act consists of five main sections: Table of Contents, Authority of the Food and Drug Administration, Tobacco Product Warnings, Constituent and Smoke Constituent Disclosure, and Prevention of Illicit Trade in Tobacco Products. The first part of the act outlines its rationale in its "Findings" section, which consists of 49 statements about tobacco, its health effects, its marketing, and other related issues. Among these findings are the following:

(1) The use of tobacco products by the Nation's children is a pediatric disease of considerable proportions that results in new generations of tobacco-dependent children and adults.

(2) A consensus exists within the scientific and medical communities that tobacco products are inherently dangerous and cause cancer, heart disease, and other serious adverse health effects.

(3) Nicotine is an addictive drug.

(4) Virtually all new users of tobacco products are under the minimum legal age to purchase such products.

(5) Tobacco advertising and marketing contribute significantly to the use of nicotine-containing tobacco products by adolescents.

(6) Because past efforts to restrict advertising and marketing of tobacco products have failed adequately to curb tobacco use by adolescents, comprehensive restrictions on the sale, promotion, and distribution of such products are needed.

(7) Federal and State governments have lacked the legal and regulatory authority and resources they need to address comprehensively the public health and societal problems caused by the use of tobacco products.

(8) Federal and State public health officials, the public health community, and the public at large recognize that the tobacco industry should be subject to ongoing oversight.

. . .

(12) It is in the public interest for Congress to enact legislation that provides the Food and Drug Administration with the authority to

regulate tobacco products and the advertising and promotion of such products. The benefits to the American people from enacting such legislation would be significant in human and economic terms.

. . .

(15) Advertising, marketing, and promotion of tobacco products have been especially directed to attract young persons to use tobacco products, and these efforts have resulted in increased use of such products by youth. Past efforts to oversee these activities have not been successful in adequately preventing such increased use.

. . .

(26) Restrictions on advertising are necessary to prevent unrestricted tobacco advertising from undermining legislation prohibiting access to young people and providing for education about tobacco use.

. . .

(30) The final regulations promulgated by the Secretary of Health and Human Services in the August 28, 1996, issue of the Federal Register (61 Fed. Reg. 44615–44618) for inclusion as part 897 of title 21, Code of Federal Regulations, are consistent with the first amendment to the United States Constitution and with the standards set forth in the amendments made by this subtitle for the regulation of tobacco products by the Food and Drug Administration, and the restriction on the sale and distribution of, including access to and the advertising and promotion of, tobacco products contained in such regulations are substantially related to accomplishing the public health goals of this division.

(31) The regulations described in paragraph (30) will directly and materially advance the Federal Government's substantial interest in reducing the number of children and adolescents who use cigarettes and smokeless tobacco and in preventing the life-threatening health consequences associated with tobacco use. . . .

(32) The regulations described in paragraph (30) impose no more extensive restrictions on communication by tobacco manufacturers and sellers than are necessary to reduce the number of children and adolescents who use cigarettes and smokeless tobacco and to prevent the life-threatening health consequences associated with tobacco use. Such regulations are narrowly tailored to restrict those advertising and promotional practices which are most likely to be seen or heard by youth and most likely to entice them into tobacco use, while affording tobacco manufacturers and sellers ample opportunity to convey information about their products to adult consumers.

. . .

(36) It is essential that the Food and Drug Administration review products sold or distributed for use to reduce risks or exposures

associated with tobacco products and that it be empowered to review any advertising and labeling for such products. It is also essential that manufacturers, prior to marketing such products, be required to demonstrate that such products will meet a series of rigorous criteria, and will benefit the health of the population as a whole, taking into account both users of tobacco products and persons who do not currently use tobacco products.

. . .

(44) The Food and Drug Administration is a regulatory agency with the scientific expertise to identify harmful substances in products to which consumers are exposed, to design standards to limit exposure to those substances, to evaluate scientific studies supporting claims about the safety of products, and to evaluate the impact of labels, labeling, and advertising on consumer behavior in order to reduce the risk of harm and promote understanding of the impact of the product on health. In connection with its mandate to promote health and reduce the risk of harm, the Food and Drug Administration routinely makes decisions about whether and how products may be marketed in the United States.

Source: Public Law 111–31—June 22, 2009. http://frwebgate.access .gpo.gov/cgi-bin/getdoc.cgi?dbname=111_cong_public_laws&docid =f:publ031.111.pdf. Accessed on August 23, 2009.

Reports and Recommendations

The Report of the National Commission on Marihuana and Drug Abuse: Marihuana: A Signal of Misunderstanding (1972)

After at least a half century of relatively severe attitudes and policies about the use of illegal substances, the attitudes of at least some Americans about the use of marijuana (and, to a much lesser extent, other illegal drugs) began to change as a result of broader cultural changes during the 1960s. At the end of that decade, government officials and policymakers began to rethink the stand that the federal government ought to take about the control of all types of drugs. One consequence of this atmosphere was the adoption by the U.S. Congress of an act that was to become Public Law 91-153, establishing a commission conduct a study of marijuana that would include "(1) the extent of use of marihuana [sic] in the United States to include number of users, number of arrests, number of convictions, amount of marihuana seized, type of user, nature of use; (2) an evaluation of the efficacy of existing marihuana laws: (3) a study of the pharmacology of marihuana and its immediate and long-term effects both physiological and psychological; (4) the relationship of marihuana use to aggressive behavior and crime; and (5) the relationship between marihuana and the use of other drugs."

In a quite remarkable result, the commission suggested that criminal penalties for the possession of small amounts of marijuana be abolished and that distinctions between legal and illegal drugs also be abolished. Some of its conclusions are as follows.

Drugs and Social Responsibility

A constant tension exists in our society between individual liberties and the need for reasonable societal restraints. It is easy to go too far in either direction, and this tendency is particularly evident where drugs are concerned.

. . .

Drugs in a Free Society

A free society seeks to provide conditions in which each of its members may develop his or her potentialities to the fullest extent. A premium is placed on individual choice in seeking self-fulfillment. This priority depends upon the capacity of free citizens not to abuse their freedom, and upon their willingness to act responsibly toward others and toward the society as a whole. Responsible behavior, through individual choice, is both the guarantor and the objective of a free society.

DRUGS AND SOCIAL RESPONSIBILITY

The use of drugs is not in itself an irresponsible act. Medical and scientific uses serve important individual and social needs and are often essential to our physical and mental well-being. Further, the use of drugs for pleasure or other non-medical purposes is not inherently irresponsible; alcohol is widely used as an acceptable part of social activities.

. . .

1. Application of the Criminal Law to Private Possession
Is Philosophically Inappropriate

With possession and use of marihuana, we are dealing with a form of behavior which occurs generally in private where a person possesses the drug for his own use. The social impact of this conduct is indirect, arising primarily in cases of heavy or otherwise irresponsible use and from the drugs symbolic aspects. We do not take the absolutist position that society is philosophically forbidden from criminalizing any kind of "private" behavior. The phrase "victimless crimes," like "public, health hazard," has become a rhetorical excuse for avoiding basic social policy issues. We have chosen a discouragement policy on the basis of our evaluation of the actual and potential individual and social impact of marihuana use. Only now that we have done so can we accord appropriate weight to the nation's philosophical preference for individual privacy.

On the basis of this evaluation we believe that the criminal law is too harsh a tool to apply to personal possession even in the effort to discourage use. It implies an overwhelming indictment of the behavior which we believe is not appropriate. The actual and potential harm of use of the drug is not great enough to justify intrusion by the criminal law into private behavior, a step which our society takes only 'with the greatest reluctance.

. . .

2. Application of the Criminal Law Is Constitutionally Suspect

The preference for individual privacy reflected in the debate over the philosophical limitations on the criminal law is also manifested in our constitutional jurisprudence. Although no court, to our knowledge, has held that government may not prohibit private possession of marihuana, two overlapping constitutional traditions do have important public policy implications in this area.

The first revolves around the concept that in a free society, the legislature may act only for public purposes. The "police powers" of the states extend only to the "public health, safety and morals."

. . .

As a matter of constitutional history, a second tradition, the application of specific provisions in the Bill of Rights, has generally replaced the notion of "inherent" limitations. The ultimate effect is virtually the same, however. The Fourth Amendment's proscription of "unreasonable searches and seizures" reflects a constitutional commitment to the value of individual privacy.

. . .

While the judiciary is the governmental institution most directly concerned with the protection of individual liberties, all policy-makers have a responsibility to consider our constitutional heritage when framing public policy. Regardless of whether or not the courts would overturn a prohibition of possession of marihuana for personal use in the home, we are necessarily influenced by the high place traditionally occupied by the value of privacy in our constitutional scheme.

Accordingly, we believe that government must show a compelling reason to justify invasion of the home in order to prevent personal use of marihuana. We find little in marihuana's effects or in its social impact to support such a determination. Legislators enacting Prohibition did not find such a compelling reason 40 years ago; and we do not find the situation any more compelling for marihuana today.

. . .

3. Total Prohibition Is Functionally Inappropriate

Apart from the philosophical and constitutional constraints outlined above, a total prohibition scheme carries with it significant institutional costs. Yet it contributes very little to the achievement of our social policy. In some ways it actually inhibits the success of that policy.

The primary goals of a prudent marihuana social control policy include preventing irresponsible use of the drug, attending to the consequences of such use, and deemphasizing use in general. Yet an absolute prohibition of possession and use inhibits the ability of other institutions to contribute actively to these objectives. For example, the possibility of criminal prosecution deters users who are experiencing medical problems from seeking assistance for fear of bring attention to themselves. In addition, the illegality of possession and use creates difficulties in achieving an open, honest educational program, both in the schools and in the home.

In terms of the social policy objective of discouraging use of the drug, the legal system can assist that objective in three ways: first, by deterring people from use; second, by symbolizing social opposition to use; and finally, by cutting off supply of the drug.

Source: National Commission on Marihuana and Drug Abuse. *Marihuana: A Signal of Misunderstanding.* Available online at http://www.druglibrary.org/Schaffer/library/studies/nc/ncrec1.htm and http://www.druglibrary.org/Schaffer/Library/studies/nc/ncrec1_9.htm. Accessed on September 2, 2009.

National Institute of Drug Abuse Reports

The National Institute of Drug Abuse is a division of the U.S. National Institutes of Health with the twofold responsibility of carrying out research on drug abuse and addiction and transmitting information gained from this research to the general public. One of the tools by which the institute carries out the latter charge is a series of research reports on individual drugs and on problems of drug abuse and addiction in general. Currently, reports are available in English and Spanish on about a dozen topics. The selections below summarize current information on the incidence and prevalence of the abuse for certain specific substances in the United States. Citations that have been omitted are designated with ellipses.

Tobacco (2009)
This report discusses a number of aspects of tobacco use, including the extent and impact of tobacco use, the addictive properties of nicotine, the medical consequences of tobacco use, smoking and pregnancy, treatments for nicotine addiction, information on current research on tobacco use, and sources of additional information about tobacco and nicotine.

What Are the Extent and Impact of Tobacco Use?

According to the 2007 National Survey on Drug Use and Health, an estimated 70.9 million Americans aged 12 or older reported current use of tobacco—60.1 million (24.2 percent of the population) were current cigarette smokers, 13.3 million (5.4 percent) smoked cigars, 8.1 million (3.2 percent) used smokeless tobacco, and 2 million (0.8 percent) smoked pipes, confirming that tobacco is one of the most widely abused substances in the United States. Although the numbers of people who smoke are still unacceptably high, according to the Centers for Disease Control and Prevention there has been a decline of almost 50 percent since 1965.

NIDA's 2008 Monitoring the Future survey of 8th-, 10th-, and 12th-graders, which is used to track drug use patterns and attitudes, has also shown a striking decrease in smoking trends among the Nation's youth. The latest results indicate that about 7 percent of 8th-graders, 12 percent of 10th-graders, and 20 percent of 12th-graders had used cigarettes in the 30 days prior to the survey—the lowest levels in the history of the survey.

The declining prevalence of cigarette smoking among the general U.S. population, however, is not reflected in patients with mental illnesses. The rate of smoking in patients suffering from post-traumatic stress disorder, bipolar disorder, major depression, and other mental illness is two- to fourfold higher than in the general population; and among people with schizophrenia, smoking rates as high as 90 percent have been reported.

Tobacco use is the leading preventable cause of death in the United States. The impact of tobacco use in terms of morbidity and mortality to society is staggering.

Economically, more than $96 billion of total U.S. health care costs each year are attributable directly to smoking. However, this is well below the total cost to society because it does not include burn care from smoking-related fires, perinatal care for low-birthweight infants of mothers who smoke, and medical care costs associated with disease caused by secondhand smoke. In addition to health care costs, the costs of lost productivity due to smoking effects are estimated at $97 billion per year, bringing a conservative estimate of the economic burden of smoking to more than $193 billion per year.

Source: Tobacco Addiction. Washington, D.C.: U.S. Department of Health and Human Services. National Institutes of Health. National Institute of Drug Abuse. Revised June 2009, 1–2.

Marijuana (2005)

This report discusses a number of aspects of marijuana use, including the extent of marijuana use, the effects of marijuana on the brain, the effects of marijuana on physical health, the effects of marijuana use on one's social life, the addictive properties of mairjuana and marijuana and and pregnancy.

What Is the Scope of Marijuana Use in the United States?

Marijuana is the Nation's most commonly used illicit drug. More than 94 million Americans (40 percent) age 12 and older have tried marijuana at least once, according to the 2003 National Survey on Drug Use and Health. . . .

Marijuana use is widespread among adolescents and young adults. The percentage of middle-school students who reported using marijuana increased throughout the early 1990s. . . . In the past few years, according to the 2004 Monitoring the Future Survey, an annual survey of drug use among the Nation's middle and high school students, illicit drug use by 8th-, 10th-, and 12th-graders has leveled off. . . . Still, in 2004, 16 percent of 8th-graders reported that they had tried marijuana, and 6 percent were current users (defined as having used the drug in the 30 days preceding the survey). . . . Among 10th-graders, 35 percent had tried marijuana sometime in their lives, and 16 percent were current users. . . . As would be expected, rates of use among 12th-graders were higher still. Forty-six percent had tried marijuana at some time, and 20 percent were current users. . . .

The Drug Abuse Warning Network (DAWN), a system for monitoring the health impact of drugs, estimated that, in 2002, marijuana was a contributing factor in over 119,000 emergency department (ED) visits in the United States, with about 15 percent of the patients between the ages of 12 and 17, and almost two-thirds male. . . .

In 2002, the National Institute of Justice's Arrestee Drug Abuse Monitoring (ADAM) Program, which collects data on the number of adult arrestees testing positive for various drugs, found that, on average, 41 percent of adult male arrestees and 27 percent of adult female arrestees tested positive for marijuana. . . . On average, 57 percent of juvenile male and 32 percent of juvenile female arrestees tested positive for marijuana.

NIDA's Community Epidemiology Work Group (CEWG), a network of researchers that tracks trends in the nature and patterns of drug use in major U.S. cities, consistently reports that marijuana frequently is combined with other drugs, such as crack cocaine, PCP, formaldehyde, and codeine cough syrup, sometimes without the user being aware of it. . . . Thus, the risks associated with marijuana use may be compounded by the risks of added drugs, as well.

Source: Marijuana Abuse. Washington, D.C.: U.S. Department of Health and Human Services. National Institutes of Health. National Institute of Drug Abuse, 1–2.

Cocaine (2009)

This report discusses a number of issues related to the use of cocaine, including the scope of cocaine use in the United States, the short- and long-term effects of cocaine use, the addictive properties of cocaine, treatments for cocaine use and addiction, and additional sources of information about cocaine.

What Is the Scope of Cocaine Use in the United States?

The National Survey on Drug Use and Health (NSDUH) estimates that in 2007 there were 2.1 million current (past-month) cocaine users, of which approximately 610,000 were current crack users. Adults aged 18 to 25 years have a higher rate of current cocaine use than any other age group, with 1.7 percent of young adults reporting past month cocaine use. Overall, men report higher rates of current cocaine use than women. Ethnic/ racial differences also occur—with the highest rates in those reporting two or more races (1.1 percent), followed by Hispanics (1.0 percent), Whites (0.9 percent), and African-Americans (0.8 percent).

The 2008 Monitoring the Future survey, which annually surveys teen attitudes and drug use, reports that while there has been a significant decline in the 30-day prevalence of powder cocaine use among 8th-, 10th-, and 12th-graders from its peak use in the late 1990s, there was no significant change in current cocaine use from 2001 to 2008; however, crack use declined significantly during this timeframe among 8th- and 12th-graders.

Repeated cocaine use can produce addiction and other adverse health consequences. In 2007, according to the NSDUH, nearly 1.6 million Americans met Diagnostic and Statistical Manual of Mental Disorders criteria for dependence or abuse of cocaine (in any form) in the past 12 months. Further, data from the 2005 Drug Abuse Warning Network (DAWN) report showed that cocaine was involved in 448,481 of the total 1,449,154 visits to emergency departments for drug misuse or abuse. This translates to almost one in three drug misuse or abuse emergency department visits (31 percent) that involved cocaine.

Source: Cocaine: Abuse and Addiction. Washington, D.C.: U.S. Department of Health and Human Services. National Institutes of Health. National Institute of Drug Abuse. Revised May 2009, 3.

Prescription Drugs (2005)

This report discusses a number of issues about the abuse of prescription drugs, including the nature and effects of opioids, CNS depressants, and stimulants; trends in the illegal use of prescription drugs among different age groups; prevention and treatment of prescription drug abuse; and the types of prescription drugs most commonly abused.

Trends in Prescription Drug Abuse

Although prescription drug abuse affects many Americans, some concerning trends can be seen among older adults, adolescents, and women. Several indicators suggest that prescription drug abuse is on the rise in the United States. According to the 2003 National Survey on Drug Use and Health (NSDUH), an estimated 4.7 million Americans used prescription drugs nonmedically for the first time in 2002-

2.5 million used pain relievers

1.2 million used tranquilizers

761,000 used stimulants

225,000 used sedatives

Pain reliever incidence increased-from 573,000 initiates in 1990 to 2.5 million initiates in 2000-and has remained stable through 2003. In 2002, more than half (55 percent) of the new users were females, and more than half (56 percent) were ages 18 or older.

The Drug Abuse Warning Network (DAWN), which monitors medications and illicit drugs reported in emergency departments (EDs) across the Nation, recently found that two of the most frequently reported prescription medications in drug abuse-related cases are benzodiazepines (e.g., diazepam, alprazolam, clonazepam, and lorazepam) and opioid pain relievers (e.g., oxycodone, hydrocodone, morphine, methadone, and combinations that include these drugs). In 2002, benzodiazepines accounted for 100,784 mentions that were classified as drug abuse cases, and opioid pain relievers accounted for more than 119,000 ED mentions. From 1994 to 2002, ED mentions of hydrocodone and oxycodone increased by 170 percent and 450 percent, respectively. While ED visits attributed to drug addiction and drug-taking for psychoactive effects have been increasing, intentional overdose visits have remained stable since 1995.

Older Adults

Persons 65 years of age and above comprise only 13 percent of the population, yet account for approximately one-third of all medications prescribed in the United States. Older patients are more likely to be prescribed long-term and multiple prescriptions, which could lead to unintentional misuse.

The elderly also are at risk for prescription drug abuse, in which they intentionally take medications that are not medically necessary. In addition to prescription medications, a large percentage of older adults also use OTC medicines and dietary supplements. Because of their high rates of comorbid illnesses, changes in drug metabolism with age, and the potential for drug interactions, prescription and OTC drug abuse and misuse can have more adverse health consequences among the elderly than are likely to be seen in a younger population. Elderly persons who take benzodiazepines are at increased risk for cognitive impairment associated with benzodiazepine use, leading to possible falls (causing hip and thigh fractures), as well as vehicle accidents. However, cognitive impairment may be reversible once the drug is discontinued.

Adolescents and Young Adults

Data from the 2003 NSDUH indicate that 4.0 percent of youth ages 12 to 17 reported nonmedical use of prescription medications in the past month. Rates of abuse were highest among the 18–25 age group (6.0 percent). Among the youngest group surveyed, ages 12–13, a higher percentage reported using psychotherapeutics (1.8 percent) than marijuana (1.0 percent).

The NIDA Monitoring the Future survey of 8th-, 10th-, and 12th-graders found that the nonmedical use of opioids, tranquilizers, sedatives/barbiturates, and amphetamines was unchanged between 2003 and 2004. Specifically, the survey found that 5.0 percent of 12th-graders reported using OxyContin without a prescription in the past year, and 9.3 percent reported using Vicodin, making Vicodin one of the most commonly abused licit drugs in this population. Past year, nonmedical use of tranquilizers (e.g., Valium, Xanax) in 2004 was 2.5 percent for 8th-graders, 5.1 percent for 10th-graders, and 7.3 percent for 12th-graders. Also within the past year, 6.5 percent of 12th-graders used sedatives/ barbiturates (e.g., Amytal, Nembutal) nonmedically, and 10.0 percent used amphetamines (e.g., Ritalin, Benzedrine).

Youth who use other drugs are more likely to abuse prescription medications. According to the 2001 National Household Survey on Drug Abuse (now the NSDUH), 63 percent of youth who had used prescription drugs nonmedically in the past year had also used marijuana in the past year, compared with 17 percent of youth who had not used prescription drugs nonmedically in the past year.

Gender Differences

Studies suggest that women are more likely than men to be prescribed an abusable prescription drug, particularly narcotics and antianxiety drugs—in some cases, 55 percent more likely.

Overall, men and women have roughly similar rates of nonmedical use of prescription drugs. An exception is found among 12- to 17-year-olds. In this age group, young women are more likely than young men to use psychotherapeutic drugs nonmedically. In addition, research has shown that women are at increased risk for nonmedical use of narcotic analgesics and tranquilizers (e.g., benzodiazepines).

Source: Prescription Drugs: Abuse and Addiction. Washington, D.C.: U.S. Department of Health and Human Services. National Institutes of Health. National Institute of Drug Abuse. Revised August 2005, 5–7.

Court Cases

Vernonia v. Acton, 515 U.S. 646 (1995)

As noted above, the U.S. Supreme Court has acted on a number of cases involving drug testing in a variety of situations. Its first decision in a school-related setting came in 1995 in the case of Vernonia School District 47J, Petitioner V. Wayne Acton, et ux. *In that case, the school board of the Vernonia (Oregon) school district decided that any student wishing to participate in athletics at the school had to sign an agreement to take a drug test. One student who declined to do so, James Acton, declined to agree to such a test, and was prohibited from joining the school's seventh grade football team. Ultimately, his parents brought suit against the school district on his behalf, claiming that suspicionless drug testing was unconstitutional. The case worked its way through the courts, with each side recording at least one favorable ruling along the way, until it reached the U.S. Supreme Court in 1995, at which time the court ruled for the school district by a vote of 6 to 3. The main arguments of the court, as provided in Justice Scalia's decision, were as follows (citations omitted, as indicated by ellipsis):*

The Fourth Amendment to the United States Constitution provides that the Federal Government shall not violate "[t]he right of the people to be secure in their persons, houses, papers, and effects, against unreasonable searches and seizures. . . . " We have held that the Fourteenth Amendment extends this constitutional guarantee to searches and seizures by state officers, . . . including public school officials. . . . In Skinner v. Railway Labor Executives' Assn., . . . , we held that state compelled collection and testing of urine, such as that required by the Student Athlete Drug Policy, constitutes a "search" subject to the demands of the Fourth Amendment. . . .

As the text of the Fourth Amendment indicates, the ultimate measure of the constitutionality of a governmental search is "reasonableness."

At least in a case such as this, where there was no clear practice, either approving or disapproving the type of search at issue, at the time the constitutional provision was enacted, . . . whether a particular search meets the reasonableness standard" 'is judged by balancing its intrusion on the individual's Fourth Amendment interests against its promotion of legitimate governmental interests.' " . . . Where a search is undertaken by law enforcement officials to discover evidence of criminal wrongdoing, this Court has said that reasonableness generally requires the obtaining of a judicial warrant. . . . Warrants cannot be issued, of course, without the showing of probable cause required by the Warrant Clause. But a warrant is not required to establish the reasonableness of all government searches; and when a warrant is not required (and the Warrant Clause therefore not applicable), probable cause is not invariably required either. A search unsupported by probable cause can be constitutional, we have said, "when special needs, beyond the normal need for law enforcement, make the warrant and probable cause requirement impracticable." . . .

We have found such "special needs" to exist in the public school context. There, the warrant requirement "would unduly interfere with the maintenance of the swift and informal disciplinary procedures [that are] needed," and "strict adherence to the requirement that searches be based upon probable cause" would undercut "the substantial need of teachers and administrators for freedom to maintain order in the schools." . . . The school search we approved in T. L. O., while not based on probable cause, was based on individualized suspicion of wrongdoing. As we explicitly acknowledged, however, " 'the Fourth Amendment imposes no irreducible requirement of such suspicion,' " " . . . We have upheld suspicionless searches and seizures to conduct drug testing of railroad personnel involved in train accidents, . . . ; to conduct random drug testing of federal customs officers who carry arms or are involved in drug interdiction. . . .

. . .

Fourth Amendment rights, no less than First and Fourteenth Amendment rights, are different in public schools than elsewhere; the "reasonableness" inquiry cannot disregard the schools' custodial and tutelary responsibility for children. For their own good and that of their classmates, public school children are routinely required to submit to various physical examinations, and to be vaccinated against various diseases. . . .

Legitimate privacy expectations are even less with regard to student athletes. School sports are not for the bashful. They require "suiting up" before each practice or event, and showering and changing afterwards. . . .

There is an additional respect in which school athletes have a reduced expectation of privacy. By choosing to "go out for the team," they voluntarily subject themselves to a degree of regulation even higher than that imposed on students generally. In Vernonia's public schools, they must submit to a preseason physical exam (James testified that his included the giving of a urine sample, App. 17), they must acquire adequate insurance coverage or sign an insurance waiver, maintain a minimum grade point average, and comply with any "rules of conduct, dress, training hours and related matters as may be established for each sport by the head coach and athletic director with the principal's approval." ... Somewhat like adults who choose to participate in a "closely regulated industry," students who voluntarily participate in school athletics have reason to expect intrusions upon normal rights and privileges, including privacy.

Having considered the scope of the legitimate expectation of privacy at issue here, we turn next to the character of the intrusion that is complained of. We recognized in Skinner that collecting the samples for urinalysis intrudes upon "an excretory function traditionally shielded by great privacy." ... We noted, however, that the degree of intrusion depends upon the manner in which production of the urine sample is monitored. ... Under the District's Policy, male students produce samples at a urinal along a wall. They remain fully clothed and are only observed from behind, if at all. Female students produce samples in an enclosed stall, with a female monitor standing outside listening only for sounds of tampering. These conditions are nearly identical to those typically encountered in public restrooms, which men, women, and especially school children use daily. Under such conditions, the privacy interests compromised by the process of obtaining the urine sample are in our view negligible.

Finally, we turn to consider the nature and immediacy of the governmental concern at issue here, and the efficacy of this means for meeting it. In both Skinner and Von Raab, we characterized the government interest motivating the search as "compelling." ...

That the nature of the concern is important-indeed, perhaps compelling-can hardly be doubted. Deterring drug use by our Nation's schoolchildren is at least as important as enhancing efficient enforcement of the Nation's laws against the importation of drugs, which was the governmental concern in Von Raab, ..., or deterring drug use by engineers and trainmen, which was the governmental concern in Skinner. ...

Taking into account all the factors we have considered above-the decreased expectation of privacy, the relative unobtrusiveness of the search, and the severity of the need met by the searchwe conclude Vernonia's Policy is reasonable and hence constitutional.

Source: Vernonia School District 47J, Petitioner V. Wayne Acton, et ux., *etc.* 515 U.S. 646 (1995). Available online at http://www.supremecourtus.gov/opinions/boundvolumes/515bv.pdf. Accessed on August 23, 2009.

Gonzalez v. Raich, 545 U.S. 1 (2005)

One of the most contentious issues related to the use of illegal drugs concerns the use of marijuana to treat a wide variety of medical conditions, such as alcohol abuse, Attention Deficit Hyperactivity Disorder (ADHD or AD/HD), various forms of arthritis, asthma, atherosclerosis, autism, bipolar disorder, colorectal cancer, depression, epilepsy, digestive diseases, hepatitis C, hypertension, leukemia, and skin tumors, to name just a few. The drug has also been recommended for the treatment of side effects of various diseases and of treatments used against those diseases, side effects such as nausea, vomiting, loss of appetite, and weight loss. While many medical professionals, laypersons, and government officials support the legalization of marijuana for use in such situations, many others argue that marijuana is still an illegal drug in the United States, and its use should be prohibited even for such "compassionate" situations as those listed above. Local, state, and federal courts have had to decide a number of cases with regard to the "compassionate use" versus "illegal drug" controversy over the past two decades. More and more of these cases have arisen as individual states have adopted laws that permit the use of marijuana in certain medical situations. As of early 2010, 13 states in the United States, as well as a number of foreign countries, including Austria, Canada, Finland, Germany, Israel, Portugal, Spain, and the Netherlands have adopted such laws. A decision in the most recent medical marijuana case by the U.S. Supreme Court was announced on June 6, 2005. In that case, the court was asked to decide whether the federal government had the authority under the U.S. Constitution to prohibit the local cultivation and use of marijuana that was approved by the state of California. The court decided in favor of the U.S. government in this case by a vote of 6 to 3. That decision did not end the controversy over the medical use of marijuana, however, as four years later the court, in an unsigned statement, rejected appeals from San Bernardino and San Diego counties in California to have the California state medical marijuana law overturned because it violated federal restrictions on the use of the drug for any purpose whatsoever. The main points in the Gonzalez v. Raich *case are cited here (citations omitted, as indicated by ellipsis).*

In the introduction to his ruling for the majority, Justice John Paul Stevens lays out the fundamental Constitutional issue and the basis for the court's decision:

The case is made difficult by respondents' strong arguments that they will suffer irreparable harm because, despite a congressional finding to the contrary, marijuana does have valid therapeutic purposes.

The question before us, however, is not whether it is wise to enforce the statute in these circumstances; rather, it is whether Congress' power to regulate interstate markets for medicinal substances encompasses the portions of those markets that are supplied with drugs produced and consumed locally. Well-settled law controls our answer. The CSA [Controlled Substances Act] is a valid exercise of federal power, even as applied to the troubling facts of this case. We accordingly vacate the judgment of the Court of Appeals.

Later in his statement, Justice Stevens highlights two essential points about the case:

First, the fact that marijuana is used "for personal medical purposes on the advice of a physician" cannot itself serve as a distinguishing factor. . . . The CSA designates marijuana as contraband for any purpose; in fact, by characterizing marijuana as a Schedule I drug, Congress expressly found that the drug has no acceptable medical uses. Moreover, the CSA is a comprehensive regulatory regime specifically designed to regulate which controlled substances can be utilized for medicinal purposes, and in what manner. Indeed, most of the substances classified in the CSA "have a useful and legitimate medical purpose." . . . Thus, even if respondents are correct that marijuana does have accepted medical uses and thus should be redesignated as a lesser schedule drug, the CSA would still impose controls beyond what is required by California law. The CSA requires manufacturers, physicians, pharmacies, and other handlers of controlled substances to comply with statutory and regulatory provisions mandating registration with the DEA, compliance with specific production quotas, security controls to guard against diversion, recordkeeping and reporting obligations, and prescription requirements. . . . Furthermore, the dispensing of new drugs, even when doctors approve their use, must await federal approval. . . . Accordingly, the mere fact that marijuana—like virtually every other controlled substance regulated by the CSA—is used for medicinal purposes cannot possibly serve to distinguish it from the core activities regulated by the CSA.

. . .

Second, limiting the activity to marijuana possession and cultivation "in accordance with state law" cannot serve to place respondents' activities beyond congressional reach. The Supremacy Clause unambiguously provides that if there is any conflict between federal and state law, federal law shall prevail. It is beyond peradventure that federal power over commerce is " 'superior to that of the States to provide for the welfare or necessities of their inhabitants,' "however legitimate or dire those necessities may be. . . . Just as state acquiescence to federal regulation cannot expand the bounds of the Commerce

Clause, . . . so too state action cannot circumscribe Congress' plenary commerce power.

Justice Stevens concludes with a brief statement about one way in which those in favor of medical marijuana can achieve their objectives:
We do note, however, the presence of another avenue of relief. As the Solicitor General confirmed during oral argument, the statute authorizes procedures for the reclassification of Schedule I drugs. But perhaps even more important than these legal avenues is the democratic process, in which the voices of voters allied with these respondents may one day be heard in the halls of Congress.

Source: Gonzales v. Raich (03-1454) 545 U.S. 1 (2005). Available online at http://www.supremecourtus.gov/opinions/boundvolumes/545bv.pdf. Accessed on August 24, 2009.

United States of America v. Philip Morris, USA, Inc., et al. Civil Action No. 99-CV-02496 (GK) (2006)

On September 22, 1999, the U.S. Department of Justice (DOJ) filed a lawsuit against nine cigarette manufacturing companies and two related industry organizations under the Racketeer Influenced and Corrupt Organizations Act (RICO) of 1970. The purpose of the lawsuit was "to recover health care costs paid for and furnished, and to be paid for and furnished, by the federal government for lung cancer, heart disease, emphysema, and other tobacco-related illnesses caused by the fraudulent and tortious conduct of defendants, and to restrain defendants and their co-conspirators from engaging in fraud and other unlawful conduct in the future, and to compel defendants to disgorge the proceeds of their unlawful conduct." The case was to become one of the longest, most complex, and most significant legal actions taken in the field of substance abuse in U.S. history. Trial began almost six years later, on September 21, 2005, before Judge Gladys Kessler (who had been involved in the case from its outset) in the U.S. District Court for the District of Columbia. On August 17, 2006, Judge Kessler found in favor of the government, ruling that "substantial evidence establishes that Defendants have engaged in and executed—and continue to engage in and execute—a massive 50-year scheme to defraud the public, including consumers of cigarettes, in violation of RICO. Moreover, Defendants' past and ongoing conduct indicates a reasonable likelihood of future violations." On May 22, 2009, a three-judge panel for the U.S. Circuit Court of Appeals for the District of Columbia circuit upheld virtually all of Judge Kessler's rulings in the case. The core of Kessler's findings (which constituted a 1683-page decision) are as follows (citations omitted, as indicated by ellipsis):

The following voluminous Findings of Fact demonstrate that there is overwhelming evidence to support most of the Government's allegations. As the Conclusions of Law explain in great detail, the Government has established that Defendants (1) have conspired together to violate the substantive provisions of RICO, pursuant to 18 U.S.C. § 1962 (d), and (2) have in fact violated those provisions of the statute, pursuant to 18 U.S.C. § 1962 (c). Accordingly, the Court is entering a Final Judgment and Remedial Order which seeks to prevent and restrain any such violations of RICO in the future.

In particular, the Court is enjoining Defendants from further use of deceptive brand descriptors which implicitly or explicitly convey to the smoker and potential smoker that they are less hazardous to health than full flavor cigarettes, including the popular descriptors "low tar," "light," "ultra light," "mild," and "natural." The Court is also ordering Defendants to issue corrective statements in major newspapers, on the three leading television networks, on cigarette "onserts," and in retail displays, regarding (1) the adverse health effects of smoking; (2) the addictiveness of smoking and nicotine; (3) the lack of any significant health benefit from smoking "low tar," "light," "ultra light," "mild," and "natural" cigarettes; (4) Defendants' manipulation of cigarette design and composition to ensure optimum nicotine delivery; and (5) the adverse health effects of exposure to secondhand smoke.

Finally, the Court is ordering Defendants to disclose their disaggregated marketing data to the Government in the same form and on the same schedule which they now follow in disclosing this material to the Federal Trade Commission. All such data shall be deemed "confidential" and "highly sensitive trade secret information" subject to the protective Orders which have long been in place in this litigation.

Unfortunately, a number of significant remedies proposed by the Government could not be considered by the Court because of a ruling by the Court of Appeals in *United States v. Philip Morris, USA, Inc., et al.,* 396 F.3d 1196 (D.C. Cir. 2005). In that opinion, the Court held that, because the RICO statute allows only forward-looking remedies to prevent and restrain violations of the Act, and does not allow backward-looking remedies, disgorgement (i.e., forfeiture of ill-gotten gains from past conduct) is not a permissible remedy.

Applying this same legal standard, as it is bound to do, this Court was also precluded from considering other remedies proposed by the Government, such as a comprehensive smoker cessation program to help those addicted to nicotine fight their habit, a counter marketing program run by an independent entity to combat Defendants' seductive appeals to the youth market; and a schedule of monetary penalties for failing to meet pre-set goals for reducing the incidence of youth smoking.

The seven-year history of this extraordinarily complex case involved the exchange of millions of documents, the entry of more than 1,000 Orders, and a trial which lasted approximately nine months with 84 witnesses testifying in open court. Those statistics, and the mountains of paper and millions of dollars of billable lawyer hours they reflect, should not, however, obscure what this case is really about. It is about an industry, and in particular these Defendants, that survives, and profits, from selling a highly addictive product which causes diseases that lead to a staggering number of deaths per year, an immeasurable amount of human suffering and economic loss, and a profound burden on our national health care system. Defendants have known many of these facts for at least 50 years or more. Despite that knowledge, they have consistently, repeatedly, and with enormous skill and sophistication, denied these facts to the public, to the Government, and to the public health community. Moreover, in order to sustain the economic viability of their companies, Defendants have denied that they marketed and advertised their products to children under the age of eighteen and to young people between the ages of eighteen and twenty-one in order to ensure an adequate supply of "replacement smokers," as older ones fall by the wayside through death, illness, or cessation of smoking. In short, Defendants have marketed and sold their lethal product with zeal, with deception, with a single-minded focus on their financial success, and without regard for the human tragedy or social costs that success exacted.

Finally, a word must be said about the role of lawyers in this fifty-year history of deceiving smokers, potential smokers, and the American public about the hazards of smoking and second hand smoke, and the addictiveness of nicotine. At every stage, lawyers played an absolutely central role in the creation and perpetuation of the Enterprise and the implementation of its fraudulent schemes. They devised and coordinated both national and international strategy; they directed scientists as to what research they should and should not undertake; they vetted scientific research papers and reports as well as public relations materials to ensure that the interests of the Enterprise would be protected; they identified "friendly" scientific witnesses, subsidized them with grants from the Center for Tobacco Research and the Center for Indoor Air Research, paid them enormous fees, and often hid the relationship between those witnesses and the industry; and they devised and carried out document destruction policies and took shelter behind baseless assertions of the attorney client privilege.*

What a sad and disquieting chapter in the history of an honorable and often courageous profession.

Toward the end of her decision, Judge Kessler added a note about the probable future behavior of the cigarette companies.

The evidence in this case clearly establishes that Defendants have not ceased engaging in unlawful activity. Even after the Complaint in this action was filed in September 1999, Defendants continued to engage in conduct that is materially indistinguishable from their previous actions, activity that continues to this day. For example, most Defendants continue to fraudulently deny the adverse health effects of secondhand smoke which they recognize internally; all Defendants continue to market "low tar" cigarettes to consumers seeking to reduce their health risks or quit; all Defendants continue to fraudulently deny that they manipulate the nicotine delivery of their cigarettes in order to create and sustain addiction; some Defendants continue to deny that they market to youth in publications with significant youth readership and with imagery that targets youth; and some Defendants continue to suppress and conceal information which might undermine their public or litigation positions. See generally Findings of Fact Section V. Significantly, their conduct continues to further the objectives of the overarching scheme to defraud, which began by at least 1953. Their continuing conduct misleads consumers in order to maximize Defendants' revenues by recruiting new smokers (the majority of whom are under the age of 18), preventing current smokers from quitting, and thereby sustaining the industry.

As Defendants' senior executives took the witness stand at trial, one after another, it became exceedingly clear that these Defendants have not, as they claim, ceased their wrongdoing or, as they argued throughout the trial, undertaken fundamental or permanent institutional change. For example, during live testimony in January 2005, more than forty years after the 1964 Surgeon General's Report, Reynolds American Executive Chairman Andrew Schindler refused to admit that smoking causes disease. . . . Nevertheless, Joint Defendants assert in their post-trial Proposed Findings of Fact

---

*It would appear this situation continues even to the present. For example, in this very litigation, a former long-time career government lawyer was so intent on representing a company aligned with the defendants that he grossly misrepresented in his pleadings and declaration to the Court the degree and substance of his earlier participation as government counsel in related litigation involving the Food and Drug Administration. As a result, he was disqualified from representing Defendant-Intervenor BATAS.

that "Reynolds Concedes That Cigarette Smoking Causes Disease." ... In reality, the RJR Web site on which Joint Defendants rely in making that statement is only a half-hearted concession with the same two conditions that Schindler made in open court: "R. J. Reynolds Tobacco Company (R. J. Reynolds) believes that smoking, in combination with other factors, causes disease in some individuals." March 18, 2005 RJR Web site printout ... "The Web site minimizes smoking as being merely "a risk factor for many chronic diseases," and states that "[m]ost, if not all, chronic diseases result from the interaction of many risk factors including genetics, diet and lifestyle choices."

RJR is not alone. Lorillard's CEO, Martin Orlowsky, likewise refused at trial to admit to the full extent of smoking's harm. He was asked, "Why hasn't Lorillard specifically stated publicly that smoking causes any diseases other than smoking emphysema, COPD or heart disease?" He responded: "We have—in certain instances, we do not know if in fact the evidence, the scientific evidence is such that it warrants saying it does cause. However, Lorillard's longstanding position, as long as I've been with the company, is that certainly smoking can, and is a risk factor for those diseases." ... Lorillard's Web site includes a July 28, 2003 press release, in which its general counsel Ronald Milstein falsely stated that, "Research has shown time and time again that willpower is the only smoking cessation aid that always works." ... At trial, Milstein specifically refused to remove his statement from the Web site. ... He made those statements notwithstanding the fact that Defendants' internal documents indicate that they recognize that it is simply false that "willpower ... always works." Clearly, then, any claim the Defendants have changed their behavior must be rejected.

Source: United States of America, et al. v. Philip Morris USA, et al. Civil Action No. 99-2496 (GK). Available online at http://www .usdoj.gov/civil/cases/tobacco2/amended%20opinion.pdf, 2–5; 1604–1605.

Data

Scheduled Drugs

Currently, more than 350 substances are classified by the Drug Enforcement Administration (DEA) and the Food and Drug Admin- istration (FDA) under provisions of the Controlled Substances Act

TABLE 6.1
Schedules of Drugs, as Defined by the Controlled Substances Act of 1970

Schedule	Examples
I	heroin, lysergic acid diethylamide (LSD), marijuana, mescaline, methaqualone, morphine, peyote, psilocybin
II	amphetamine, cocaine, codeine, fentanyl, hydrocodone, meperidine, methadone, methamphetamine, morphine, opium and its extracts, phencyclidine (PCP)
III	anabolic steroids (including testosterone and derivatives), barbituric acid derivatives ("barbiturates"), some codeine and hydrocodone products, ketamine, lysergic acid
IV	alprazolam (Xanax), chlordiazepoxide (e.g., Librium), chloral hydrate, diazepam (e.g., Valium), mepromabate (e.g., Miltown), phenobarbital (e.g., Luminal), zolpidem (e.g., Ambien), zopiclone (e.g., Lunesta)
V	codeine and derivatives preparations, diphenoxylate preparations (e.g., Lomotil), opium preparations (e.g., Parapectolin)

Source: Office of Diversion Control, Drug Enforcement Administration, U. S. Department of Justice. "Controlled Substances Schedule." Available online. http://www.deadiversion.usdoj.gov/schedules/schedules.htm. Accessed on August 23, 2009.

of 1970. Table 6.1 shows examples of substances presently listed in each of the five categories available to the DEA and FDA.

Nonmedical Use of Prescription-type Psychotherapeutics in Lifetime, Past Year, and Past Month among Persons Aged 12 or Older, 2002–2004

One aspect of substance abuse that is sometimes neglected is the misuse of prescription drugs for purposes other than those for which a prescription is written. For example, a son may use drugs from a prescription written for his mother to treat his own medical problem or just "to get high" or to have some other psychoactive experience. The Substance Abuse and Mental Health Services Administration (SAMHSA) conducts regular surveys on this issue, the most recent of which was published in 2006. That survey reported on the number of individuals who used a prescription drug "simply for the experience or feeling the drug caused" during the month preceding the survey, the year preceding the survey, or at any time in his or her lifetime. The data collected by SAMHSA is segregated in its report by age, ethnicity, sex, and other factors; only the general summary for the report is listed in Table 6.2.

TABLE 6.2
Nonmedical Use of Prescription-type Psychotherapeutics in Lifetime, Past Year, and Past Month among Persons Aged 12 or Older, 2002–2004

2002	Lifetime		Past Year		Past Month	
Drug	Number[1]	Percent	Number[1]	Percent	Number[1]	Percent
Prescription psychotherapeutics	46,558	19.8	14,680	6.2	6,210	2.6
Pain relievers	29,611[3]	12.6	10,992	4.7	4,377	1.9
OxyContin®	1,924[4]	0.8[4]	_[2]	_[2]	_[2]	_[2]
Tranquilizers	19,267	8.2	4,849	2.1	1,804	0.8
Stimulants	21,072	9.0[3]	3.181	1.4	1,218	0.5
Methamphetamine	12,383	5.3	1,541	0.7	597	0.3
Sedatives	9,960	4.2	981	0.4	436[3]	0.2[3]

2003	Lifetime		Past Year		Past Month	
Drug	Number[1]	Percent	Number[1]	Percent	Number[1]	Percent
Prescription psychotherapeutics	47,882	20.1	14,986	6.3	6,336	2.7
Pain relievers	31,207	13.1	11,671	4.9	4,693	2.0
OxyContin®	2,832	1.2	_[2]	_[2]	_[2]	_[2]
Tranquilizers	20,220	8.5	5,051	2.1	1,830	0.8
Stimulants	20,798	8.8	2,751	1.2	1,191	0.5
Methamphetamine	12,303	5.2	1,315	0.6	607	0.3
Sedatives	9,510	4.0	831	0.3	294	0.1

2004	Lifetime		Past Year		Past Month	
Drug	Number[1]	Percent	Number[1]	Percent	Number[1]	Percent
Prescription psychotherapeutics	48,013	20.0	14,643	6.1	6,007	2.5
Pain relievers	31,768	13.2	11.256	4.7	4,404	1.8
OxyContin®	3,072	1.3	1,213	0.5	325	0.1
Tranquilizers	19,852	8.3	5,068	2.1	1,616	0.7
Stimulants	19,982	8.3	2,751	1.2	1,189	0.5
Methamphetamine	11,726	4.9	1,440	0.6	583	0.2
Sedatives	9,891	4.1	737	0.3	265	0.1

[1]Number in thousands
[2]Data not available
[3]Significantly different from 2004 data at the 0.5 level
[4]Significantly different from 2004 data at the 0.1 level

Source: Colliver, James D., et al. Misuse of Prescription Drugs: Data from the 2002, 2003, and 2004. National Surveys on Drug Use and Health. Washington, D.C.: Department of Health and Human Services, Substance Abuse and Mental Health Services Administration Office of Applied Studies, September 2006, Appendix D, Table 2.1AB.

Illicit Drug Use in the Lifetime, Past Year, and Past Month among Persons Aged 12 or Older: Percentages, 2006 and 2007

The Office of Applied Statistics of SAMHSA periodically conducts very detailed surveys about the use and abuse of legal and illegal drugs of all types, covering a range of demographic characteristics, such as age, sex, and ethnicity. The most recent general survey of this kind was published in September 2008. The most general findings of that study are reproduced in Table 6.3.

TABLE 6.3

Illicit Drug Use in the Lifetime, Past Year, and Past Month among Persons
Aged 12 or Older: Percentages, 2006 and 2007

Time Period/Demographic characteristic	Illicit Drugs		Illicit Drugs other than Marijuana	
	2006	2007	2006	2007
LIFETIME	45.43	46.11	29.63	29.65
Age				
12–17	27.60	26.23	19.49	18.37
18–25	58.98	57.42	39.52	38.36
26 and older	45.48	46.80	29.28	29.65
Gender				
Male	50.29	50.65	33.47	33.46
Female	40.86	41.83	26.02	26.07
PAST YEAR	14.54	14.40	8.64	8.53
Age				
12–17	19.58	18.72	12.39	11.55
18–25	34.37	33.19	20.24	19.46
26 and older	10.41	10.59	6.11	6.25
Gender				
Male	17.40	17.38	10.01	9.87
Female	11.85	11.59	7.35	7.27
PAST MONTH	8.27	8.01	3.91	3.74
Age				
12–17	9.77	9.54	4.93	4.68
18–25	19.80	19.75	8.87	8.07
26 and older	6.06	5.78	2.91	2.87
Gender				
Male	10.51	10.40	4.69	4.60
Female	6.17	5.76	3.17	2.93

Source: Results from the 2007 National Survey on Drug Use and Health: National Findings. Washington, D.C.: Department of Health and Human Services, Substance Abuse and MentalHealth Services Administration Office of Applied Studies, September 2008, Table B11.

Prevalence of Illegal Drug Use in the United States, 2002–2007

A number of the many questions asked in the 2007 National Survey on Drug Use and Health was the frequency with which respondents used illegal drugs. Table 6.4 summarizes the major findings obtained by asking that question.

TABLE 6.4

Prevalence of Illegal Drug Use in the United States, Percentages, 2002–2007

Substance/Time Period	Ages 12–17					
	2002	2003	2004	2005	2006	2007
Marijuana						
Lifetime	20.6	19.6	19.0	17.4	17.3	16.2
Past Year	15.8	15.0	14.5	13.3	13.2	12.5
Past Month	8.2	7.9	8/7	6.8	6.7	6.7
Cocaine						
Lifetime	2.7	2.6	2.4	2.3	2.2	2.1
Past Year	2.1	1.8	1.6	1.7	1.6	1.5
Past Month	0.6	0.6	0.5	0.6	0.4	0.4
Ecstasy						
Lifetime	3.3	2.4	2.1	1.6	1.9	1.8
Past Year	2.2	1.3	1.2	1.0	1.2	1.3
Past Month	0.5	0.4	0.3	0.3	0.3	0.3
LSD						
Lifetime	2.7	1.6	1.2	1.1	0.9	0.8
Past Year	1.3	0.6	0.6	0.6	0.4	0.5
Past Month	0.2	0.2	0.2	0.1	0.1	0.1
Inhalants						
Lifetime	10.5	10.7	11.0	10.5	10.1	9.6
Past Year	4.4	4.5	4.6	4.5	4.4	3.9
Past Month	1.2	1.3	1.2	1.2	1.3	1.2
Alcohol						
Lifetime	43.4	42.9	42.0	40.6	40.4	39.4
Past Year	34.6	34.3	33.9	33.3	32.9	31.8
Past Month	17.6	17.7	17.6	16.5	16.6	15.9
Cigarettes						
Lifetime	33.3	31.0	29.2	26.7	25.8	23.7
Past Year	20.3	19.0	18.4	17.3	17.0	15.7
Past Month	13.0	12.2	11.9	10.8	10.4	9.8

Substance/Time Period	Ages 18–25					
	2002	2003	2004	2005	2006	2007
Marijuana						
Lifetime	53.8	53.9	52.8	52.4	54.4	50.8
Past Year	29.8	28.5	27.8	28.0	28.0	27.5
Past Month	17.3	17.0	16.1	16.6	16.3	16.4
Cocaine						
Lifetime	15.4	15.0	15.2	15.1	15.7	15.0
Past Year	6.7	6.6	6.6	6.9	6.9	6.4
Past Month	2.0	2.2	2.1	2.6	2.2	1.7
Ecstasy						
Lifetime	15.1	14.8	13.8	13.7	13.4	12.8
Past Year	5.8	3.7	3.1	3.1	3.8	3.5
Past Month	1.1	0.7	0.7	0.8	1.0	0.7
LSD						
Lifetime	15.9	14.0	12.1	10.5	8.9	7.3
Past Year	1.8	1.1	1.0	1.0	1.2	1.1
Past Month	0.1	0.2	0.3	0.2	0.2	0.2
Inhalants						
Lifetime	15.7	14.9	14.0	13.3	12.5	11.3
Past Year	2.2	2.1	2.1	2.1	1.8	1.6
Past Month	0.5	0.4	0.4	0.5	0.4	0.4
Alcohol						
Lifetime	86.7	87.1	86.2	85.7	86.5	85.2
Past Year	77.9	78.1	78.0	77.9	78.8	77.9
Past Month	60.5	61.4	60.5	60.9	61.9	61.2
Cigarettes						
Lifetime	71.2	70.2	68.7	67.3	66.6	64.7
Past Year	49.0	47.6	47.5	47.2	47.0	45.1
Past Month	40.8	40.2	39.5	39.0	38.4	36.2

Source: *Results from the 2007 National Survey on Drug Use and Health: National Findings.* Washington, D.C.: Department of Health and Human Services, Substance Abuse and Mental Health Services Administration Office of Applied Studies, September 2008, Tables 9.1 and 9.2.

Cigarette Consumption in the United States, 1900–2007

The pattern in cigarette consumption in the United States over the past century has been remarkably consistent. Between 1900 and the 1960s, consumption rose slowly, but steadily, in almost every year. Consumption then leveled off until the mid-1970s, when it began to decline, which it has continued to do ever since. This trend is reflected in Table 6.5.

TABLE 6.5
Cigarette Consumption, in Billions, in the United States, 1900–2007

Year	1900	1901	1902	1903	1904	1905	1906	1907	1908	1909
Total cigarettes	2.5	2.5	2.8	3.1	3.3	3.6	4.5	5.3	5.7	7.0
Cigarettes per capita	54	53	60	64	66	70	86	99	105	125

Year	1910	1911	1912	1913	1914	1915	1916	1917	1918	1919
Total cigarettes	8.6	10.1	13.2	15.8	16.5	17.9	25.2	35.7	45.6	48.0
Cigarettes per capita	151	173	223	260	267	285	395	551	697	727

Year	1920	1921	1922	1923	1924	1925	1926	1927	1928	1929
Total cigarettes	44.6	50.7	53.4	64.4	71.0	79.8	89.1	97.5	106.0	118.6
Cigarettes per capita	665	742	770	911	982	1,085	1,191	1,279	1,366	1,504

Year	1930	1931	1932	1933	1934	1935	1936	1937	1938	1939
Total cigarettes	119.3	114.0	102.8	111.6	125.7	134.4	152.7	162.8	163.4	172.1
Cigarettes per capita	1,485	1,399	1,245	1,334	1,483	1,564	1,754	1,847	1,830	1,900

Year	1940	1941	1942	1943	1944	1945	1946	1947	1948	1949
Total cigarettes	181.9	208.9	245.0	284.3	296.3	340.6	344.3	345.4	358.9	360.9
Cigarettes per capita	1,976	2,236	2,585	2,956	3,039	3,449	3,446	3,416	3,505	3,480

Year	1950	1951	1952	1953	1954	1955	1956	1957	1958	1959
Total cigarettes	369.8	397.1	416.0	408.2	387.0	396.4	406.5	422.5	448.9	467.5
Cigarettes per capita	3,552	3,744	3,886	3,778	3,546	3,597	3,650	3,755	3,953	4,073

Year	1960	1961	1962	1963	1964	1965	1966	1967	1968	1969
Total cigarettes	484.4	502.5	508.4	523.9	511.3	528.8	541.3	549.3	545.6	528.9
Cigarettes per capita	4,171	4,266	4,266	4,345	4,194	4,258	4,287	4,280	4,186	3,993

Year	1970	1971	1972	1973	1974	1975	1976	1977	1978	1979
Total cigarettes	536.5	555.1	566.8	589.7	599.0	607.2	613.5	617.0	616.0	621.5
Cigarettes per capita	3,985	4,037	4,043	4,148	4,141	4,122	4,091	4,043	3,970	3,861

Year	1980	1981	1982	1983	1984	1985	1986	1987	1988	1989
Total cigarettes	631.5	640.0	634.0	600.0	600.4	594.0	583.8	575.0	562.5	540.0
Cigarettes per capita	3,849	3,836	3,739	3,488	3,446	3,370	3,274	3,197	3,096	2,926

Year	1990	1991	1992	1993	1994	1995	1996	1997	1998	1999
Total cigarettes	525.0	510.0	500.0	485.0	486.0	487.0	487.0	480.0	465.0	435.0
Cigarettes per capita	2,834	2,727	2,647	2,543	2,524	2,474	2,445	2,422	2,275	2,101

Year	2000	2001	2002	2003	2004
Total cigarettes	430.0	425.0	415.0	400.0	388.0
Cigarettes per capita	2,049	2,051	1,982	1,890	1,814

Source: Centers for Disease Control and Prevention. "Smoking and Tobacco Use: Consumption Data." Available online at http://www.cdc.gov/tobacco/data_statistics/tables/economics/consumption/index.htm. Accessed on August 26, 2009.

Alcohol-related Vehicular Accident Fatalities, United States, 1982–2004

Alcohol abuse is a profound problem for individuals, whose physical, mental, and emotional health is likely to suffer from overuse or misuse of alcohol. It is also a serious problem, however, for innocent individuals who suffer from another person's misuse of alcohol. One ongoing problem in this regard is the number of vehicular accidents caused by people who have consumed more alcohol than will allow them to drive safely. Table 6.6 summarizes the number and percentage of alcohol-related deaths over the 20-year period from 1984 to 2004.

TABLE 6.6
Alcohol-related Vehicular Accident Fatalities, United States, 1982–2004

Year	Traffic Crashes	Traffic Fatalities	Alcohol-related Traffic Crash Fatalities	Percent Alcohol-related Traffic Crash Fatalities
1982	39,092	43,945	26,172	59.6
1983	37,976	42,589	24,634	57.8
1984	39,631	44,257	24,761	55.9
1985	39,195	43,825	23,166	52.9
1986	41,090	46,087	25,017	54.3
1987	41,438	46,390	24,093	51.9
1988	42,130	47,087	23,833	50.6
1989	40,741	45,582	22,423	49.2

Year	Traffic Crashes	Traffic Fatalities	Alcohol-related Traffic Crash Fatalities	Percent Alcohol-related Traffic Crash Fatalities
1990	39,836	44,599	22,587	50.6
1991	36,937	41,508	20,159	48.6
1992	34,942	39,250	18,290	46.6
1993	35,780	40,150	17,908	44.6
1994	36,254	40,716	17,308	42.5
1995	37,241	41,817	17,732	42.4
1996	37,494	42,065	17,749	42.2
1997	37,324	42,013	16,711	39.8
1998	37,107	41,501	16,673	40.2
1999	37,140	41,717	16,572	39.7
2000	37,526	41,945	17,380	41.4
2001	37,862	42,196	17,400	41.2
2002	38,491	43,005	17,524	40.7
2003	38,477	42,884	17,105	39.9
2004	38,444	42,836	16,919	39.5

A crash is considered alcohol-related if either a driver or a nonoccupant (pedestrian or pedalcyclist) had a blood alcohol concentration (BAC) of 0.01 g/dl or greater. When alcohol tests were not done or test results are unknown, imputed BAC data provided by NHTSA are used.

Source: Yi, Hsiao-ye Yi, Chiung M. Chen, and Gerald D. Williams. *Surveillance Report #76: Trends in Alcohol-related Fatal Traffic Crashes, United States, 1982–2004.* Washington, D.C.: National Institute on Alcohol Abuse and Alcoholism, Division of Epidemiology and Prevention Research, Alcohol Epidemiologic Data System, August 2006, 30, Table 8.

Emergency Room Visits Involving Nonmedical Use of Selected Pharmaceuticals

While there may be some reason for cautious optimism about a reduction in the use of illegal substances in the United States in recent years, one trend is in the opposite direction: the abuse of legal prescription medicines. A number of surveys have suggested that both adolescents and adults are increasingly using prescription medicines, such as stimulants and depressants, for purposes other than those intended. In June 2009, the Substance Abuse and Mental Health Services Administration issued an update on its 2004 publication summarizing the number of emergency room admissions for the nonmedical use of certain pharmaceuticals. The summary data for that report is reprinted in Table 6.7.

TABLE 6.7
ED Visits Involving Nonmedical Use of Selected Pharmaceuticals

Drug	Estimated Visits	Percent of All Visits[1]
Opiates/opioids	172,726	32.2
Oxycodone and combinations	41,701	7.8
Hydrocodone and combinations	39,844	7.4
Methadone	38,806	7.2
Benzodiazepines	143,546	26.8
Alprazolam	46,526	8.7
Clonazepam	28,178	5.2
Muscle relaxants	25,934	4.8
Carisoprodol	14,736	2.7
Cyclobenzaprine	6,183	1.2
All ED visits involving nonmedical use of pharmaceuticals	536,247	100

[1]Percentages for subcategories calculated by author; not present in original report.
Source: *Emergency Department Visits Involving Nonmedical Use of Selected Pharmaceuticals.* Washington, D.C.: Substance Abuse and Mental Health Services Administration, July 2006; Revised June 2009, 3 (Table 1).

Treatment Admissions for Substance Abuse (2007)

Each year, the Substance Abuse and Mental Health Services Administration (SAMHSA) collects data on the number of admissions to health and treatment facilities in the United States for various legal and illegal drugs. These data are reported by state health departments to SAMHSA, who collates and disseminates the information. Selected data from the most recent report available are provided in Table 6.8.

TABLE 6.8
Treatment Admissions for Substance Abuse (2007)

Substance	1997	1999	2001	2003	2005	2007
Total	1,607,957	1,725,885	1,780,239	1,867,796	1,885,507	1,817,577
Alcohol	796,674	824,641	788,259	776,091	741,987	732,925
Alcohol only	455,699	461,532	433,620	430,990	408,422	406,038
Alcohol with secondary drug	350,975	363,109	354,639	345,101	333,565	326,887
Opiates	251,417	280,145	315,869	326,836	329,730	337,387
Heroin	235,143	257,508	277,653	273,996	259,462	246,871
Other opiates/synthetics	16,274	22,637	38,216	52,840	70,268	90,516

Substance	1997	1999	2001	2003	2005	2007
Non-R$_X$ methadone	1,209	1,606	2,050	2,719	4,070	5,094
Other opiates/synthetics	15,065	21,031	36,166	50,121	66,198	85,422
Cocaine	236,770	242,143	230,870	254,687	266,420	234,772
Smoked cocaine	174,900	176,507	168,890	184,846	191,973	167,914
Non-smoked cocaine	61,870	65,636	61,980	69,841	74,447	66,858
Marijuana/hashish	197,840	232,105	265,975	291,470	301,263	287,933
Stimulants	68,166	73,568	97,358	135,063	173,081	143,921
Methamphetamine	53,694	58,801	78,390	114,451	154,447	137,154
Other amphetamines	13,737	13,890	17,527	19,327	17,667	5,870
Other stimulants	735	877	1,441	1,285	967	897
Other drugs	18,942	26,702	33,324	29,821	28,167	25,823
Tranquilizers	4,796	5,913	7,447	8,164	8,458	9,949
Benzodiazepine	3,835	5,048	6,497	7,402	7,928	9,491
Other tranquilizers	961	865	950	762	530	458
Sedatives/hypnotics	3,240	3,459	3,998	4,277	4,456	4,210
Barbiturates	1,278	1,148	1,274	1,337	1,380	1,013
Other sedatives/hypnotics	1,962	2,311	2,724	2,940	3,076	3,197
Hallucinogens	2,672	2,789	3,149	2,236	2,006	1,502
PCP	1,896	2,321	3,193	4,177	2,861	3,124
Inhalants	1,819	1,423	1,259	1,217	1,372	992
Over-the-counter	506	1,091	624	708	768	802
Other	4,013	9,706	13,654	9,042	8,246	5,244
None reported	38,148	46,581	48,584	53,828	44,859	54,816

Source: Treatment Episode Data Set (TEDS) Highlights-2007. Rockville, MD: Substance Abuse and Mental Health Services Administration, February 2009, 5, Table 1a.

7

Directory of Organizations

A large number of local, regional, state, national, and international organizations are interested in the subject of substance abuse and addiction. For some of these organizations, that topic is the sole reason for their existence, while other organizations have more general missions, in which substance abuse is one of many concerns. The organizations listed in this chapter are only a sample of the many groups concerned with the issue of substance abuse. They have been categorized in the chapter according to their sponsorship: governmental, professional, academic, or private.

Governmental

Drug Enforcement Administration (DEA)
Web site: http://www.usdoj.gov/dea

The U.S. Drug Enforcement Administration was established as a division of the U.S. Department of Justice in July 1973 by an executive order issued by President Richard M. Nixon. Nixon conceived of the DEA as a single, unified organization to deal with the "war on drugs" that he had recently declared. At its founding, the DEA had 1,470 agents in 43 offices in 31 countries and a budget of less than $75 million. Today, it has 5,235 agents in 87 offices in 63 countries, with a budget of $2.3 billion. The agency's primary mission is to enforce the nation's drug laws and bring to justice any individual who is involved in the illegal manufacture, transportation, or distribution of illicit drugs. DEA has a wide-ranging group of programs and activities that involve topics and problems such as money-laundering, asset forfeiture, cannabis education, demand reduction, diversion control, forensic sciences, high intensity drug trafficking areas, organized crime drug enforcement forces, and the Southwest border initiative. The agency's Web site is a valuable resource of information on a number of topics, such as drug abuse prevention, drug policy, diversion control, legislative resources, and law enforcement.

Publications: "Checklist for Veterans and Reservists Called To Active Military Duty" (pamphlet); *A Tradition of Excellence* (history of the DEA; book); *Drugs of Abuse* (book); *Get It Straight* (book); *Guidelines for Law Enforcement for the Cleanup of Clandestine Drug Laboratories-2005 Edition* (manual); *Microgram Bulletin* (newsletter); *Microgram Journal* (journal); "Speaking Out" (pamphlet); *What Americans Need to Know about Marijuana* (booklet).

European Monitoring Centre for Drugs and Drug Addiction (EMCDDA)

Web site: http://www.emcdda.europa.eu/

The European Monitoring Centre for Drugs and Drug Addiction was established in 1993 to provide member state of the European Union with a comprehensive and coordinated system for collecting, organizing, and distributing information about substance abuse issues within the EU. Prior to that time, various countries had different methods of collecting and analyzing these data—and a poorly developed system for exchanging information with each other. Today, EMCDDA employs 90 specialists in the field of drug information and analysis, with the responsibility of providing member states with the scientific information they need for the development of sound drug policies. As of early 2010, the agency has organized its work under five primary rubrics: drugs and driving, neuroscience, research, women, and young people. It has announced additional organizational themes for the future, such as cannabis, cocaine, crime, death and mortality, infectious diseases, country-by-country, opioids, prison, recreational settings, synthetic drugs, and trafficking.

Publications: Reports, booklets, brochures, and other print publications categorized by type, such as thematic papers, risk assessments, work programs, methodological studies, monographs, and joint publications. Examples include "Methamphetamine: A European Union Perspective in the Global Context,"

"Internet-based Drug Treatment Interventions," "Neurobiological Research on Drugs: Ethical and Policy Implications," "Addiction Neurobiology: Ethical and Social Implications," "2009 Annual Report: The State of the Drugs Problem in Europe," "Women's Voices—Experiences and Perceptions of Women Facing Drug Problems," "EMCDDA Overview Brochure," and "Drug Use: An Overview of General Population Surveys in Europe."

Health Canada
Web site: http://www.hc-sc.gc.ca/

Health Canada is the Canadian government's department responsible for helping Canadian citizens to maintain and improve their health. The agency's Web site provides a host of valuable information about substance abuse on a variety of pages. A good beginning point is the page on Drug Prevention and Treatment, at http://www.hc-sc.gc.ca/hc-ps/drugs-drogues/index-eng.php. The department's major emphasis on the control of drug abuse in the country is currently outlined in the nation's National Anti-Drug Strategy, adopted by the federal government in 2007. The purpose of this program is to reduce both supply and demand for illegal drugs in Canada. Detailed information about the initiative is available online at http://www.national antidrugstrategy.gc.ca/.

Publications: Health Canada provides a wide array of publications on a variety of health-related topics under the general headings of *Assisted Human Reproduction, Children, It's Your Health, Sun Safety,* and *Women's Health.* Some excellent online publications on substance abuse can be found at http://www.hc-sc.gc.ca/hc-ps/drugs-drogues/learn-renseigne/index-eng.php.

National Institute on Alcohol Abuse and Alcoholism (NIAAA)
Web site: http://www.niaaa.nih.gov/

The National Institute on Alcohol Abuse and Alcoholism was established in 1970 as a provision of the Comprehensive Alcohol Abuse and Alcoholism Prevention, Treatment, and Rehabilitation Act of 1970 (P.L. 91-616). The new organization was charged in the act with developing and conducting health, education, training, research, and planning programs for the prevention and treatment of alcohol abuse and alcoholism. NIAAA supports extramural research on alcoholism and alcohol abuse and conducts its own intramural research on the same topics, providing about 90 percent of all research in the field in the United States. Much of its work is currently subsumed within five sponsored programs: Health Disparities Initiatives 2005; Leadership to Keep Children Alcohol Free; College Drinking Prevention; Initiative on Underage Drinking; and Interagency Coordinating Committee on FAS [Fetal Alcohol Syndrome].

Publications: *NIAAA Newsletter*; *NIAAA Alcohol Alert* (quarterly bulletin); *Alcohol Research and Health* (journal); *Helping Patients Who Drink Too Much: A Clinician's Guide*; manuals, monographs, reports, pamphlets, brochures, fact sheets, and posters on a variety of topics related to alcoholism and alcohol abuse.

National Institute on Drug Abuse (NIDA)
Web site: http://www.nida.nih.gov/

The National Institute on Drug Abuse was established in 1974 as the leading federal agency for research on drug abuse and addiction. The agency was transferred to the National Institutes of Health in 1992. NIDA has two primary functions: (1) sponsoring of basic research on drug use and abuse, and (2) dissemination of new information on these topics to professionals and the general public. It carries out its functions through four research centers (Epidemiology, Services and Prevention Research, Basic Neuroscience and Behavioral Research, Clinical Neuroscience and Behavioral Research, and Pharmacotherapies and Medical Consequences of Drug Abuse), the Center for Clinical Trials Network, three major programs (AIDS Research Program, International Program, and Intramural Research), and a number of workgroups, dealing with topics such as genetics, neuroscience, research training, minority concerns, health disparities, children and adolescents, and women and sex/gender differences.

Publications: *NIDA Notes* (newsletter); *Research Reports*; *Topics in Brief* (newsletter); *NIDA InfoFacts* (fact sheets); *NIDA Addiction Science & Clinical Practice* (journal); *Drugs, Brains, and Behavior–The Science of Addiction* (booklet); *Principles of Drug Addiction Treatment: A Research Based Guide*, Second Edition (booklet); and *Principles of Drug Abuse Treatment for Criminal Justice Populations* (booklet).

National Women's Health Information Center (NWHIC)
Web site: http://womenshealth.gov/

The National Women's Health Information Center is a service of the Office on Women's Health of the U.S. Department of Health and Human Services. In was established in 1991 for the purpose of providing leadership to bringing about equity in health programs with gender-specific activities. It provides information on a host of issues of special interest to women and girls as well as men, such as body image, breast cancer, breastfeeding, fitness and nutrition, girls' health, healthy aging, heart health and stroke, HIV/AIDS, men's health, menopause, mental health, minority women's health, pregnancy, preventive health, smoking and how to quit, and violence against women. The agency sponsors a variety of special programs, which change from time to time. They currently include topics such as "BodyWorks—A Toolkit for Healthy Girls and Strong Women," "For Your Heart," "The Heart Truth," "Could I Have Lupus?," "Powerful Girls have Powerful Bones," and "Woman Activity Tracker."

Publications: *The Healthy Woman: A Complete Guide for All Ages* (book); *A Lifetime of Good Health: Your Guide to Staying Healthy* (booklet); *An Easy Guide to Breastfeeding* (booklet); *BodyWise Handbook*; many fact sheets, pamphlets, and brochures on topics such as "Common Screening and Diagnostic Tests," "How to Get a Second Opinion," "How to Talk to Your Doctor or Nurse," "Symptoms of Serious Health Conditions," "Screening Tests and Immunizations Guidelines for Women," "Menopause Resource Guide," and "State Domestic Violence Resources."

Office of National Drug Control Policy (ONDCP)
Web site: http://www.whitehousedrugpolicy.gov/

The Office of National Drug Control Policy was established in 1988 as one provision of the Anti-Drug Abuse Act of 1988. It is the primary agency in the Executive department for developing and executing policy on the use and abuse of illegal drugs in the United States. It is responsible for developing the National Drug Control Strategy, which outlines national policy on drug control, establishes a budget for this effort, and coordinates the work of federal, state, and local authorities in the fight against substance abuse. The office uses a three-prong attack on drug abuse that focuses on prevention, treatment, and interdiction of drug sources.

Publications: Over 1,000 pamphlets, brochures, reports, and other publications dealing with virtually every aspect of the substance abuse problem in the United States and other parts of the world, such as "2007 National Money Laundering Strategy"; "ADAM [Arrestee Drug Abuse Monitoring] II Report Fact Sheet 2008"; "Afghanistan Opium Winter Rapid Assessment Survey 2008"; "The DASIS [Drug and Alcohol Services Information System] Report: Adolescent Admissions Reporting Inhalants, 2006"; "The NSDUH [National Survey on Drug Use and Health] Report: Risk & Protective Factors for Substance Use among American Indian or Alaska Native Youths"; and "The War on Meth in Indian Country."

Substance Abuse and Mental Health Services Administration (SAMHSA)
Web site: http://www.samhsa.gov/

The Substance Abuse and Mental Health Services Administration was created in 1992 during the reorganization of the federal government's agencies responsible for mental health services. It assumed most of the responsibilities of the Alcohol, Drug Abuse, and Mental Health Administration (ADAMHA), which was disbanded in the reorganization. The organization is charged with developing and supporting programs that improve the quality and availability of prevention, treatment, and rehabilitation for abusers of both legal and illegal drugs. Its work is divided among four major divisions, the Center for Mental Health Service, Center for Substance Abuse Prevention, Center for Substance Abuse Treatment, and Office of Applied Studies. Some of the programs the agency has recently funded include conferences for the dissemination of new knowledge about substance abuse, campus suicide prevention programs, community mental health services programs for children and their parents, jail diversion and trauma recovery programs (with special preference for veterans), supportive housing services, drug-free community programs, offender reentry programs, and state and community prevention programs.

Publications: Many reports on a variety of substance-abuse related topics, such as *Characteristics of Substance Abuse Treatment Facilities Offering Acupuncture, Treatment for Substance Abuse and Depression among Adults by Race/Ethnicity,* and *Fiscal Year 2008 Annual SYNAR Reports: Youth Tobacco Sales; SAMHSA Newsletter;*

informational brochures, pamphlets, flyers, and posters, such as those in the "Tips for Teens" series (about marijuana, methamphetamines, inhalants, heroin, steroids, club drugs, etc.) as well as "Keeping Your Teens Drug-Free: A Family Guide," "Get the Facts on Drugs," and "Good Mental Health is Ageless."

United Nations Office on Drugs and Crime (UNODC)
Web site: http://www.unodc.org/

The United Nations Office on Drugs and Crime was established in 1997 through the merger of the United Nations Drug Control Programme and the Centre for International Crime Prevention. The agency's mission is to assist member states in their battles against illegal substance abuse, crime, and terrorism. The three primary components of UNODC's work are providing technical assistance to member states in dealing with drug abuse, crime, and terrorism; conducting research to collect up-to-date information on these topics; and assisting member states in the ratification and implementation of various regional and international treaties dealing with drug use and crime. The agency currently conduct four major campaigns dealing with illegal substance abuse and crime: World Drug Day, International Anti-Corruption Day, World AIDS Day, and the Blue Heart Campaign against human trafficking. Much of the agency's work is carried out through two commissions. The Commission on Narcotic Drugs is the primary policymaking agency for the United Nations in the area of illegal substance abuse. The Commission on Crime Prevention and Criminal Justice provides the United Nations with guidance on policies and practices in these two fields.

Publications: *World Drug Report*, an annual survey of the status of substance abuse throughout the world; periodic reports on the status of drug abuse and crime worldwide, such as *United Nations Surveys on Crime Trends and the Operations of Criminal Justice Systems* and *International Homicide Statistics*; a periodic journal, *Bulletin on Narcotics*; a popular magazine, *Perspectives*; an annual report of the agency's activities in the preceding year; and reports on a variety of specific topics, such as "Addiction Crime and Insurgency" (the threat posed by opium from Afghanistan), "Colombia Coca Survey," "Handbook for Parliamentarians on Combating Trafficking in Persons," "Handbook on Prisoners with Special Needs," and "HIV and AIDS in Places of Detention."

Working Partners for an Alcohol- and Drug-Free Workplace
Web site: http://www.dol.gov/workingpartners/

Working Partners for an Alcohol- and Drug-Free Workplace is an initiative of the U.S. Department of Labor whose purpose it is to raise awareness among employers and employees about the impact that alcohol and drugs can have on working conditions and to provide information about ways in which workplaces can be kept free of these substances. Some elements of the programs efforts are training of supervisors and employees, drug testing resources, provision of resources for employers and employees, and crisis management tools for workplaces that do not have alcohol- and drug-free policies.

Publications: Email updates; "Working Partners for an Alcohol and Drug-Free Workplace" (brochure); "Steps to a Drug-Free Workplace" (brochure); "Methamphetamine in the Workplace" (Power-Point presentation); "Top 12 Reasons Why a Good Drug-Free Workplace Program Goes Bad" (PowerPoint presentation); fact sheets on Symptoms and Intervention Techniques, General Workplace Impact, Construction Industry, General Services Industry, Health Care Industry, Hospitality Industry, High-Tech Industry, Manufacturing Industry, Retail Industry, Transportation Industry, and Wholesale Industry.

World Health Organization (WHO)
Web site: http://www.who.int/en/

The World Health Organization was founded on April 7, 1948, a day now observed as World Health Day, as an agency of the United Nations. The agency's current efforts are guided by a six-point agenda that focuses on promoting development to improve the health status of people in developing countries; fostering health security against epidemics and other outbreaks of disease; strengthening health systems; promoting research to gain better information on health issues on which policies can be based; enhancing partnerships among WHO, other international, national, and regional agencies and private organizations; and improving the efficiency of existing health agencies throughout the world.

Publications: Many books, reports, articles, and other publications on a large variety of issues related to substance abuse, such as *Global Status Report on Alcohol 2004* (book), *Global Status*

Report: Alcohol Policy (book), *Neuroscience of Psychoactive Substance Use and Dependence* (book), *International Guidelines for Estimating the Costs of Substance Abuse* (book), "What Do People Think They Know about Substance Dependence" (leaflet), *Evaluation of Psychoactive Substance Use Disorder Treatment* (series of workbooks), *Costs and Effects of Treatment for Psychoactive Substance Use Disorders: a Framework for Evaluation* (report), and *Brief Intervention for Hazardous and Harmful Drinking* (manual).

Academic Organizations

Many state colleges and universities both in the United States and other nations have departments, centers, or other entities that conduct research, training, and education on the subject of substance abuse. The list below contains a sampling of such agencies.

Center for Education and Drug Abuse Research (CEDAR)
University of Pittsburgh
Web site: http://www.pitt.edu/~cedar/

The Center for Education and Drug Abuse Research was founded in 1989 with a grant from the National Institute for Drug Abuse. Its mission is to study the factors involved in the process by which an individual transitions from being a non-user to demonstrating the characteristics of substance abuse disorder (SUD). The results of this research will provide suggestions for prevention methodologies that can be instituted to reduce the risk of a person converting from substance non-use to substance use. As of early 2010, CEDAR has identified more than two dozen factors involved in the conversion process, all of which are listed on the center's Web site.

Publications: Many scholarly papers for refereed journals reporting the results of specific research studies by CEDAR members.

Center for Substance Abuse Research (CESAR)
University of Maryland
Web site: http://www.cesar.umd.edu/cesar/about.asp

The Center for Substance Abuse Research was established at the University of Maryland in 1990 upon recommendation of the Governor's Alcohol and Drug Abuse Commission. As a division of the College of Behavioral and Social Sciences, CESAR conducts basic research on substance abuse, collects statistical data on the topic, and trains students in the fields of criminal justice, public health, psychology, and sociology. The center also does research and collects data that can be used in the development of public policies on substance abuse prevention, treatment, and education.

Publications: Many publications, such as *Need for Substance Abuse Treatment in Maryland* (report); *CESAR Fax* (weekly newsletter); *DEWS Fax* (bimonthly newsletter); *Incidence and Persistence of Cannabis Dependence Among College Students* (report); *Youth and Drugs in Washington, D.C., 1999–2006* (report); *Heavy Drinking and Polydrug Use in College Students* (report); and *Social Context of Drinking and Alcohol Problems Among College Students* (report).

Division of Alcoholism and Drug Abuse
New York University Medical Center/New York
University School of Medicine
Web site: http://www.med.nyu.edu/substanceabuse/

The NYU Division of Alcoholism and Drug Abuse is located within the Department of Psychiatry at the NYU Medical Center and School of Medicine. Its purpose is to draw on research, some of which is conducted at the division, to develop new ideas for training, research, and clinical care in substance abuse and to develop new models that can be implemented nationwide.

National Center on Addiction and Substance Abuse
at Columbia University
Web site: http://www.casacolumbia.org/

The National Center on Addiction and Substance Abuse at Columbia University (CASA) was founded in 1992 by former Secretary of Health, Education, and Welfare, Joseph Califano, Jr., for the purpose of informing the American public about the social and economic costs of substance abuse. CASA claims to be "the only nation-wide organization that brings together under one roof all the professional disciplines needed to study and combat abuse of all substances—alcohol, nicotine as well as illegal, prescription and performance enhancing drugs—in all sectors of society." The center's work is organized into five separate areas: health and treatment, policy research and analysis, youth programs, policy to practice, and Join Together, a program designed to help community leaders to make the best possible use of recent research advances to prevent and treat substance abuse.

Publications: Three books, *Women under the Influence, High Society: How Substance Abuse Ravages America and What to Do About It*, and *How to Raise a Drug-Free Kid: The Straight Dope for Parents*; a number of reports, such as *National Survey of American Attitudes on Substance Abuse* (conducted and issued annually), *Shoveling Up: The Impact of Substance Abuse on Federal, State and Local Budgets, CASA-SARDsm: Intensive Case Management for Substance-Dependent Women Receiving Temporary Assistance for Needy Families, Non-Medical Marijuana: Rite of Passage or Russian Roulette?, Tobacco: The Smoking Gun*, and *The Importance of Family Dinners*; *CASAInside* (newsletter).

Tobacco Control Legal Consortium (TCLC)
Web site: http://tclconline.org/

The Tobacco Control Legal Consortium has its headquarters at the Tobacco Law Center (TLC) at the William Mitchell College of Law at St. Paul, Minnesota. TLC was founded in 2000 as a consequence of the massive legal settlement between the nation's largest tobacco companies and the attorneys general of nearly all 50 states. At its founding, the center consisted of a single attorney working at Mitchell. Today, it consists of seven full-time attorneys who also coordinate the efforts of the Tobacco Control Legal Consortium, which consists of attorneys from a number of states involved in the original 2000 lawsuit decision. TCLC is involved in a wide variety of activities involved in providing smoke-free environments, including the drafting of model smoke-free legislation, legal actions to enforce existing smoke-free laws and regulations, responding to challenges to smoke-free laws and other clean air legislation, writing amicus curiae briefs in smoking and clean air cases, and conducting legal research on tobacco and smoking issues.

Publications: *Tobacco Law and Policy: A Database of Law Review and Journal Articles* (online database); *The Verdict Is In: Findings from United States v. Philip Morris* (booklet containing selected quotes from 2006 tobacco decision); *Going Too Far? Exploring the Limits of Tobacco Regulation* (symposium proceedings); many law synopses, such as *Regulating Cigarettes for Fire Safety, Secondhand Smoke and Casinos, There Is No Constitutional Right to Smoke*, and *The Americans with Disabilities Act: Effective Legal Protection Against*

Secondhand Smoke Exposure; Legal Resources for Tobacco Control; many PowerPoint presentations; *Legal Update* (newsletter).

UCLA Integrated Substance Abuse Programs (ISAP)
Web site: http://www.uclaisap.org/

The UCLA [University of California at Los Angeles] Integrated Substance Abuse Programs was established in 1999 as a way of coordinating the efforts of a number of different programs for research on substance abuse at the university. It is currently located within the Department of Psychiatry and Biobehavioral Sciences at the David Geffen School of Medicine at UCLA. The program currently has four major objectives: (1) developing and evaluating new approaches for the treatment of substance abuse; (2) transferring newly developed treatments into mainstream applications; (3) promoting the empirical understanding of substance abuse and supporting efforts to deal with related problems; and (4) investigating the epidemiology, neurobiology, consequences, treatment, and prevention of substance abuse. Some current programs at ISAP include Clinical Trial Networks, Center for Advancing Longitudinal Drug Abuse Research (CALDAR), Criminal Justice Drug Abuse Treatment Studies, Los Angeles County Evaluation System (LACES), and Friends LaBrea.

Publications: A large number of papers, book chapters, and reports describing the work and findings of ISAP staff and researchers; *Methamphetamine Treatment: A Practitioner's Reference 2007* (manual): *Treating Addicted Offenders: A Continuum of Effective Practices* (manual); *Once In A Blue Moon: Toward a Better Understanding of Hetero-sexually Identified Men who have Sex with Men and/or Preoperative Transgender Women* (report); *Getting Off: A Behavioral Treatment Intervention For Gay and Bi-sexual Male Methamphetamine Users* (manual); and *Evaluation of the Substance Abuse and Crime Prevention Act 2004* (report).

Private

Addiction Technology Transfer Center (ATTC)
Web site: http://www.attcnetwork.org/

The Addiction Technology Transfer Center is a network of a national office and 14 regional offices that serve all 50 states, the

District of Columbia, Puerto Rico, the U.S. Virgin Islands, and the Pacific Islands of Guam, American Samoa, Palau, the Marshal Islands, Micronesia, and the Mariana Islands. ATTC was established in 1993 by a grant from the U.S. Substance Abuse and Mental Health Services Administration (SAMHSA) for the purpose of translating the results of basic research into practical recommendations for prevention and treatment services. The center achieves this objective in a three-step program that includes dissemination of recent advances in research on substance abuse, training of workers to put new knowledge into practice, and incorporating new knowledge and technology into everyday use in treatment centers and recovery programs. ATTC is still funded by SAMHSA, who most recently extended the program to 2012 in 2007.

Publications: Many books, book chapters, pamphlets, brochures, and educational materials, such as *Building Resilience, Wellness and Recovery: A Shift from an Acute Care to a Sustained Care Recovery* (book, electronic book); *Clinical Supervision I-Building Chemical Dependency Counselor Skills* (book); *Clinical Supervision II: Addressing Supervisory Problems in Addictions Treatment* (book); *Healing the Stigma of Addiction: A Guide for Treatment Practitioners* (book); "Toolbox Training: A Substance Abuse Educational Series for Helping Professionals" (pamphlet); "Buprenorphine" (pamphlet); "Addictions Recovery: When Knowing the Facts Can Help" (brochure); "How to Set Up an Effective Mobile Outreach Prevention Program" (brochure); "Native American Curriculum for Non-Tribal Substance Abuse Programs" (brochure); and *Adolescent Treatment Issues: Understanding & Managing Youth Training of the Trainers (TOT) Manual* (curriculum).

Al-Anon/Alateen
Web site: http://www.al-anon.alateen.org/

Al-Anon was founded in 1951 by Lois W., wife of Bill W., founder of Alcoholics Anonymous, and Anne B. The organization grew rapidly and was incorporated in 1954 under the name of Al-Anon Family Group Headquarters, Inc. The purpose of the organization was to assist family members in dealing with the problems they faced as loved ones of alcoholics. A year later, the group published its first book, *The Al-Anon Family Groups, A Guide for the Families of Problem Drinkers*. In 1957, a similar support group was formed for and by the children of men and women with alcohol problems, a group that was given the name Alateen. A year later, the board of directors of Al-Anon decided to establish an Alateen Committee and in 1964, a special staff person was hired to work with Alateen groups. As of early 2010, there are more than 24,000 Al-Anon/Alateen groups in 130 countries around the world, with an average membership of about 13 individuals per group. The organization's publications have been printed in more than 30 different languages.

Publications: Many books, booklets, kits, and other publications, such as *Discovering Choices* (book); *Dilemma of the Alcoholic Marriage* (book); *The Al-Anon Family Groups* (book); *One Day at a Time in Al-Anon* (book); *Lois Remembers* (book); *Blueprint for Progress* (booklet); *Al-Anon/Alateen Service Manual* (booklet); *When I Got Busy, I Got Better* (booklet); *The Best of Public Outreach* (booklet); "Al-Anon is for Men" (pamphlet); "Alcoholism: The Family Disease" (pamphlet); "So You Love an Alcoholic" (pamphlet); "The Twelve Steps and Tradition" (pamphlet); "Alateen Newcomer Packet" (kit); "Courage to Change" (CD-ROM).

Alcoholics Anonymous
Web site: http://www.aa.org/

Alcoholics Anonymous was founded by two men attempting to deal with their alcoholism, William Griffith ("Bill") Wilson and Robert Holbrook ("Bob") Smith. The traditional date for the founding of the organization is set at June 10, 1935, the date on which Smith had his last drink. Although the organization keeps no formal records, it estimated that as of January 1, 2007, it had at least 1,248,000 members in over 55,000 groups in the United States, and an almost equal number of groups overseas, with just over 700,000 members. The total number of groups worldwide was estimated at 116,773. The organization is very simple in concept, with no membership dues or requirements, other than the desire to quit drinking. It is perhaps best known for its twelve-step program for dealing with problems of alcoholism.

Publications: More than 150 books, pamphlets, guides, and other materials, including *Alcoholics Anonymous* (book); *Experience, Strength, and Hope* (book); *Twelve Steps and Twelve Traditions* (book); *As Bill Sees It* (book); *Living Sober* (book); *Young People and A.A.* (book); "44 Questions" (pamphlet); "Do You Think You're Different?" (pamphlet); "A.A. and the Armed Services" (pamphlet); "A Newcomer Asks" (pamphlet); "A.A. and the Gay/Lesbian Alcoholic" (pamphlet); and *Box 4-5-9* (newsletter).

American Council for Drug Education (ACDE)
Web site: http://www.acde.org/

The American Council for Drug Education was founded in 1977 in response to the growing problem of substance abuse in the United States. The organization's primary mission is to ensure that accurate, scientifically-based information about drug abuse prevention programs is easily available to the general public. In 1995, ACDE became an affiliate of the Phoenix House Foundation, which calls itself "the largest, private, non-profit drug abuse service agency in the country." ACDE operates the Web site, www.drughelp.com, which provides information on drugs, drugs abuse, drug abuse prevention, and drug abuse treatment, with referrals to public and private treatment facilities, self-help resources, crisis centers, and family assistance groups throughout the nation.

Publications: *Working it Out: Adult Children of Alcoholics in the Workplace* (user's guide, video, and handouts); *Support Groups that Work* (manual); *The Feel Better Book* (workbook); *Faces of Addiction Kit for Schools* (video and ancillary materials); "Know Your Strengths, Know Your Risks" (pamphlet); and "Ties that Bind" (fact sheets).

Americans for Nonsmokers' Rights (ANR)
Web site: http://www.no-smoke.org/

Americans for Nonsmokers' Rights was founded in 1976 for the purpose of protecting nonsmokers from the hazards posed by secondhand cigarette smoke, to prevent young people from becoming addicted to tobacco products, and to act as a counter force to the tobacco industry in efforts to reduce the use of tobacco products in the United States. The organization is primarily member-supported and works to support all types of regulation of secondhand smoke, including voluntary, legislative, and regulatory policies. It also works to support legislative and regulatory efforts to limit the influence of the tobacco industry in the development of national policies on smoking and tobacco use. ANR's sister organization, the American Nonsmokers' Rights Foundation (ANRF) was founded in 1982 to develop programs for school-age youth on the importance of smoke-free spaces in American society.

Publications: A quarterly newsletter, *UPDATE!*; numerous electronic fact sheets on topics such as secondhand smoke, economic impact of secondhand smoke, ventilation, preemption by the tobacco industry, going smoke-free at home, work, and in the community; smoke-free travel; legal issues; and target populations.

Americans for Safe Access (ASA)
Web site: http://www.safeaccessnow.org/

Americans for Safe Access calls itself the "largest national member-based organization of patients, medical professionals, scientists and concerned citizens promoting safe and legal access to cannabis for therapeutic use and research." The organization has more than 30,000 members and chapters in 40 states. Founded in 2002, ASA lists a number of important accomplishments in its brief history, including organizing legal support for more than 30 individuals being accused of illegal marijuana use, conducting training tours on individual rights in the field of medical marijuana, organizing protest rallies against state and local actions against the medical uses of marijuana, filing suit against laws prohibiting the cultivation of marijuana for medical purposes, and working on the sponsorship of legislation to protect the rights of individuals who use marijuana for medical purposes.

Publications: "Condition" books on topics such as aging, arthritis, cancer, chronic pain, and HIV/AIDS; a legal manual specifically for the state of California; and Know Your Rights cards.

Association for Medical Education and Research in Substance Abuse (AMERSA)
Web site: http://www.amersa.org/

The Association for Medical Education and Research in Substance Abuse has more than 300 physician members from a number of specialty areas, along with nurses, social workers, psychologists, pharmacologists, dentists, and other professionals. The organization was founded in 1976 by members of the Career Teachers Program, which was then funded by the National Institute on Alcohol Abuse and Alcoholism and the National Institute on Drug Abuse for the purpose of developing faculty members with special training in the area of substance abuse. Members of AMERSA have developed, implemented, and evaluated curricula, educational programs, and faculty development programs and clinical and research measures for substance abuse services and professional education and have conducted research related to substance abuse education, clinical service, and prevention. AMERSA sponsors an annual conference on substance abuse education, provides a speakers' bureau on the topic, and currently has a task force on physician education in the field of substance abuse.

Publications: *Substance Abuse* (journal); *About AMERSA* (newsletter).

Center on Addiction and the Family (COAF)
Phoenix House
Web site: http://www.coaf.org/

The Center on Addiction and the Family was founded in 1982 as the Children of Alcoholics Foundation. It became part of Phoenix House in 1997 and expanded its mission to include all forms of substance abuse. The organization's mission is to help children of substance abusers to escape from the model established by their parents and reach their own full potential in life. COAF attempts to achieve this goal by developing curricula and other educational materials, writing reports about substance abuse, promoting research on the topic, and providing information to professionals and the general public about substance abuse issues. The center currently carries out much of its work through eight major programs: Collaborations (involving work with other substance abuse agencies); Transitions (a prevention program for older adolescents); Facts on Tap (an alcohol and other drug education program for college campuses); Building Bridges (a program designed to help parents in treatment cope with family issues); Ties That Bind (helping individuals deal with issues of kinship care and parental substance abuse); Pandora's Box (an online educational program for professionals dealing with children of substance abusers); Changing Our View (revamping Phoenix House protocols to strengthen its outreach efforts); and Trainings, Consultation and Technical Assistance (working with organizations to provide customized staff development programs on issues).

Publications: Same as those listed for American Council for Drug Education; see above.

Drug Policy Alliance Network (DPAN)
Web site: http://www.drugpolicy.org/

The Drug Policy Alliance was formed in 2000 when The Lindesmith Center merged with the Drug Policy Foundation. DPAN is committed to searching for alternatives to current drug policies in the United States, an effort that is based on the belief that the present "war on drugs" is ineffective and actually does more harm than good. The core of DPAN activities is organized within seven major initiatives: Safety First, a "reality-based" program to provide parents and students with education about drugs that promotes their safety and health; Marijuana Law Reform, an effort to change the attitudes of policymakers and legislators about the legal status of marijuana; National Policy, an initiative by the organization's national office to educate legislators and policymakers about the need for new ways of thinking about substance abuse policy in the United States; Legal Affairs, operated out of the DPAN Berkeley (California) office, which writes model legislation, assists in litigation, and trains legal professionals; Organizing and Policy Project, which attempts to make national drug policy a part of community-based organization agendas; Health Policy Project, based in Sacramento, California, which works to reduce the health effects and other damage caused by substance abuse; and International Efforts, the organization's campaign to change drug policy and laws in other parts of the world.

Publications: Many books, booklets, pamphlets, and electronic publications, including "About Methadone and Buprenorphine" (booklet); "Beyond Zero Tolerance" (pamphlet); *Cocaine: Global Histories* (book); *Just4Teens* (DVD); *How To Legalize Drugs* (booklet); "Making Sense of Student Drug Testing" (pamphlet); *Marijuana Myths; Marijuana Facts* (booklet); and *On Liberty and Drugs: Essays on the Free Market and Prohibition* (booklet).

Harm Reduction Coalition (HRC)
Web site: http://www.harmreduction.org/

Harm Reduction Coalition was founded in 1993 by a coalition of drug users, advocates, and needle exchange providers.

The organization's goal is to challenge the persistent stigma on users of illegal substances and to work for reform of national, state, and local drug laws. HRC accepts as a reality that substance abuse is and always will be a part of human society, and that rather than working to completely eliminate this problem, governments should work to reduce the harm produced by substance abuse. The organization conducts most of its work through about a dozen specific programs, including the California Syringe Access Project, which promotes efforts to expand syringe exchange programs in the state; opiate overdose prevention projects, which provides educational programs in shelters, jails, treatment programs, and other facilities designed to serve substance abusers; Harm Reduction Training Institute, which offers training programs in Oakland and New York City for professionals and volunteers who work with substance abusers; and the Brick Rebuilding Project, which focuses on educating at-risk youth about the risks and dangers of substance abuse.

Publications: Brochures, booklets, pamphlets, videos, and posters in English and Spanish, such as "H Is for Heroin," "Hepatitis ABC," "Overdose: Prevention and Survival," "HRC Hepatitis C Reader," "9 Tips for Treating Hepatitis C in Current and Former Substance Users." and "To Do No Harm."

International Council on Alcohol and Addictions (ICAA)
Web site: http://www.icaa.ch/

The International Council on Alcohol and Addictions is one of the oldest—if not *the* oldest—international nongovernmental organization devoted to issues of alcoholism and substance abuse. It was organized in 1907 during the 11th International Conference Against Alcoholism in Stockholm, Sweden. It was originally called the International Bureau Against Alcoholism (IBAA), and was formed because attendees at the conference realized that there was a need for a formal, ongoing, international resource of reliable information about the dangers of alcoholism. In 1964, the organization changed its name to the International Council on Alcohol and Alcoholism (ICAA), and four years later, it changed its name again, this time to recognize its interest in issues of substance abuse and addiction, to the International Council on Alcohol and Addictions. ICAA's main activity is its annual international conference, at which a wide variety of papers and sessions on alcohol and substance abuse are offered. It also offers training sessions for specialists working in the field. The council is also joint sponsor with the German Archive for Temperance and Abstinence Literature of the Archer Tongue Collection for cultural studies on alcohol, currently located at the University of Applied Sciences Magdeburg–Stendal, at Magdeburg, Germany.

Publications: None

International Harm Reduction Association (IHRA)
Web site: http://www.ihra.net/

The International Harm Reduction Association is the international counterpart of the Harm Reduction Coalition (see above), which works to reduce the harm caused to individuals by substance abuse and by the stigmatization that such individuals experience in the general society. The first meeting to deal with this issue was held in Liverpool, England, in 1990, and the IHRA itself was formed five years later to provide a means of continuing the dialogue among professionals interested in harm reduction between regular meetings on the topic. Today, the organization sponsors conferences around the world on harm reduction, acts as an advocate for the concept of harm reduction before legislative bodies and the general public, coordinates activities of regional harm reduction groups, and develops and disseminates information in particular about harm reduction for individuals addicted to alcohol or troubled with alcoholism.

Publications: *International Journal of Drug Policy*, presentations and articles by IHRA staff, "50 Best" collections of the best articles on harm reduction each year, "HR2 Reports" on developments in harm reduction research, and media releases.

Mothers Against Drunk Driving (MADD)
Web site: http://www.madd.org/

Mothers Against Drunk Driving was founded in 1980 by Irving, Texas, resident Candace ("Candy") Lightner after her 13-year-old daughter was killed in a hit-and-run accident by a man who already had previously been convicted of drunk driving. The organization went through a period of internal debate in the mid-1980s over the question as to whether drunk driving or the consumption of alcohol itself was the core issue with which it was concerned. At that point, in 1984, the organization changed its name from Mothers Against Drunk Drivers to Mothers Against Drunk Driving to reflect its broader concerns. (In disagreement with this revised view, Lightner resigned from the organization she had founded.) Over the years, MADD has sponsored a number of campaigns to reduce drunk driving, including an effort to change the drinking age to 21 in all states, a recommendation for widespread use of random roadblocks to catch drinking drivers, and the creation of a victim/survivor help line. Its current emphasis is on a Campaign to Eliminate Drunk Driving that consists of four basic elements: high-visibility law enforcement, ignition interlocks for convicted drunk drivers, advanced automotive technologies to prevent drunk driving, and expanded grassroots support for the organization and its programs.

Publications: Press kits on topics such as the 2008 National Impaired Driving Crackdown campaign, Pennsylvania lobby day for H.B. 2019, and State Progress Report for 2008; fact sheets on topics such as the alcohol ignition interlock system, the Campaign to Eliminate Drunk Driving, and emerging technology; *MADDvocate* magazine; grief brochures; legal brochures; financial brochures; children's brochures; adolescent brochures; intervention brochures; and *DRIVEN* magazine.

National Asian Pacific American Families Against Substance Abuse (NAPAFASA)
Web site: http://www.napafasa.org/

The National Asian Pacific American Families Against Substance Abuse was formed in 1987 to deal with the growing problem of substance abuse in Asian American, Native Hawaiian, and other Pacific Islander populations. NAPAFASA works with its own members, with service providers, and with the general public to provide information, referrals, research results, advocacy programs, technical assistance, policy analysis, and other services for dealing with substance abuse issues. It is part of a network of more than 200 Asian and Pacific Islander service organizations. Some current and past programs offered by the organization are the Asian and Pacific Islander Substance Abuse Technical Assistance and Training Project for the State of California; Problem Gambling Prevention Technical Assistance and Training Project for the State of California; Recovery Month; Asian American and Pacific Islander Impaired Driving Prevention Project for the State of California; Parent Corps; and the Pacific Island Initiative Project.

Publications: *NAPAFASA Newsletter* (electronic newsletter; available to members only).

National Council on Alcoholism and Drug Dependence (NCADD)
Web site: http://www.ncadd.org/

The National Council on Alcoholism and Drug Dependence was formed in 1944 as the National Committee for Education on Alcoholism by Marty Mann, reputed to be the first woman to stay sober under the Alcoholics Anonymous program. Mann's primary objective was to publicize the message that alcoholism is not a moral failing but a disease. There is no more stigma to being an alcoholic, she believed, than to having cancer. For this reason, she urged that medical facilities and treatments, rather than prison terms and fines, be provided for alcoholics. The organization's current logo reflects this mission; it consists of the caduceus symbol that represents medical science with a key, symbolizing the gateway to knowledge and understanding. NCADD organizes its efforts around three major programs and services: awareness activities such as press releases, public service announcements, and community activities; prevention and treatment programs; and Registry of Addiction Recovery (ROAR), a program by which recovering alcoholics can "go public" about their alcoholism and recovery.

Publications: Booklets, brochures, pamphlets, fact sheets, videos, DVDs, kits, and other materials, including *Ask Dr. Bob: Questions and Answers on Alcoholism* (booklet); "Alcohol-Related Birth Defects" (fact sheet); "Youth and Alcohol" (fact sheet); "Underage Drinking" (fact sheet); *I Ran Out of People to Blame* (brochure); *I Wasn't Having Fun Anymore* (brochure); "Past These Walls" (DVD); *What Should I Tell My Children about Drinking?* (video); and "Drinking Too Much Too Fast Can Kill You" (poster).

National Inhalant Prevention Coalition (NIPC)
Web site: http://www.inhalants.org/

The National Inhalant Prevention Coalition was founded in 1992 by Synergies, a nonprofit corporation based in Austin, Texas. The organization began two years earlier as a statewide program called Texas Prevention Partnership, as an effort to educate school children in Texas about the dangers of inhalant abuse. Today, NIPC is operated by a branch of Synergies in Chattanooga, Tennessee. Currently, the organization sponsors the National Inhalants & Poisons Awareness Week during the third week in March to better educate students and the general public about the dangers of using inhalants for the purpose of recreation. NIPC also provides an array of information about the medical, social, economic, and other risks of using inhalants on its Web site.

Publications: None

NORML (National Organization for the Reform of Marijuana Laws)
Web site: http://norml.org/

NORML is one of the relatively few organizations much better known by its acronym than by its full and official name, the National Organization for the Reform of Marijuana Laws. The group was formed in 1970 with an original grant of $5,000 from the Playboy Foundation. Founder of the organization was Keith Stroup, an attorney and a strong advocate of the legalization of marijuana, the cause for which NORML has worked for almost 40 years. Stroup served as executive director of the organization until 1979, a period during which 11 states decriminalized the use of marijuana and other states significantly reduced penalties for its use. NORML currently claims to have 135 chapters throughout the country and a legal staff of more than 500 attorneys to assist with the writing of legislation and legal action on behalf of its primary mission, the decriminalization of marijuana use nationwide. In addition to providing information about marijuana and its legalization to the general public, the organization lobbies state and federal legislators, sponsors an annual national conference, and has spawned a nonprofit foundation, the NORML Foundation, which is committed to educating the general public about marijuana and its legalization.

Publications: Reviews of surveys and polls; a compilation of domestic and international laws; many reports on topics such as hemp, medical marijuana, marijuana crop reports, driving and marijuana, and arrest records; and *Legislative Alerts, News & Analysis from NORML*, an online newsletter.

Partnership for a Drug-Free America®
Web site: http://www.drugfree.org/

The Partnership for a Drug-Free America® was formed in 1986 with a grant provided by the American Association of Advertising Agencies (AAAA). The plan originally was to conduct a three-year effort to deal with the growing problem of substance abuse and addiction in the United States by way of an aggressive and sophisticated advertising campaign. At the end of that three-year period, however, a decision was made to continue the program. Perhaps the most famous element of the Partnership advertising program was its now-famous "fried egg" ad, which showed an egg before and during frying with the message "This is your brain; This is your brain on drugs." The centerpiece of the Partnership's current efforts is a Web site, drugfree.org, which attempts to translate the latest and most reliable information produced by research into tips and suggestions for teenagers about the risks posed by substance abuse. The organization also operates a number of specific educational campaigns, such as the Parent Campaign; Check Yourself, for teenagers; Get Help for Drug Problems; RX/OTC Abuse; Meth; Inhalants; Cough Medicine Abuse; and Steroids. Detailed information about all of these programs is available on the organization's Web site.

Publications: An online guide to drugs.

The RAND Corporation
Web site: http://www.rand.org/

The RAND Corporation was founded in 1945 as a freestanding division within the Douglas Aircraft Corporation for research and development (from which it got its name) on issues of interest not only to the U.S. Air Force, one of its original sponsors, but also on topics of interest to scientists and engineers on the RAND staff. The organization was created in order to continue a lively tradition of interest in a variety of intellectual issues that had arisen as a result of the needs of World War II. Today, the institution carries on a very wide variety of research topics for the U.S. government, foreign governments, state and local governments, colleges and universities, foundations, industries, professional organizations, and other nonprofit groups. It has produced well over 300 publications dating to 1981 on a variety of issues related to substance abuse.

Publications: Many research reports on topics such as the afford-
ability of alcoholic beverages in the European Union, changes in
global drug problems, the costs of amphetamine use in the United
States, the effects of substance abuse on workplace injuries, the
unintended consequences of drug use policies, inpatient costs
associated with marijuana comorbidity, and reducing alcohol
harm from an international perspective.

Substance Abuse Librarians and Information Specialists (SALIS)
Web site: http://www.salis.org/

Substance Abuse Librarians and Information Specialists was
formed in 1978 with the assistance of the U.S. National Institute
on Drug Abuse and the National Institute on Alcohol Abuse and
Alcoholism. SALIS merged with its Canadian counterpart, Librarians and Information Specialists in Addictions, in 1986. The organization's goals are to disseminate accurate information about the
use and misuse of drugs; to provide a communications network
for specialists working in the field of alcohol, tobacco, and other
drug use and abuse; to serve as an advocate for members on issues
of common interest; and to support programs for professional
development. SALIS sponsors an annual national convention and
provides a small number of scholarships for students in the field.

Publications: *SALIS News* (quarterly newsletter); *ATOD Serials
Database* (online database); *How To Organize and Operate an ATOD
Information Center: A Guide* (manual); *New Books List* (online database); *Alcohol, Tobacco and Other Drug Databases* (United States
and non-U.S. lists; online databases).

Women's Christian Temperance Union (WCTU)
Web site: http://www.wctu.org/

The Women's Christian Temperance Union was founded in 1874
by a group of women concerned about the destructive effects of
alcoholism and alcohol abuse in their own families and those of
friends and neighbors. These women initially devoted their
efforts in 1873 to congregating at taverns, praying against the
abuse of alcohol, and urging tavern owners to close their businesses. After about a year of such effort, these women decided
that a more formal organization was needed to achieve the goals
for which they worked, that organization being the WCTU.

Today, the organization has expanded its concerns to include—in addition to alcohol)—tobacco, illegal drugs, pornography, and gambling. One of the WCTU's current campaigns is opposition to the so-called Amethyst Initiative, an effort by a number of prominent Americans to have the drinking age reduced to 18.

Publications: *The Union Signal*, the official journal of the WCTU; *National Happenings*, a quarterly newsletter; *Signal Press Catalog* (Signal Press is the publishing arm of the WCTU), which contains about 600 items, including books, booklets, brochures, leaflets, flyers, posters, activity sheets, "think and do" sheets, pictures to color, lesson sheets, story and puzzle pages, and a wide variety of supplies.

Professional Organizations

American Academy of Family Physicians (AAFP)
Web site: http://www.aafp.org/

The American Academy of Family Physicians was founded in 1947 as the American Academy of General Practice. It changed its name to its current form in 1971 to more accurately represent the nature of the primary health care function of practitioners. The original purpose of the organization, and still one of its main missions, is to promote and encourage high standards among primary physicians in the United States. It also has a number of other objectives, including promoting cost-effective health care, preserving the right of family physicians to engage in medical and surgical practices for which they are trained, to serve as advocates for family medicine, and to ensure an optimal supply of family physicians. Substance abuse is an issue of significant concern to AAFP, which has issued position papers on topics such as marijuana, tobacco and smoking, alcohol advertising and youth, and drug use by physicians.

Publications: A number of articles in the organization's journal, *American Family Physician*, which can be accessed on its Web site at http://www.aafp.org/online/en/home/publications.html.

American Psychological Association (APA)
Web site: http://www.apa.org/

The American Psychological Association was founded in 1892 at Clark University by a group of 26 professionals in the field.

The organization today has a membership of about 150,000 individuals who specialize in fields such as evaluation, measurement,
and statistics, behavioral neuroscience, social psychology, devel-
opmental psychology, clinical psychology, education psychology,
industrial and organizational psychology, military psychology,
adult development and aging, child psychology, rehabilitation
psychology, consumer psychology, behavior analysis, trauma psychology, addictions, and psychopharmacology and substance
abuse. The section most interested in issues of substance abuse is
Division 28, Psychopharmacology and Substance Abuse. Members
of the division are especially interested in the interaction of drugs,
behavior, and other environmental factors in humans and other
animals. The group promotes teaching and research about the
effects of psychoactive substances on animal behavior. The home
page for the division is http://www.apa.org/divisions/div28/.

Publications: *Psychopharmacology and Substance Abuse News*, newsletter published three times a year. APA itself has published a
very large collection of books, pamphlets, booklets, and other
print materials and many journals, ranging from *American
Psychologist* and *Asian American Journal of Psychology* to *Journal of
Counseling Psychology* and *Journal of Family Psychology* to *Review
of General Psychology* and *School Psychology Quarterly*.

American Public Health Association (APHA)
Web site: http://www.apha.org/

The American Public Health Association was founded in 1872
during a period when researchers were first discovering the
causes of many infectious diseases, causes that could be controlled
by the development of an enlightened approach to public health
issues. The two guiding principles of the early association are
essentially the same as those that guide it today: an understanding
that governmental decisions about public health policy need to be
guided by the latest information on prevention and treatment of
disease, and that an aggressive program of public education about
such issues is needed. Today, APHA conducts much of its work
through 25 special sections on topics such as Alcohol, Tobacco,
and Other Drugs, Community Health Planning and Policy Development, Disability, Environment, Epidemiology, Food and Nutrition, Gerontological Health, Health Administration, HIV/AIDS,
Injury Control and Emergency Health Services, International

Health, and Maternal and Child Health. The association also makes available certain special interest groups which members may join. Currently there are groups for alternative and complementary health practices, community health workers, ethics, health informatics information technology, health law, laboratory, physical activity, and veterinary public health.

Publications: *The Nation's Health* (newspaper); *American Journal of Public Health*; *Inside Public Health* (monthly newsletter); many books, such as *Health Issues in the Black Community, Ethics in Epidemiology for Public Health Practice, Disability and Public Health*, and *Case Studies in Public Health Ethics*; and reports and issues briefs on topics such as "Creating a Safe Food System for America," "The Role of Community-Based Programs in Ensuring Access to Care Under Universal Coverage," "Shifting the Course of Our Nation's Health: Prevention and Wellness as National Policy," "Holes in the Net: Surveying the Impact of the Current Economic Recession on the Health Care Safety Net," "America Breathing Easier: Working Together, We Can Alleviate the Burden of Asthma and Keep America Breathing Easier," and "Evaluating the Economic Causes and Consequences of Racial and Ethnic Health Disparities."

American Society of Addiction Medicine (ASAM)
Web site: http://www.asam.org/

The American Society of Addiction Medicine was first accepted by the American Medical Association in 1988 as a national medical specialist society. ASAM grew out of earlier state organizations, beginning with the New York City Medical Committee on Alcoholism in 1951. The organization has a fivefold mission that includes improving information about and access to addiction treatment; educating physicians and other medical professionals about addictions; supporting research and prevention programs; promoting the appropriate role of the physician in the care of patients with addiction; and establishing addiction medicine as a well-recognized medical specialty among professionals, government officials, purchasers and consumers of health care services, and the general public. ASAM offers courses and sponsors conferences and other meetings on addiction medicine.

Publications: *Principles of Addiction Medicine* (textbook); *Patient Placement Criteria* (guidelines); *ASAM News* (newsletter); *Journal of Addiction Medicine* (journal); Review Course CD-ROM (study guide).

Association for Addiction Professionals (NAADAC)
Web site: http://www.naadac.org/

The National Association for Addiction Professionals was founded in 1972 as the National Association of Alcoholism Counselors and Trainers (NAACT). A decade later, the organization changed its name to reflect its broader range of concerns, to the National Association for Alcoholism and Drug Abuse Counselors (NAADAC). It changed its name once more in 2001 to the Association for Addiction Professionals, while keeping its earlier acronym. The association currently has more than 10,000 members in 43 states, consisting of substance abuse counselors, educators, health care professionals, and others interested in the field. NAADAC's mission is "to achieve excellence through education, advocacy, knowledge, standards of practice, ethics, professional development and research." To this end, the organization sponsors an annual conference, other seminars and meetings, and a program for the certification of professionals in addiction treatment and education.

Publications: Books and pamphlets on a variety of topics, such as *Buprenorphine's Role in Opiate Treatment*, *Conflict Resolution Kit*, *Counseling Lesbian, Gay, and Bisexual Clients*, *Critical Incidents*, *How to Advocate: A Call to Action*, and *Medication Management for Addiction Professionals*.

8

Resources

The use and misuse of alcohol, tobacco, prescription drugs, marijuana, cocaine, heroin, and other legal and illegal drugs have been the subject of a vast quantity of literature over the past century. Literally thousands of books, articles, reports, pamphlets, brochures, and electronic commentaries have been produced on the subject. This chapter can list only a sample of those resources. The items shown here are classified first as print or nonprint resources, with the former including books, articles, and reports, and the latter consisting of Web sites dealing with substance abuse. The items have also been classified as those dealing with substance abuse in general, with legal drugs (tobacco, alcohol, and prescription drugs primarily), and with illegal drugs (such as marijuana, cocaine, heroin, amphetamines, and the like). Some overlap among topics does occur, however, since many resources listed may mention more than one topic.

Print

General
Books
Abadinsky, Howard. *Drug Use and Abuse: A Comprehensive Introduction*, 6th ed. Belmont, CA: Wadsworth Publishing, 2007.

The author, an expert in criminology, discusses the issue of substance abuse from the standpoint of law enforcement, with chapters on the impact of drugs on society, the history of drug use and abuse, the pharmacological impact of drugs on the human body, drug policy considerations, drug abuse as a law enforcement issue, the treatment and prevention of drug abuse, theories of substance abuse, and the drug business.

Connors, Gerard J., Dennis M. Donovan, and Carlo C. DiClemente. *Substance Abuse Treatment and the Stages of Change: Selecting and Planning Interventions.* **New York: Guilford Press, 2004.**

This text is intended for specialists in the field and for students preparing for careers in which substance abuse is an important topic. The book focuses on methods of treatment; issues with special populations; individual, couple, and group treatment; and relapse issues.

Fisher, Gary L., and Thomas C. Harrison. *Substance Abuse: Information for School Counselors, Social Workers, Therapists, and Counselors,* **4th ed. Boston: Pearson, 2009.**

This book is designed for the general reader as well as for use in educational settings. It covers the complete range of substance abuse issues with which professionals named in the title are likely to deal. It presents useful background information, as well as suggestions for diagnosis, prevention, and treatment of substance abuse issues.

Gahlinger, Paul. *Illegal Drugs: A Complete Guide to their History, Chemistry, Use, and Abuse.* **New York: Plume, 2004.**

This superb overview of virtually all aspects of substance abuse includes chapters on the history of specific drugs, such as opium, marijuana, and heroin; a history of legal efforts to control substance abuse; drug testing; the pharmacological effects of drugs; the business of illegal drugs; and a review of legal psychoactive drugs.

Hanson, Glen, Peter Venturelli, and Annette Fleckenstein. *Drugs and Society,* **10th ed. Boston: Jones and Bartlett, 2008.**

This widely used textbook opens with a general discussion of substance abuse issues, along with an explanation of the way drugs affect the nervous system. The main body of the book is then devoted to detailed discussions of the major drugs of concern, including alcohol, narcotics, stimulants, hallucinogens, inhalants, marijuana, and over-the-counter and prescription drugs.

Inaba, Darryl, and William E. Cohen. *Uppers, Downers, All Arounders: Physical and Mental Effects of Psychoactive Drugs,* 6th ed. Ashland, OR: CNS Publications, 2007.

This book covers in detail almost every legal and illegal drug of interest to the general public, from whom it receives generally very positive reviews. Chapters deal with topics such as the history of drug use and abuse, classification of drugs, the pharmacology of drugs, stimulants, depressants, alcohol, hallucinogens, drug treatment, and drug use and mental health.

Johnson, Jerry L., and George Grant. *Casebook: Substance Abuse.* Boston: Allyn & Bacon, 2004.

As with other casebooks in this series, *Substance Abuse* opens with a general introduction to the topic, followed by four detailed case studies to which students are expected to develop responses.

Julien, Robert M. *A Primer of Drug Action: A Concise, Non-Technical Guide to the Actions, Uses, and Side Effects of Psychoactive Drugs.* New York: Holt Paperbacks, 2001.

This book is designed for the general reader. It provides a technical and detailed description of the biochemistry and pharmacology of drug action, beginning with a description of the nervous system and its response to psychoactive substances, followed by detailed explanations of the actions of specific drugs and drug classes, including alcohol and inhalants of abuse; barbiturates; benzodiazepines; cocaine, amphetamines, and other stimulants; caffeine and nicotine; opioids; and hallucinogenics.

Karch, Steven B. *Drug Abuse Handbook,* 2nd ed. Boca Raton, FL: CRC Press, 2006.

This book includes the contributions of more than 80 specialists on substance abuse in a wide variety of fields. Individual chapters deal with a number of drug-related issues, many of which do not appear in standard substance or drug abuse books, such as medical complications of drug abuse, drug abuse in sports, drug testing, postmortem toxicology, and criminalistics and controlled substances.

Kuhn, Cynthia, Scott Swartzwelder, and Wilkie Wilson. *Buzzed: The Straight Facts About the Most Used and Abused Drugs from Alcohol to Ecstasy,* 3rd ed. New York: W. W. Norton, 2008.

The title somewhat misrepresents the content of the book, which is less "streetwise" than it is technical and academic, although still easily accessible to the general reader. Part I of the book contains chapters on individual drugs and drug groups, ranging from herbal concoctions and coffee and tea to ecstasy and hallucinogens of all types. Part II of the book deals with more general topics, such as the nature of addiction, the neurological effects of drugs, legal issues, and drug treatment and recovery.

Lynch, Timothy, ed. *After Prohibition: An Adult Approach to Drug Policies in the 21st Century.* **Washington, D.C.: The Cato Institute, 2000.**

Eleven of the twelve papers in this volume present reasons that drugs that are currently illegal should be legalized, while the final paper argues against this position. The arguments presented for legalizing drugs are economic, legal, social, political, and ethical.

Maisto, Stephen A., Mark Galizio, and Gerard J. Connors. *Drug Use and Abuse,* **5th ed. Belmont, CA: Wadsworth Publishing, 2007.**

This textbook takes a broad-range view of the issue of drug use and abuse, drawing on information from biology, medicine, history, psychology, and sociology. Introductory chapters deal with pharmacology and psychopharmacology, while middle chapters focus on specific drugs, such as heroin, cocaine, caffeine, alcohol, and opiates. The final two chapters discuss prevention and treatment of substance abuse.

Miller, William R., and Kathleen M. Carroll, eds. *Rethinking Substance Abuse: What the Science Shows, and What We Should Do about It.* **New York: Guilford Press, 2006.**

The editors argue that the practice of substance abuse counseling has lagged significantly behind new information obtained from research. They consider in this book what counseling programs would actually look like if they were based on our use of the best research results currently available.

Musto, David. *Drugs in America: A Documentary History.* **New York: New York University Press, 2002.**

This fascinating book collects speeches, sermons, policy statements, laws, personal letters, and other documents that describe all facets of the use and abuse of drugs in the United States.

Newton, David E. *Chemistry of Drugs*. New York: Facts On File, 2007.

The author presents factual information on a variety of drug types, including natural products, designer drugs, and rationale-design drugs, with a consideration of social, political, and ethical issues related to drug use and abuse.

Perrine, Daniel M. *The Chemistry of Mind-Altering Drugs: History, Pharmacology, and Cultural Context*. Washington, D.C.: American Chemical Society, 1996.

The primary focus of this book is on the pharmacological and biochemical effects of drugs on the human nervous system, with some mention made of almost every legal and illegal drug of interest. The author also places the issue of substance abuse in a broader perspective, however, reviewing the history of drug use and its impact on the general culture, for example, in literature.

Rotgers, Frederick, Jonathan Morgenstern, and Scott T. Walters, eds. *Treating Substance Abuse: Theory and Technique*, 2nd ed. New York: Guilford Press, 2006.

This book is a revised edition of a widely popular textbook in the field of substance abuse that deals with topics such as twelve-step programs for recovery, a psychoanalytic theory of substance abuse, family therapy techniques, behavioral treatments for drug abusers, and contingency management in dealing with substance abuse.

Savelli, Lou. *Street Drugs*. Flushing, NY: Looseleaf Law Publications, Inc., 2007.

Written by a New York drug division officer, this book provides basic, down-to-earth information about illegal drugs sold and used on the streets, including their technical names, street names, risk for addiction, symptoms of abuse, physical appearance, related paraphernalia, effects of use, methods of ingestion, packaging, and price. The book covers not only the most common illegal drugs, such as cocaine, ecstasy, and heroin, but also prescription drugs.

Schuckit, Marc A. *Drug and Alcohol Abuse: A Clinical Guide to Diagnosis and Treatment*, 6th ed. New York: Springer, 2005.

For three decades, this book has been a standard reference for clinicians working with substance abusers. The latest edition has 14 chapters on major drugs and drug groups, such as alcohol, stimulants, cannabinols, inhalants, over-the-counter drugs, and xanthines and nicotines, as well as multidrug abuse and dependence, emergency problems, and rehabilitation.

Stevens, Patricia, and Robert L. Smith. *Substance Abuse Counseling: Theory and Practice*, **4th ed. Upper Saddle River, NJ: Prentice Hall, 2008.**

This book is widely used in courses for counseling students, with extensive use of case studies and a review of recent research and developments in the field.

Velasquez, Mary, Gaylyn Gaddy Maurer, Cathy Crouch, and Carlo C. DiClemente. *Group Treatment for Substance Abuse: A Stages-of-Change Therapy Manual.* **New York: Guilford Press, 2001.**

This book is designed for practitioners who are dealing with patients having substance abuse and addiction problems. It includes a theoretical introduction to the topic along with a variety of handouts and exercises that counselors can use in working with such individuals.

Journals and Periodicals
Journal of Substance Abuse Treatment. **ISSN: 0740–5472.**

Published eight times a year, this journal is concerned with substance abuse treatment specifically.

Substance Abuse. **ISSN: 0889–7077.**

This quarterly journal is one of the premier publications for the most recent research and opinion on substance abuse issues.

Substance Abuse Treatment, Prevention, and Policy. **ISSN: 1747–597X.**

This journal is especially important to students of substance abuse issues because many of its articles are available though its Open Access policy, which allows readers the right to copy, distribute, and display articles; to make derivative works from an article; and to use an article for commercial purposes.

Articles

Backett-Milburn, Kathryn, et al. "Challenging Childhoods: Young People's Accounts of 'Getting By' in Families with Substance Use Problems." *Childhood* 15 (4): 461–479.

A number of studies have attempted to discover and interpret the health, social, and other issues faced by substance abusers. Much less attention has been paid to the children of adult substance abusers. In this review, researchers explore the methods that such individuals develop to survive in the real world with parents who are often incapable of taking care of themselves, let alone their children. They discuss a number of survival strategies that those children develop and use in their everyday lives.

Bullington, Bruce. "Drug Policy Reform and its Detractors: The United States as the Elephant in the Closet." *Journal of Drug Issues* 34 (3): 687–721.

This excellent article reviews some significant changes that have been taking place in national drug policies in Central and Western Europe since the beginning of the twenty-first century. It suggests that the growth of a centralized European community may lead to even greater changes in the policies of individual nations, but that drug policies in the United States will still have a significant influence over such policies in Europe.

Council on School Health and Committee on Substance Abuse. "The Role of Schools in Combating Illicit Substance Abuse." *Pediatrics* 120 (6; December 2007): 1379–1384.

The American Academy of Pediatrics has issued this policy statement about the role of schools in working with families to identify individuals who may be at risk for substance abuse and for developing practices that will help prevent such developments.

Dunn, Michael S. "The Relationship Between Religiosity, Employment, and Political Beliefs on Substance Use among High School Seniors." *Journal of Alcohol and Drug Education* 49 (1; March 2005): 73–88.

One might expect that a number of personal, social, cultural, religious, and other factors are involved in the tendency of an adolescent to become involved in illegal substance use. This study attempts to determine how a number of those factors are related to alcohol, cigarette, marijuana, and cocaine use among a group of high school seniors. The author summarizes those factors which appear to be related to the use of each drug, and the strength with which each factor operates.

Haggerty, Kevin P., et al. "Long-term Effects of the Focus on Families Project on Substance Use Disorders Among Children of Parents in Methadone Treatment." *Addiction* **103 (12; December 2008): 2008–2016.**

The authors report on an experimental study designed to assist parents in a methadone treatment program in improving their parenting skills, with the objective of reducing the risk of their children also developing substance abuse problems. The study found that the experimental treatment, now called the Families Facing the Future project, was significantly more effective for preventing substance abuse among male children than among female children.

Hornik, Robert, et al. "Effects of the National Youth Anti-Drug Media Campaign on Youths." *American Journal of Public Health* **98 (12; December 2008): 2229–2236.**

In 1998, U.S. Congress created the National Youth Anti-Drug Media Campaign in an effort to reduce drug abuse by young Americans. This study attempted to determine the effect of that campaign on the target audience in the period between 1999 and 2004. Researchers concluded that "[m]ost analyses showed no effects from the campaign."

Kendler, Kenneth S., et al. "Genetic and Environmental Influences on Alcohol, Caffeine, Cannabis, and Nicotine Use from Early Adolescence to Middle Adulthood." *Archives of General Psychiatry* **65 (6; June 2008): 674–682.**

There is evidence that both heredity and environment are involved in a person's tendency to begin or not begin the use of psychoactive drugs, such as alcohol, nicotine, and cannabis. The extent to which each factor is important at various stages has not, however, been well studied. In this research, Kendler and his colleagues found that environmental factors, such as family influences and peer pressure, were especially influential during the early years of adolescence in leading (or not leading) one to begin using psychoactive drugs, while genetics was a more important factor in such decisions later in adolescence and in early adulthood.

Kilpatrick, Dean G., et al. "Risk Factors for Adolescent Substance Abuse and Dependence: Data from a National Sample." *Journal of Consulting and Clinical Psychology* 68 (1; February 2000): 19–30.

The authors of this article attempted to isolate factors which predispose a person to become addicted to legal and/or illegal substances, such as alcohol, marijuana, and cocaine. They found that adolescents who witnessed or were involved in family violence of almost any kind and those who had experienced some other form of post-traumatic stress disorder were most inclined to develop a dependence on "hard" drugs. This pattern was significantly less apparent among African Americans, but not among Hispanics and Native Americans, than among Caucasians.

King, Ryan S., and Marc Mauer. "The War on Marijuana: the Transformation of the War on Drugs in the 1990s." *Harm Reduction Journal* 3 (6; February 2006): 3–6.

The authors review U.S. policy and practices with regard to marijuana use in the 1990s and find that 82 percent of the increase of 450,000 drug arrests made between 1900 and 2002 were for marijuana use, and, of that number, 79 percent were for possession alone. They also found that an estimated $4 billion is spent annually for the arrest, prosecution, and incarceration of marijuana offenders. They argue that the effort and expense devoted to the control of marijuana could be more efficiently spent on other types of drug enforcement.

Lubman, Dan I., et al. "Intervening Early to Reduce Developmentally Harmful Substance Use among Youth Populations." *MJA* [*Medical Journal of Australia*] 187 (7 Suppl.; October 2007): S22–S25.

The authors discuss the growing risk of substance abuse and addiction among adolescents and point out that a number of policies and practices are need to prevent at-risk individuals from becoming involved in the use of legal and illegal substances early in their lives.

Nadelman, Ethan A., and Courtwright, David T. "Should We Legalize Drugs? History Answers." *American Heritage* 44 (1; February/March 1993): 41–56.

Nadelman and Courtwright debate one of the oldest and most fundamental questions in the field of substance abuse: how and to what extent would legalization of drugs affect this social problem? Although somewhat dated, the arguments presented on both sides are still cogent and relevant to the present day.

Nighswonger, Todd. "Just Say Yes to Preventing Substance Abuse." *Occupational Hazards* 62 (April 2000): 39–42.

The author points out the importance of having a workforce that is entirely drug-free to guarantee the safety and efficiency of business operations. He recommends a five-part program for adoption by a company.

Steiker, Lori K. Holleran. "Making Drug and Alcohol Prevention Relevant: Adapting Evidence-based Curricula to Unique Adolescent Cultures." *Family and Community Health* 31 (1 Suppl.; January/March 2008): S52–S60.

The author argues for drug prevention programs that are more relevant to the real everyday lives of adolescents and that take into consideration their cultural backgrounds. She describes experimental programs that have been developed to achieve these aims, and cites data that suggest that such programs are more effective at preventing substance abuse among adolescents than other, more traditional but less relevant programs.

Wittchen, H. U., et al. "What Are the High Risk Periods for Incident Substance Use and Transitions to Abuse and Dependence? Implications for Early Intervention and Prevention." *International Journal of Methods in Psychiatric Research* 17 (Special Issue 1; 2008): S16–S29.

This team of researchers attempted to discover the time period during which individuals transitioned from first exposure to a drug to becoming addicted to that drug for a number of substances, including alcohol, nicotine, cannabis, and other illicit drugs. They found that, except for alcohol, that transition occurs quite rapidly and, as a result, "the time windows for targeted intervention to prevent progression to malignant patterns in adolescence are critically small, leaving little time for targeted intervention to prevent transition."

Reports

2008 Florida Youth Substance Abuse Survey. Tallahassee, FL: Executive Office of the Governor. Florida Department of Education. Florida Department of Children and Families. Florida Department of Health. Florida Department of Juvenile Justice. Florida Alcohol and Drug Abuse Association, Inc., December 2008.

Many cities, states, and regions conduct surveys and studies of substance abuse issues in their own geographic region. This study is included here as an example of such studies. The extensive report deals with topics such as the survey methodology; findings on alcohol, tobacco, and other drug use; other antisocial behaviors (such as carrying a handgun or attempting to steal a vehicle); risk and protective factors; special topics; and extensive tables and charts.

Caulkins, Jonathan P., et al. *How Goes the War on Drugs? An Assessment of U.S. Drug Programs and Policy.* Santa Monica, CA: RAND Drug Policy Research Center, 2005.

For more than 15 years, the RAND Corporation has been studying the U.S. "war on drugs." This report is an effort to "stand back" and take an overview of the progress (or lack of it) during that period of time. The main topics considered in the report are how effective the war on drugs has been thus far (the answer: not very); why the "war" has not been more successful; what side effects there have been from the "war"; why there has been no course correction in programs with such modest successes; and an alternative view of how drug policy might evolve.

Epidemiological Trends in Drug Abuse. Bethesda, MD: U.S. Department of Health and Human Services. National Institutes of Health. Division of Epidemiology, Services and Prevention Research. National Institute on Drug Abuse, January 2009.

The Community Epidemiology Work Group consists of 21 researchers from around the nation who meet on a regular basis to report on and discuss problems of drug abuse in their respective regions. This publication consists primarily of the reports of these researchers, with additional input from experts in Canada and Mexico, and additional information from forensic laboratories and other sources about characteristics of a number of illegal substances.

Morrall, Andrew R., et al. *The Relative Effectiveness of 10 Adolescent Substance Abuse Treatment Programs in the United States.* **Santa Monica, CA: The RAND Corporation, 2006.**

This report was prepared at the request of the Substance Abuse and Mental Health Administration and other agencies to determine the effectiveness of various possible methods of treating adolescent substance abusers in the United States, of whom there are about 150,000 under the age of 18 each year. Researchers compared the effectiveness of three long-term care facilities, four short-term facilities, and three outpatient programs. They found relatively modest differences among the programs they studied and considered some reasons for this possibly surprising result.

National Survey of American Attitudes on Substance Abuse XIV: Teens and Parents. **New York: National Center on Addiction and Substance Abuse at Columbia University, August 2009.**

The National Center on Addiction and Substance Abuse at Columbia University conducts an annual survey to determine attitudes of adolescents and their parents toward substance abuse, with the goal of providing data that will allow teachers, counselors, and other professionals concerned about substance abuse to develop better programs for preventing the illegal use of drugs among teenagers.

Results from the 2007 National Survey on Drug Use and Health: National Findings. **Washington, D.C.: Office of Applied Studies, Substance Abuse & Mental Health Services Administration, U.S. Department of Health & Human Services, September 2008.**

The Substance Abuse and Mental Health Services Administration annually conducts an exhaustive survey of the civilian, noninstitutionalized population of the United States to gather data on substance abuse in the United States. This report covers data collected in 2007 through interviews with 67,500 individuals. It contains information on virtually any topic in the field of substance abuse in the United States in which a person might be interested.

Trends in Substance Use, Dependence or Abuse, and Treatment among Adolescents: 2002 to 2007. Washington, D.C.: Office of Applied Studies, Substance Abuse & Mental Health Services Administration, U.S. Department of Health & Human Services, December 4, 2008.

This report is one of a series published as part of the National Survey on Drug Use and Health. It summarizes trends in the use of alcohol, cigarettes, and illicit drugs by adolescents in the United States between 2002 and 2007.

Van Gundy, Karen. *Substance Abuse in Rural and Small Town America*. **Durham, NH: Carsey Institute, 2006.**

This report is an effort to learn more about and report on the status of substance abuse in rural areas and small towns of the United States. It begins by reviewing and summarizing the results of previous studies and reporting current trends nationally and by state and region. It then discusses patterns of substance abuse by various groups, such as age, sex, race, income, education, and employment status. It then focuses on the special problem of methamphetamine production and consumption in rural areas and small towns before concluding with a number of recommendations for dealing with substance abuse in such regions.

World Drug Report. **Geneva, Switzerland: United Nations Office on Drugs and Crime, 2007 (issued annually).**

This report purports to review the state of drug use and control throughout the world and is issued annually by the United Nations Office on Drugs and Crime. The 2007 report, which runs 282 pages, contains a vast amount of information on production, trafficking, and abuse of opium, cocaine, cannabis, and amphetamines. This report is an invaluable resource for anyone interested in a comprehensive overview of the status of illegal drugs throughout the world.

Legal Substances
Books
AA Services. *Alcoholics Anonymous: The Big Book*, 4th ed. Akron, OH: Alcoholics Anonymous, 2001.

First published in 1939, the "Big Book" has long been regarded as the gold standard of reference materials for alcoholics and recovering alcoholics. It provides a fundamental introduction to the problem of alcoholism, with special messages to the alcoholic and his or her family, friends, neighbors, employers, and coworkers. A key feature of the book has always been a number of personal success stories from men and women who have begun to overcome the disorder and have moved from being alcoholic to a recovering alcoholic.

Burroughs, Augusten. *Dry: A Memoir.* **New York: St. Martin's Press, 2003.**

Burroughs is author of the best-selling memoir, *Running with Scissors*, describing his difficult childhood. This follow-up book discusses the alcoholism into which he has descended, outlining the day-to-day existence of an otherwise apparently successful businessman.

Carr, Allen. *The Easy Way to Stop Drinking.* **New York: Sterling Publications, 2005.**

This book is typical of a host of books currently available for alcoholics, in which an author offers a seemingly simple and straightforward approach to overcoming the problem of alcoholism. The system he recommends is called the Easyway method.

Colvin, Rod. *Overcoming Prescription Drug Addiction: A Guide to Coping and Understanding.* **Omaha, NE: Addicus Books, 2008.**

Abuse of and addiction to legal prescription drugs is a topic that is sometimes ignored in discussions of substance abuse. This book considers principles and methods of coping with such addictions, methods by which fraudulent prescriptions are obtained, and legal methods that have been developed to monitor and control the illegal use of prescription drugs.

Hester, Reid K., and William R. Miller. *Handbook of Alcoholism Treatment Approaches,* **3rd ed. Boston: Allyn & Bacon, 2002.**

This scholarly work reviews a number of models that have been developed to explain alcoholism and then chosen those strategies which appear to have been most effective, based on those models.

Jay, Jeff, and Debra Jay. *Love First: A Family's Guide to Intervention*, 2nd ed. **Center City, MN: Hazelden, 2008.**

Just as there are dozens of books aimed at helping alcoholics overcome their addiction, so there are many books designed to help family, friends, and colleagues to overcome their loved one's addiction. This book is an example of such books. The authors recommend a host of procedures, including developing a plan, building a team, and writing an intervention letter, seeking a treatment center as essential elements in a plan of recovery.

Ketcham, Katherine, and William F. Asbury. *Beyond the Influence: Understanding and Defeating Alcoholism*. **New York: Bantam Books, 2000.**

The authors present the case for alcoholism as a "genetically transmitted neurological disease" rather than a personality disorder or character flaw. They suggest a program of recovery based on this principle, drawing on the latest research available at the time the book was written.

Müller, Richard, and Harald Klingemann, eds. *From Science to Action? 100 Years Later—Alcohol Policies Revisited*. **Dordrecht, Netherlands; Norwell, MA: Kluwer Academic Publishers, 2004.**

This collection of essays focuses on alcohol policy in the states of the European Union during the twentieth century. It was issued to commemorate the hundredth anniversary of the founding of the Swiss Institute for the Prevention of Alcohol and Other Drug Problems. Papers in the collection deal with the history of alcohol policy in Western Europe, policies and practices in specific nations, and the ethics and politics of alcohol policies.

Olson, Nancy. *With a Lot of Help from Our Friends: The Politics of Alcoholism*. **New York: Writers Club Press, 2003.**

The author, a recovering alcoholic, served on the staff of Senator Harold Hughes (D–IA), also a recovering alcoholic, with special responsibility for alcohol-related problems. She wrote this book at Senator Hughes' suggestion, shortly before his death in 1996. The book discusses the politics of alcohol-related issues in the United States during the period between 1970 and 1980, one in which such issues were probably of greater concern than at any time since Prohibition.

Plant, Martin, and Moira Plant. *Binge Britain.* **New York: Oxford University Press, 2006.**

As the title suggests, this book focuses on current drinking problems in Great Britain, but it also offers a broader perspective on the history of alcohol-related issues over an extended period of time. The authors also discuss current British policies on drinking, and the possible direction of their evolution in the future.

Rotskoff, Lori. *Love on the Rocks: Men, Women, and Alcohol in Post-World War II America.* **Chapel Hill: The University of North Carolina Press, 2001.**

The author presents a fascinating review and analysis of the role of alcohol in the American family in the years following World War II, with chapters on the growth of problem drinking among returning war veterans, the growth of Alcoholics Anonymous as a major service for dealing with alcoholism, the "dilemma of the alcoholic marriage," and alcoholism and consumerism in the postwar period.

Royce, James E., and David Scratchley. *Alcoholism and Other Drug Problems.* **New York: The Free Press, 2002.**

This book is an updated and revised version of Royce's original 1996 work that focuses on the physiology, pharmacology, and social aspects of addiction to alcohol and other drugs (although the focus is on alcohol). Part 2 of the book deals with some specialized issues of alcohol addition, including its causality, its status as a disease, and its effects on other family members and other concerned individuals. Part 3 of the book focuses on prevention and treatment of the condition.

Thoburn, Doug. *Alcoholism Myths and Realities: Removing the Stigma of Society's Most Destructive Disease.* **Northridge, CA: Galt Publishers, 2005.**

The author attempts to dispel more than 100 myths about alcoholism and help readers understand the true nature of the condition, thereby allowing for a more informed and rational plan for recovery for those troubled with the problem.

Tracy, Sarah W. *Alcoholism in America: From Reconstruction to Prohibition*, rev. ed. Baltimore, MD: Johns Hopkins University Press, 2007.

The author limits her story to the history of alcohol consumption in the United States for the 50-year period between 1870 (the founding of the American Society for the Cure of Inebriates) to 1920 (the beginning of Prohibition). She considers the story of alcoholism at least in part as a personal and community issue, but also on the much larger scale as a national social, economic, political, and ethical issue.

Tracy, Sarah W., and Caroline Jean Acker, eds. *Altering American Consciousness: The History of Alcohol and Drug Use in the United States, 1800–2000*. Amherst: University of Massachusetts Press, 2004.

This work is an extension of the first editor's original book on alcoholism in the United States in the period of 1870–1920 (see above), consisting of 14 papers dealing with the way alcoholism in particular and drug addiction in general have been defined and treated over a period of two centuries.

Zernig, Gerald, et al., eds. *Handbook of Alcoholism*. Boca Raton, FL: CRC Press, 2000.

This important standard reference on alcoholism deals with all major aspects of the subject, including screening and diagnosis, acute treatment, treatment of alcohol abuse and dependence, treatment of non-psychiatric alcohol-related disorders, research, and useful data and definitions.

Articles

Bailey, J. Elise, Elizabeth Campagna, and Richard C. Dart. "The Underrecognized Toll of Prescription Opioid Abuse on Young Children." *Annals of Emergency Medicine* 53 (4; April 2009): 419–424.

The authors argue that the accidental poisoning of children by prescription opioids is a poorly recognized and underreported problem in the United States. Their research suggests that

9,179 children in their study, conducted between January 2003 and June 2006, were exposed to such prescriptions, resulting in 8 deaths and 43 "major effects." The drug most frequently responsible for such accidents was naloxone, obtained from a parent supply of the drug in more than 99 percent of all cases.

Blanke, D. Douglas, and Kerry Cork. "Exploring the Limits of Smoking Regulation." *William Mitchell Law Review* **34 (4; May 2008): 1587–1593.**

This paper reviews a discussion held at the William Mitchell Law School on October 23, 2007, with regard to recent regulation on smoking in a number of venues. The question raised at this meeting was whether and to what extent recent laws had "crossed the line" in attempting to restrict the use of a legal product by the general product. The meeting was sponsored by the Tobacco Control Legal Consortium.

Blocker, Jack S. "Did Prohibition Really Work? Alcohol Prohibition as a Public Health Innovation." *American Journal of Public Health* **96 (2; February 2006): 233–243.**

The author presents a somewhat different view of the campaign for Prohibition in the United States and its ultimate effects on problems of alcoholism and on the population in general.

Culberson, John W., and Martin Ziska. "Prescription Drug Misuse/Abuse in the Elderly." *Geriatrics* **63 (9; September 2008): 22–31.**

The authors review current evidence on the misuse of prescription drugs by the elderly and find that the rate of misuse may be as high as 11 percent among this group. Major factors associated with the abuse of prescription drugs among the elderly are gender (elderly women are more likely to abuse prescription drugs than men), social isolation, depression, and history of substance abuse.

Denisco, Richard A., Redonna K. Chandler, and Wilson M. Compton. "Addressing the Intersecting Problems of Opioid Misuse and Chronic Pain Treatment." *Experimental and Clinical Psychopharmacology.* **16 (5; October 2008): 417–428.**

The authors note the significant increase in the misuse of prescription drugs over the past decade or so and attribute this change to the confluence of two factors: the increase in misuse per capita in the United States and the increase in the number of prescriptions being written for pain-relievers. The best available evidence suggests that the latter factor may be the more important of the two in the growth of this problem.

Ford, Jason A. "Nonmedical Prescription Drug Use Among Adolescents: The Influence of Bonds to Family and School." *Youth and Society* 40 (3; March 2009): 336–352.

Prescription drug abuse has now become the second most important substance abuse problem among adolescents, following the use of marijuana. The author explores this issue in some detail and concludes from data in the 2005 National Survey on Drug Use and Health that social bonds to the family is one of the strongest indicators as to an adolescent's tendency (or lack of it) to misuse prescription drugs.

Herring, Rachel, Virginia Berridge, and Betsy Thom. "Binge Drinking Today: Learning Lessons from the Past." *Drugs: Education, Prevention, and Policy* 15 (5; October 2008): 475–486.

The authors point out that binge drinking is a serious social problem in the United States, but that it is not a new problem. They review the literature on binge drinking in the past and explore possible lessons for the present epidemic of binge drinking.

Ibrahim, Jennifer K., and Stanton A. Glantz. "The Rise and Fall of Tobacco Control Media Campaigns, 1967–2006." *American Journal of Public Health* 97 (8; August 2007): 1383–1396.

Research has shown that public media campaigns to limit smoking have been very successful. The tobacco industry, however, has contested these campaigns in a number of ways, by preventing their creation, limiting or eliminating their funding, contesting their content, or preventing their existence by legal action. The authors have documented the existence of these efforts and have pointed out their effectiveness in the continuation of public media campaigns against smoking. They conclude that "[t]obacco control advocates must learn from the past and continue to confront the tobacco industry and its third-party allies to defend antitobacco media campaigns or, despite evidence of their effectiveness, they will be eliminated."

McCabe, Sean Esteban, James A. Cranford, and Brady T. West. "Trends in Prescription Drug Abuse and Dependence, Co-occurrence with Other Substance Use Disorders, and Treatment Utilization: Results from Two National Surveys." *Addictive Behaviors* 33 (10; June 2008): 1297–1305.

The authors use data from two large national surveys, the 1991–1992 National Longitudinal Alcohol Epidemiologic Survey and the 2001–2002 National Epidemiologic Survey on Alcohol and Related Conditions to explore patterns of prescription drug abuse and co-occurrence of such use with abuse of other substances among adolescents. They conclude that further research is needed in this field, and that existing treatment services are not being sufficiently used to help adolescents with co-occurrent dependence.

Österberg, Esa L., and Salme K. Ahlström. "International Perspectives on Adolescent and Young Adult Drinking." *Alcohol Research and Health* 28 (4; 2004/2005): 258–268.

The authors report on an extensive study of patterns of alcohol consumption among adolescents and young adults in a number of countries. They find, not surprisingly, that patterns of behavior and factors related to the use and abuse of alcohol vary widely from nation to nation.

Spiller, Henry, et al. "Epidemiological Trends in Abuse and Misuse of Prescription Opioids." *Journal of Addictive Diseases* 28 (2): 130–136.

The authors explore a number of possible factors that may be correlated with increasing misuse of prescription drugs and find that two in particular are correlated with the problem: poverty and unemployment. They suggest that their finding may assist in directing limited funds for the treatment of substance abusers who fit these categories.

Stolberg, Victor B. "A Review of Perspectives on Alcohol and Alcoholism in the History of American Health and Medicine." *Journal of Ethnicity in Substance Abuse* 5 (4): 39–106.

The author provides an extended review of the way Americans have viewed alcohol—in both positive and negative terms, as it turns out—throughout the nation's history. He pays special attention to the conflicted attitudes of the medical profession toward alcohol and alcohol abuse.

"Towards a Europe Free from Tobacco Smoke: Policy Options at EU Level." n.p.: European Commission, Health & Consumer Protection Directorate-General, 2007.

The risks posed to public health of secondhand smoke are being increasingly recognized in various European countries, many of which have responded with legislation specific to their own situation. This Green Paper explores the possibility of developing a European Union-wide policy built on scientific evidence regarding the health risks of environmental smoke.

Wakefield, Melanie, et al. "Impact of Tobacco Control Policies and Mass Media Campaigns on Monthly Adult Smoking Prevalence." *American Journal of Public Health* **98 (8; August 2008): 1443–1450.**

The authors studied the effects of a variety of smoking cessation initiatives for the period of 1995 to 2006. These initiatives included increasing the price of cigarettes, media campaigns promoting reduction in smoking, antismoking laws in public places, and increased availability of nicotine replacement therapies. They found that only the first two initiatives were effective and concluded that "[i]ncreases in the real price of cigarettes and tobacco control mass media campaigns broadcast at sufficient exposure levels and at regular intervals are critical for reducing population smoking prevalence."

Zajdow, Grazyna. "Alcoholism's Unnatural History: Alcoholism Is Not a 'Health' Issue, but One of Personal and Existential Pain. Recognising this Would Force Us to Acknowledge One of the Most Successful Methods of Dealing with Alcohol Addiction." *Arena* **70 (April 2004): 41–43.**

The author discusses the implications of thinking about alcohol addiction as a health problem versus a very personal psychological problem, and how these two different models have vastly different implications for treatment of the condition.

Reports

Emergency Department Visits Involving Nonmedical Use of Selected Pharmaceuticals. Washington, D.C.: Substance Abuse and Mental Health Services Administration, July 2006; Revised June 2009.

This report is part of the SAMHSA's Drug Abuse Warning Network (DAWN) series on trends in the use of legal and illegal substances in the United States. This report summarizes trends in the reporting of nonmedical uses of prescription drugs as the reason for emergency room visits in 2004, updated to 2008. According to the report, there were 536,247 such visits in 2008, of which the use of opiates and benzodiazepines were the most common drugs mentioned, accounting for 32.2 percent and 26.8 percent of all visits respectively.

Prescription and Over-the-Counter Medications. Washington, D.C.: National Institute on Drug Abuse, June 2009.

This report is a part of the National Institute on Drug Abuse's NIDA InfoFacts series. It provides a general overview of the issue of prescription drug abuse, the drugs involved, current trends of abuse among adolescents and adults, and methods for preventing and treating the problem.

Teens and Prescription Drugs. Washington, D.C.: Office of National Drug Control Policy, February 2007.

This report provides a general overview of the problem of prescription drug abuse by adolescents in the United States. It considers issues such as prevalence and incidence of the problem, availability and accessibility of prescription drugs to adolescents, gender differences for the problem, type of drugs used by teenagers, and dependence and treatment programs.

Trends in Nonmedical Use of Prescription Pain Relievers: 2002 to 2007. Washington, D.C.: U.S. Department of Health and Human Services. Substance Abuse and Mental Health Services Administration. Office of Applied Studies, February 5, 2009.

This report is part of the National Survey on Drug Use and Health. It provides data and statistics on the trends in the nonmedical use of prescription drugs among the general population and specialized groups in the United States.

Illegal Substances

Books

Brick, John, ed. *Handbook of the Medical Consequences of Alcohol and Drug Abuse,* 2nd ed. New York: Haworth Medical Press, 2008.

This book is intended for professionals in the field of substance abuse, with detailed technical information on some major drugs of abuse, including alcohol, marijuana, opiates, cocaine, and inhalants. The authors of individual chapters consider issues such as the effects of these drugs on the nervous system, acute and chronic toxic effects, direct and indirect medical effects, and effects on pregnant women and the fetus.

Bulter, Carol A. *100 Interactive Activities for Mental Health and Substance Abuse Recovery.* Plainview, NY: Wellness Reproductions, 2001.

This spiral-bound activity book is designed to help recovering addicts and abusers from ages eight and up to deal with issues such as self-esteem, anger management, assertion, stress management, and problem solving.

Conyers, Beverly. *Addict in the Family: Stories of Loss, Hope, and Recovery.* Center City, MN: Hazelden, 2003.

The author, a mother of three, writes of her family's experiences in dealing with their youngest son, a heroin addict.

Dasqupta, Amitava. *Drugs of Abuse Testing.* Boston: Jones & Barlett, 2009.

Drug testing has become an issue of some controversy in the United States today. This book provides a general background to the problems posed by substance abuse and the role of testing in dealing with those issues. The author begins with a brief historical review of substance abuse in the United States and legal efforts to deal with the problem, as well as the pharmacology of major drugs. He then discusses the evolution of workplace drug testing, legal issues related to the practice, methodologies of testing protocols, and attempts by individuals to "beat" testing practices.

Dorsman, Jerry. *How to Quit Drugs for Good: A Complete Self-Help Guide.* **New York: Three Rivers Press, 1998.**

The author outlines a method by which someone addicted to drugs can develop his or her own program for withdrawal and recovery. In the section on "Planning your own personal approach to quitting," he discusses methods for breaking a habit, the importance of changes in diet, and "30 additional ways to renew yourself."

Huggins, Laura E., ed. *Drug War Deadlock: The Policy Battle Continues.* **Stanford, CA: Hoover Institution Press, 2005.**

This book consists of six major sections, dealing with background to the U.S. "war" over drug policy; philosophical and historical bases for this conflict; perspectives of various individuals about the status of the conflict; points of view about specific features of the drug war; the special situation of marijuana; a review of the situation in Europe and its significance for American drug policy; and a conclusion that includes a "blueprint for peace" that would end the war over drugs.

Lookadoo, Justin. *The Dirt on Drugs.* **Grand Rapids, MI: Revell: Hungry Planet, 2005.**

This book is intended for children and teenagers and takes an aggressive approach to pointing out the serious problems associated with substance abuse. It focuses on 10 specific drugs and drug groups, including alcohol, tobacco, marijuana, cocaine, inhalants, and steroids.

McGinnis, Sheryl Letzgus, and Heiko Ganzer. *I Am Your Disease: The Many Faces of Addiction.* **Denver, CO: Outskirts Press, 2006.**

This book is intended as a cautionary statement for teenagers who are considering the abuse of drugs, or who are already involved in such activities. The authors present a number of true-life stories about children and adolescents, and their families, as they fact the consequences of becoming addicted to one or another illegal drugs.

Robinson, Matthew B., and Renee G. Scherlen. *Lies, Damned Lies, and Drug War Statistics: A Critical Analysis of Claims Made by the Office of National Drug Control Policy.* **Albany: State University of New York, 2007.**

The White House Office of National Drug Control Policy (ONDCP) annually issues a report reviewing national drug policy and its effects on drug use in the United States. Robinson and Scherlen review reports of the ONDCP for 2000 through 2005 and conclude that the agency consistently misrepresents the status of substance abuse in the United States and on the government's ability to exert control over the problem. They suggest that government programs have thus far had little or no effect on the production and consumption of illegal drugs in the United States.

Salant, James. *Leaving Dirty Jersey: A Crystal Meth Memoir.* **New York: Simon Spotlight Entertainment, 2007.**

The author writes of his efforts—and those of his parents—to free himself from his crystal meth addiction, first in a rehabilitation center in California, and later, on his own on the streets. The book does not present an academic, dispassionate analysis of the substance abuse problem in the United States, but it does give an intense review of the problems faced by one individual drug addict.

Storm, Jennifer. *Blackout Girl: Growing Up and Drying Out in America.* **Center City, MN: Hazelden, 2008.**

This memoir was written by a young woman who regularly experienced "blackouts" because of alcohol abuse beginning at the age of 12, after which she moved on to other drugs. She was fortunate to recover from her addictions and told of her history in this moving book.

Toner, Patricia Rizzo. *Substance Abuse Prevention Activities.* **Just for the Health of It!, Unit 6. West Nyack, NY: Center for Applied Research in Education, 1993.**

This set of puzzles, worksheets, skits, and other activities is designed for students in grades 7 through 12 who are dealing with substance abuse issues, either in an academic setting or in their own lives.

Vigna, Judith. *My Big Sister Takes Drugs.* **Niles, IL: Albert Whitman & Company, 1995.**

This illustrated book is intended for children ages four through eight and tells the story of a young boy who learns that his older sister is taking drugs and reports her to his family. The daughter is then placed in a rehabilitation center, which has its own effects on the life and relationships of the storyteller.

Articles

Bretteville-Jensen, Anne Line. "To Legalize or Not To Legalize? Economic Approaches to the Decriminalization of Drugs." *Substance Use and Misuse* 41 (4; April 2006): 555–565.

Discussion about decriminalizing the use of certain currently illegal substances often focuses on ethical and social issues. In this paper, the author considers the economic implications of legalizing drugs such as marijuana, cocaine, and heroin, the first and primary effect probably being a significant decrease in prices. In this event, the number of drug users may increase.

Committee on Substance Abuse and Committee on Adolescence. "Policy Statement: Legalization of Marijuana: Potential Impact on Youth." *Pediatrics* 113 (6; June 2004): 1825–1826.

This brief report concludes with two recommendations. First, the American Academy of Pediatrics opposes the legalization of marijuana. Second, the organization supports further research into the use of cannabis-containing products for the alleviation of medical problems not amenable to treatment by other means.

Costa Dias, Andréa, et al. "Follow-Up Study of Crack Cocaine Users: Situation of the Patients After 2, 5, and 12 Years." *Substance Abuse* 29 (3; August 2008): 71–79.

This study is of particular interest because it follows a cohort of 131 crack cocaine users over a period of 12 years to determine their status as drug users and their general health. Researchers found that the largest group of individuals had become abstinent and had been very successful in remaining so in succeeding years. The death rate among the original sample, however, was very high, amounting to 27 individuals at the 12-year point. Researchers noted, however, that it was not drug use, but general socioeconomic factors that were more likely to be responsible for these mortalities.

Denton, J. Scott, et al. "An Epidemic of Illicit Fentanyl Deaths in Cook County, Illinois: September 2005 through April 2007." *Journal of Forensic Sciences* 53 (2; March 2008): 452–454.

Fentanyl is probably not one of the most widely known illegal drugs to most individuals in the United States, but it has been implicated in a number of serious cases of abuse resulting in severe medical disorders and death in some cases. This article describes an epidemic that struck Cook County, Illinois between September 2005 and April 2007 and resulted in the death of 350 individuals. It discusses the forensic issues involved in tracing the laboratory responsible for the epidemic and its ultimate closure.

Fazey, Cindy. "International Policy on Illicit Drug Trafficking: the Formal and Informal Mechanisms." *Journal of Drug Issues* 37 (4; September 2007): 755–779.

Over the last decade, a number of nations around the world have developed new official, semi-official, and unofficial policies and practices for dealing with international trafficking in illegal drugs. The need for this change has arisen because of the problems in getting more formal agencies, such as those within the United Nations, to adopt policies and practices that are accepted to large numbers of states with differing viewpoints and objectives. The author reviews some of the new policies and practices being used to control the international flow of illegal substances.

Hendricksen, Lisa, et al. "Receptivity to Alcohol Marketing Predicts Initiation of Alcohol Use." *Journal of Adolescent Health* 42 (1; January 2008): 28–35.

One of the methods commonly recommended for reducing the tendency of children and adolescents to begin drinking and smoking is limiting or eliminating advertising on television, in newspapers and magazines, and in other media. Hendricksen and her colleagues asked whether research supported the notion that such efforts do have measurable effects on an individual's tendency to begin drinking. They found that it did, and suggested that limitations on advertising could help reduce the number of adolescents who begin drinking alcohol.

Khatapoush, Shereen, and Denise Hallfors. "Sending the Wrong Message": Did Medical Marijuana Legalization in California Change Attitudes about and Use of Marijuana?" *Journal of Drug Issues* 34 (4; October 2004): 751–770.

Some critics of the legalization of marijuana use for medical purposes proposed by California's Proposition 215 in 1996 argued that passage of the proposition would increase the use of marijuana in the general public. The authors of this study test that argument by surveying a sample of California residents before and after the vote on the proposition (which passed) and find that its enactment appears to have had no measurable effect on marijuana use among the general public.

Kritikos, P. G., and S. P. Papadaki. "The History of the Poppy and of Opium and Their Expansion in Antiquity in the Eastern Mediterranean Area." *Bulletin on Narcotics* **19 (3; 1967): 17–38.**

This article provides a detailed history of the use of opium from the earliest known times (about 3500 BCE) to the first century CE. It is nicely illustrated with a number of depictions of the way the poppy and opium were included in the arts and crafts of ancient peoples. The article originally appeared in Greek in the *Journal of the Archæological Society of Athens*, but was later reprinted in the UN *Bulletin on Narcotics*. It is also available on the Internet in English at http://www.poppies.org/news/99502023966018 .shtml#bf127.

Maag, Verena. "Decriminalisation of Cannabis Use in Switzerland from an International Perspective: European, American and Australian Experiences." *International Journal of Drug Policy* **14 (3; June 2003): 279–281.**

The Swiss government commissioned a study of the possible effects of decriminalizing marijuana use, using as its basis three national studies previously conducted in the United States, Australia, and Italy. Those studies found no consistent relationship between government policy and marijuana use, but that legalization does have some measurable and positive benefits to the general society in terms of reduced law enforcement costs and negative effects on those arrested for the crime.

McNeese, C. Aaron. "After the War on Drugs Is Over: Implications for Social Work Education." *Journal of Social Work Education* **39 (2; Summer–Spring 2003): 193–212.**

The author considers a proposal for "a free market for drugs unfettered by government intervention" and considers the impact such a program would have for the harm currently produced by government policies on drug users. He suggests that such a change would have significant implications for social policy and practice.

Rasmussen, Nicolas. "America's First Amphetamine Epidemic 1929–1971: A Quantitative and Qualitative Retrospective with Implications for the Present." *American Journal of Public Health* 98 (6; June 2008): 974–985.

The author reviews an amphetamine epidemic that swept the United States in the 1940s through the 1960s and concludes that current amphetamine abuse patterns are similar to those of the earlier period. He suggests that lessons can be learned about the control of the present-day epidemic from the earlier experience.

Reports

Bachman, Jerald G., Lloyd D. Johnston, and Patrick M. O'Malley. *Monitoring the Future: Questionnaire Responses from the Nation's High School Seniors.* Ann Arbor: The University of Michigan Institute for Social Research, Survey Research Center, 2008.

Since 1975, the Survey Research Center at the University of Michigan has been conducting an annual survey of practices of and attitudes about substance abuse among seniors at about 130 selected high schools throughout the United States. This volume is the latest in that series, which provides an invaluable overview of changing opinions about drug use among high school students in the country. With more than 200 pages of data, these reports are arguably the most complete picture available of the status of substance abuse among American teenagers currently available.

Club Drugs—2002 Update. Washington, D.C.: U.S. Department of Health and Human Services. Substance Abuse and Mental Health Services Administration. Office of Applied Studies, July 2004.

This report is part of the Substance Abuse and Mental Health Services Administration's Drug Abuse Warning Network Series. It summarizes the status of so-called "club drugs" in the United States, a term that includes (for this report) GHB (gamma-hydroxy-butyrate), ketamine, LSD (lysergic acid diethylamide), and MDMA (methylenedioxymethamphetamine, also known as

Ecstasy). The report notes that the four drugs together accounted for about 8,100 emergency room visits in 2002, about one percent of the total number of visits for all forms of legal and illegal drug abuse.

Heroin and Other Opiate Admissions to Substance Abuse Treatment. **Washington, D.C.: U.S. Department of Health and Human Services. Substance Abuse and Mental Health Services Administration. Office of Applied Studies, August 27, 2009.**

This report is part of the Treatment Episode Data Set (TEDS) series of the Office of Applied Studies, which assesses the current status of various legal and illegal substances monitored by the Substance Abuse and Mental Health Services Administration. The report notes that heroin is by far the opiate most likely to be responsible for hospital admissions, accounting for about one-fifth of all substance abuse admissions in 2007.

The Partnership Attitude Tracking Study (PATS). **New York: Partnership for a Drug-Free America, May 16, 2006.**

Since 1987, the Partnership for a Drug-Free America has been conducting annual surveys about attitudes of adolescents and their parents about the use of a variety of legal and illegal substances, ranging from tobacco and cough medicine to ketamine and crack cocaine. In the latest study, data suggest that the use of drugs by teenagers has continued to decline in the country for all drugs except prescription medicines and inhalants. The most common reason for adolescents' use of prescription drugs was that they are readily available from medicine cabinets at home and from other sources, they are not illegal, and they are easy to get by using someone else's prescription.

Robinson, Jeffrey. *Who's Really in Prison for Marijuana?* Washington, D.C.: Office of National Drug Control Policy, 2005.

This report was issued by the Office for National Drug Control Policy in response to claims from supporters of the legalization of marijuana that U.S. prisons are filled with individuals convicted of minor drug offenses, such as possession of small amounts of marijuana. The report concludes that "the vast majority of drug prisoners are violent criminals, repeat offenders, traffickers, or all of the above."

Senate Special Committee on Illegal Drugs. *Cannabis: Our Position for a Canadian Public Policy.* **Ottawa, September 2002.**

The Special Committee on Illegal Drugs of the Canadian Senate conducted an extensive study of the problem of cannabis use in the nation, whose results are summarized in this report. The committee concluded the government's existing policies and practices with regard to cannabis use have been an expensive failure and that drastic revisions in those policies and practices were needed. Specifically, they recommend the development of a system by which individuals over the age of 16 would be able to procure legally small amounts of marijuana for personal use through licensed facilities. The report concludes with 11 recommendations for changing the fundamental approach to dealing with cannabis in the nation.

Nonprint

Web Sites

Literally hundreds of Web sites provide information, advice, and/ or opinions about substance abuse. Some of these sites are maintained by governmental agencies or private organizations that are well known and highly respected. Other sites bear no mention of their sponsors or are operated by individuals or groups about whom little information is available. Users are cautioned to confirm the legitimacy of sites for which sponsorship is unlisted or questionable. The list below provides a sample of some of the many apparently reliable resources available on the Internet.

AddictionSearch.com. "Welcome to AddictionSearch.com." http://addictionsearch.com. Accessed on August 30, 2009.

This Web site is operated by a group of private professionals with background in substance abuse and interest in providing assistance to those faced with related problems. The site contains general information on addictions, statistics on adult and adolescent substance abuse, special information on specific topics (age, sex, ethnicity, etc.), treatment methods, articles on various aspects of substance abuse, treatment centers, prevention methods, social issues, and organizations interested in substance abuse.

Borio, Gene. "The Tobacco Timeline." http://www.tobacco.org/History/Tobacco_History.html. Accessed on August 31, 2009.

This outstanding review of the history of the use and regulation of tobacco products begins in the prehistory era and continues through 2007. It is a superb review of the role of tobacco in human society.

Campaign for Tobacco-Free Kids. "Smoking and Other Drug Use." http://www.tobaccofreekids.org/research/factsheets/pdf/0106.pdf. Accessed on August 31, 2009.

This brief leaflet outlines the association between smoking and other types of drug use, abuse, and addiction.

Canadian Institute of Neurosciences. "The Brain from Top to Bottom." http://thebrain.mcgill.ca/flash/index_i.html. Accessed on September 17, 2009.

This Web site is one of the best sources of information on the mechanisms by which drugs produce their effects on the brain. The site is an interactive page that allows users to see precisely the events that occur in the central nervous system with and without the presence of drugs.

Christie, Alice, Ph.D. "EMC 675 Class Web Quest: Substance Abuse." http://www.west.asu.edu/achristie/675wq2.html. Accessed on August 31, 2009.

This online learning activity presents an interesting and useful way for students to think through the issues involved in substance abuse, with an excellent (if somewhat outdated) list of links to web pages with more information on the topic.

Clinco Communications, Inc. Addiction Treatment Forum. http://www.atforum.com/index.php. Accessed on August 30, 2009.

This Web site is by Clinco Communications, Inc., an independent medical communications agency, and is supported by a grant from the Covidien Mallinckrodt company of St. Louis, Missouri. It provides a variety of sources of information, including a quarterly newsletter, *Addiction Treatment Forum*; news and updates; links to a number of resources with information on substance abuse; special information on methadone (manufactured by

Covidien Mallinckrodt); frequently asked questions about substance abuse; patient brochures on a number of topics, available for downloading from the Web site; a list of conferences, meetings, and other events; and a locator for methadone clinics.

DMOZ Open Directory Project. "Substance Abuse." http://www .dmoz.org/Health/Addictions/Substance_Abuse/. Accessed on August 31, 2009.

The Open Directory Project describes itself as "the largest, most comprehensive human-edited directory of the Web." On the "Substance Abuse" page, it lists 2,300 links to Web pages with information about this topic, subdivided into categories such as alcohol, centers and counseling services, drugs, support groups, tobacco, books, organizations, prevention, resources, treatment, and methadone maintenance.

eMedicineHealth.com. "Substance Abuse." http://www.emedi cinehealth.com/substance_abuse/article_em.htm. Accessed on August 30, 2009.

This excellent health resource provides a broad and accurate review of the general topic of substance abuse with links to many specialized topics, including specific drugs, health disorders, medical terms, and links to other organizations.

Film Ideas. "Smoking and Substance Abuse." http://www .filmideas.com/substance.html. Accessed on August 30, 2009.

Film Ideas is a private company that develops films for educational institutions, libraries, and other non-theatrical settings on a number of topics of interest, substance abuse being one of them. This Web site contains brief descriptions of the films available on this topic.

Focus Adolescent Services. "Drug and Teen Substance Abuse." http://www.focusas.com/SubstanceAbuse.html. Accessed on August 30, 2009.

This Web site claims to be the "largest and most comprehensive Internet site of information and resources on teen and family issues." It provides online information on a number of important features of substance abuse, including drugs that teens abuse, warning signs, drug treatment and recovery, counseling and therapy, and self-help and support groups.

Healthfinder.gov. "Substance Abuse." http://www.healthfinder .gov/scripts/SearchContext.asp?topic=827&refine=1. Accessed on August 31, 2009.

The U.S. Department of Health and Human Services maintains this superb Web site, which summarizes government publications and Web sites on a host of health topics. The "Substance Abuse" page lists advisories, alerts, and bulletins; databases; decision support tools; disease management; educational games; frequently asked questions; general information; grants; media campaigns; newsletters; online checkups; policies; practice guidelines; quick tips; regulations; research; risk factors; self-help; statistics; support groups; and treatments and procedures.

HelpGuide.org. "Abuse and Addictions." http://www.helpguide .org/mental/drug_substance_abuse_addiction_signs_effects _treatment.htm. Accessed on August 31, 2009.

HelpGuide is a privately operated Web site designed to help people understand, prevent, and resolve "life's challenges," which include issues such as anxiety, bipolar disorder, eating disorders, grief and loss, as well as drug and alcohol abuse. The section on the last of these topics includes information on alcoholism and alcohol abuse and treatment, drug abuse and drug addiction and treatment, and substance abuse and mental health.

Maxwell, Jane Carlisle. "Trends in the Abuse of Prescription Drugs." http://www.utexas.edu/research/cswr/gcattc/documents/ PrescriptionTrends_Web.pdf. Accessed on August 28, 2009.

This excellent article reviews 10 of the most recent studies on the illegal use of prescription drugs and concludes with some general observation about the extent and seriousness of the problem.

Medline Plus. "Pregnancy and Substance Abuse." http:// www.nlm.nih.gov/medlineplus/pregnancyandsubstanceabuse .html. Accessed on August 31, 2009.

This Medline page focuses on one important aspect of substance abuse, the health effects it may have on pregnant women and the fetuses they are carrying.

Medline Plus. "Substance Abuse Problems." http://www.nlm .nih.gov/medlineplus/substanceabuseproblems.html. Accessed on August 30, 2009.

This Web page is a service of the U.S. National Library of Medicine and the National Institutes of Health. It provides an index to more than 50 topics in the general area of substance abuse, such as alcohol, anabolic steroids, cocaine, drug abuse, inhalants, marijuana, methamphetamine, prescription drug abuse, and prescription drug abuse. The page is also available directly from the National Institutes of Health at "Substance Abuse," http://health .nih.gov/category/SubstanceAbuse.

MentalHelp. net. "Addictions: Alcohol and Substance Abuse." http://www.mentalhelp.net/poc/view_doc.php?type=doc&id =28899&w=5&cn=14. Accessed on August 30, 2009.

This Web site, maintained by Dr. Allan Scwartz, contains more than two dozen articles on a number of drug- and alcohol-related issues, such as introduction to alcohol and substance abuse, important diagnostic concepts regarding alcohol and substance abuse, abused drug categories, central nervous system stimulants, opiates, cannabinols, hallucinogens, solvents, symptoms of alcohol or substance abuse, alcohol and substance abuse treatment overview, medications for alcohol and substance abuse symptom and relapse reduction, and psychotherapy overview for alcohol and substance abuse.

National Clearing House for Alcohol and Drug Information. "Straight Facts about Drugs and Alcohol." http://ncadi.samhsa .gov/govpubs/rpo884/. Accessed on August 31, 2009.

This audio program provides extensive information on the problem of substance abuse in general, along with detailed information about the abuse of a number of specific drugs, including marijuana, methamphetamine, cocaine, alcohol, and cigarette smoking.

National Inhalant Prevention Coalition. "Frequently Asked Questions." http://www.inhalants.org/. Accessed on August 31, 2009.

This Web site is an excellent source of information on all aspects of the abuse of inhalants, with sections on general information on inhalants, frequently asked questions about inhalants, the Inhalant Prevention Campaign, and news about inhalant abuse.

National Institute on Alcohol Abuse and Alcoholism. "FAQs for the Public." http://www.niaaa.nih.gov/FAQs/General -English/default.htm. Accessed on August 31, 2009.

The National Institute on Alcohol Abuse and Alcoholism offers this web page with answers to frequently asked questions about alcoholism and alcohol abuse, such as "Is alcoholism a disease?", "Is alcoholism inherited?", "Can alcoholism be cured?", "What medications treat alcoholism?", "Is alcohol good for your heart?", and "Is it safe to drink during pregnancy?".

New York Times. "Drug Abuse." http://health.nytimes.com/ health/guides/specialtopic/drug-abuse/overview.html. Accessed on August 30, 2009.

As part of its online Health Guide, *The New York Times* offers a collection of articles it has published on a variety of substance abuse topics, such as alternative names of drugs; marijuana; phencyclidine; hallucinogens; stimulants; amphetamines; inhalants; opiates, opioids, and narcotics; stages of juvenile drug use; and treatment overview.

Occupational Safety and Health Administration, U.S. Department of Labor. "Workplace Substance Abuse." http://www.osha.gov/ SLTC/substanceabuse/index.html. Accessed on August 31, 2009.

This web page deals with the special issues of substance abuse in the workplace and deals with questions such as OSHA standards that apply; materials available for the training of supervisors and workers; relevant state and federal laws about substance abuse in the workplace; and basic information about substance abuse, prevention, and treatment.

"Pathology of Drug Abuse." http://library.med.utah.edu/ WebPath/TUTORIAL/DRUG/DRUG.html. Accessed on August 31, 2009.

This tutorial from the University of Utah Medical School contains many photographs of the effects of tobacco, alcohol, and other drugs on the human body.

PreventionNet. "Prevention Highlights." http://www.preventionnet .com/. Accessed on November 15, 2009.

PreventionNet is a program supported by a grant from the National Institute on Drug Abuse for disseminating information about drug abuse prevention programs that have been found to work. Currently, the it includes 11 programs in its database, including Life Skills Training, Project Star, Seattle Social Development Project, Project Family, Focus on Family, and Adolescent Transitions Program. The Web site also provides links to research centers, professional organizations, prevention Web sites and newsletters, and print resources.

Project CORK. http://www.projectcork.org/database_search/. Accessed on August 29, 2009.

Project CORK was founded at the Dartmouth Medical School in 1977 through a grant from Operation Cork, an arm of the Kroc Foundation. The purpose of the project is to provide up-to-date information on a host of drug-related issues for users of the Internet. The project's database currently contains more than 90,000 items in a searchable format on its Web site. It is very user-friendly, with an extensive listing of more than 200 topics that are continually updated.

Schaffer Library of Drug Policy. http://www.druglibrary.org/ schaffer/. Accessed on September 2, 2009.

The documents in this web page originally appeared in an exhibit at the Pelletier Library of Allegheny College, Pennsylvania, from October 15, 1999 through March 1, 2000. They deal with virtually every issue related to the use and abuse of all kinds of drugs. It may well be the largest single source of articles of substance abuse available to the general public.

School Mental Health Project, University of California at Los Angeles Department of Psychology. "Substance Abuse." http:// smhp.psych.ucla.edu/pdfdocs/Substance/substance.pdf. Accessed on August 31, 2009.

This "tool kit" is designed for use by professionals for use in staff training and for student/family interventions. It includes basic fact sheets on substance abuse; a guide to assessment tools; information on prevention; treatment strategies; and print, electronic, and organizations resources.

Substance Abuse and Mental Health Services Administration. "SAMHSA Health Information Network (SHIN)." http://www .samhsa.gov/shin/moreaboutshin.aspx. Accessed on August 30, 2009.

This Web site combines the services of two information sources, the National Clearinghouse for Alcohol and Drug Information (NCADI) and the National Mental Health Information Center (NMHIC). It provides four types of services to the general public: (1) a contact center that operates 24 hours a day, 7 days a week, to provide information on substance abuse and mental health in English and Spanish by trained professionals in the field, (2) access to more than 1,600 publications on substance abuse and mental health issues, (3) access via the Web site and email that typically draws about 1.5 million contacts per month, and (4) outreach and collaboration resources for conferences, exhibits, meetings, and other events related to substance abuse and mental health.

Substance Abuse and Mental Health Services Administration. "Substance Abuse Treatment Facility Locator." http://dasis3 .samhsa.gov/. Accessed on August 30, 2009.

This web page is a service of the U.S. Substance Abuse and Mental Health Services Administration. It provides a list of facilities available for treatment of substance abuse problems in all 50 states.

teAchnology. "Substance Abuse Teaching Plans." http://www .teach-nology.com/teachers/lesson_plans/health/substance/. Accessed on August 31, 2009.

This Web site provides access to a number of lesson plans for teaching about substance abuse at almost all levels. Some topics are "Drugs and Alcohol," "Safe Use of Medicine," "Steroids and the Body," "Tendon Damage from Steroids," and "Just Say No."

TeenDrugAbuse. "Teen Drug Abuse." http://www.teendrugabuse .us/index.html. Accessed on August 30, 2009.

The TeenDrugAbuse Web site is sponsored by Teen Help, LLC, to spread information about drug abuse among adolescents in the United States. This Web site offers a general overview of the problem, a review of the relationship between drug abuse and school, and between drug abuse and the family. Resources for dealing with substance abuse and addiction are also provided.

TeensHealth. "Drugs and Alcohol." http://kidshealth.org/teen/ drug_alcohol/. Accessed on August 31, 2009.

This presentation is decided for teenagers and covers basic information on smoking, alcohol use, and drug abuse, along with a section on getting help for an addiction.

Wired In. Daily Dose.net. http://dailydose.net. Accessed on August 30, 2009.

Daily Dose was created in January 2001 by the parent Web site Wired In which, in turn, was established to empower people to deal with their drug and alcohol abuse problems. Daily Dose provides access to news, research studies and results, blogs, podcasts, films, and audio resources on substance abuse issues. The site also has links to more than 150 other Internet resources with interests similar to its own.

World Health Organization. "Management of Substance Abuse." http://www.who.int/substance_abuse/en/. Accessed on August 30, 2009.

The World Health Organization (WHO) is a division of the United Nations, with responsibility for collecting information about substance abuse in nations around the world and to provide information to individuals and groups wishing to know more about this issue. WHO has three primary responsibilities in this field: (1) preventing and reducing the negative health and social consequences of substance abuse, (2) reducing the demand for nonmedical uses of psychoactive substances, and (3) assessing psychoactive substances so as to be able to advise the United Nations on regulation of these substances. This Web site includes a list of current WHO programs related to substance abuse, terminology and classification used in discussions of substance abuse, facts and figures, publications, latest research results, and links to other sites dealing with substance abuse.

Glossary

Discussions of substance abuse often involve terminology which is unfamiliar to the average person. In some cases, the terms used are scientific or medical expressions used most commonly by professionals in the field. In other cases, the terms may be part of the so-called "street slang" that users themselves employ in talking about the drugs they consume, the paraphernalia associated with drugs, or the kind of experiences that accompany drug use. This chapter lists and defines some of the most common terms from each group.

addiction   A long-lasting and typically recurring psychological and/or physiological need for one or more substances, such as alcohol or tobacco, that generally results in permanent or long-lasting changes in the neurochemistry of the brain.

alcohol   In discussions of substance abuse, a term that refers to the chemical's correct chemical name is ethanol or ethyl alcohol. In chemistry, the term has a different and more general meaning, referring to a class of organic compounds that contains the hydroxyl functional group, –OH.

alcoholism   Physical dependence on alcohol such that discontinuing the use of alcohol results in withdrawal symptoms. Alcoholism is typically accompanied by the development of social and/or health problems serious enough to require professional help.

alkaloid   A naturally occurring organic compound containing one or more basic nitrogen atoms found in plants often displaying medicinal properties.

analgesic   A drug capable of relieving pain.

analog   (also **analogue**) A chemical compound similar in structure to some other chemical compound.

anorectic   A substance that reduces the appetite.

antidepressant   A drug that reduces or moderates depression, resulting in an elevation in one's mood.

antitussive   A cough suppressant.

ataxia   Loss of control of muscular movement, manifested in an unsteady gait, unsteady movements, and clumsiness; a common symptom of mild drug overdose.

BAC   Acronym for *blood alcohol content* or *blood alcohol concentration*, a measure of the amount of alcohol present in a person's body, usually represented as percent content or percent concentration, as 0.08 (i.e., 0.08%).

barbiturate   A substance derived from the chemical barbituric acid ($C_4H_4N_2O_3$). Some examples of barbiturates are barbital (Veronal®), phenobarbital (Luminal®), pentobarbital (Nembutal®), and sodium pentothal.

bhang   A concoction or infusion made with leaves and flowers from the hemp plant, widely used on the Indian subcontinent as a recreational drug and as a drug for religious and ceremonial purposes.

binge drinking   Excessive consumption of alcohol over a relatively brief period of time, which typically results in nausea, vomiting, loss of control over one's bodily functions and, in extreme cases, more serious symptoms, such as coma and death.

blackout   Loss of memory about a particular event, such as the taking of a drug or overconsumption of alcohol.

bronchodilator   A drug that relaxes and dilates the bronchial passages, allowing for easier breathing.

caffeine   A mildly addictive alkaloid stimulant found in coffee, tea, kola nuts, and many synthetic beverages, such as soda drinks.

cannabinoid   Any one of the substances found in the cannabis plant, *Cannibis sativa*, or, more generally, that has a chemical structure similar to that of tetrahydrocannabinol (THC) or that binds to cannabinoid receptors in the body.

cannabis   The botanical name for the plant from which marijuana comes. Its correct botanical name is *Cannibis sativa*.

chemical dependence   A condition that develops when one's body undergoes changes that result in a continual physiological need for a particular drug or other substance.

cirrhosis   A medical condition in which normal tissue in the liver is replaced by scar tissue; the most serious consequence of alcoholism or alcohol abuse.

club drug   *See* **designer drug**.

cocaine   A powerful stimulant extracted from the leaves of the coca plant (*Erythroxylon coca*).

codeine   An addictive alkaloid narcotic derived from opium, used a and antitussive and analgesic, and also abused as a recreational drug.

codependency   A relationship in which a non-substance abuser is controlled by the behavior of a second person who is a substance abuser, generally resulting in devastating consequences for both members of the partnership.

controlled substance analog   *See* **designer drug**, definition 2.

crack   A highly addictive form of cocaine, made by mixing cocaine with baking soda and water.

cross-addiction   Addiction to two substances belonging to different classes, such as alcohol and cocaine.

delirium   A medical condition characterized by severe confusion; rapid changes in brain function; rambling or incoherent speech; sensory misperceptions; sleep disruption; drowsiness; memory loss; and disorientation with respect to time, place, or persons.

delirium tremens   A medical condition associated with withdrawal of alcohol among chronic alcoholics, characterized by uncontrollable trembling, hallucinations, severe anxiety, excessive sweating, and feelings of terror.

dependence   A condition in which an individual develops a fixation on or craving for a drug that is not necessarily so severe as to be classified as an addiction but that may, nonetheless, require professional help to overcome.

designer drug   (1) A synthetic chemical compound developed for the treatment of a specific disease or group of diseases; (2) A psychoactive chemical deliberately synthesized to avoid antidrug laws that mimics the effects of a banned drug. Also known as a controlled substance analog, club drug, or rave drug.

dissociative drug   A substance that produces feelings of analgesia, disconnection, and alienation.

drug   A chemical used in the diagnosis, cure, mitigation, treatment, or prevention of disease or to bring about an alternation in one's mental or emotional state.

dysphoria   A condition of unusually severe depression and/or anxiety, mental and/or physical discomfort, and general malaise.

ecstasy   A street name for 3-4 methylenedioxymethamphetamine (also known as Adam or MDMA).

empathogen   A drug capable of producing strong emotional features, such as emotional closeness, love, and affection. The term *entactogen* has been suggested as a synonym for the word.

enabling   The act of supporting or contributing to the destructive behavior of a substance abuser, sometimes based on the enabler's best intentions of helping that person.

endogenous   Produced naturally within the body.

entactogen   *See* **emphathogen**.

flashback   Recurring emotional or sensory experiences that take place independently, and often at much later times, than an initial experience which, in the case of drugs, was the occasion of having consumed those drugs.

freebasing   A method of consuming cocaine by mixing it with ether so that it can be smoked.

hallucinogen   A drug that causes profound distortions in a person's perceptions of reality, causing an individual to see images, hear sounds, and feel sensations that seem real but do not exist.

heroin   An analgesic drug derived from morphine, also known as diacetylmorphine, with legitimate medical use as a painkiller, but whose recreational use may result in feelings of extreme euphoria that can become addictive.

inhalant   A substance of low volatility, such that it can be easily absorbed through the respiratory system.

intervention   An event in which a group of individuals confront an alcoholic or a substance abuser with the demand for specific action by that person to begin dealing with his or her addiction.

laudanum   A tincture of opium, that is, opium powder dissolved in alcohol.

LSD   *See* **lysergic acid diethylamine**.

lysergic acid diethylamine   A semisynthetic chemical compound with very strong hallucinogenic effects, often known by its common names of *LSD* or *acid*.

mainlining   Taking a drug by injection into a vein.

MAOI   Acronym for *monamine oxidase inhibitor*, a class of drugs used to treat cases of severe depression, insomnia, panic attack, and anxiety because they provide a sense of well-being and euphoria. They are often used as drugs of last resort, however, because of serious interactions with a number of foods and, for that reason, pose a special risk when used as recreational drugs.

methamphetamine   A highly addictive psychoactive drug belonging to the family of phenylethylamines, easily made by amateur chemists, and known by a variety of common names, depending in part on the form in which it is consumed, as "chalk," "crank," "crystal," "ice," glass," "meth," and "speed."

narcotic   Any drug that, in small doses, produces insensitivity to pain, dulls the senses, and induces deep sleep, but in larger doses may result in numbness, convulsions, and coma.

neuron   A nerve cell.

neurotransmitter   A chemical that carries a nerve impulse between two neurons.

nicotine   A very addictive alkaloid compound that occurs naturally in plants belonging to the genus Solanaceae, which includes the tobacco plant, of which it constitutes about 0.6–3.0 percent by dry weight.

oneirogen   A substance that produces a dreamlike state of consciousness.

opiate   Any drug or other substance derived from or chemically related to opium.

opiate receptor   Specialized receptor cells in neurons that bind to natural analgesic molecules present in the body.

opium   An addictive narcotic extracted from the seeds of the opium poppy, *Papaver somniferum*.

OTC drug   *See* **over-the-counter drug**.

over-the-counter drug   A drug that can be purchased without a prescription.

overdose   (verb) To take an excessive, risky, and potentially fatal quantity of a harmful substance.

paranoia   A psychological disorder characterized by delusions of persecution or grandeur.

pharmacopoeia   A catalog of drugs, chemicals, and medicinal preparations.

phenylethylamines   A class of drugs whose members contain three functional groups—the phenyl group ($-C_6H_5$), ethyl group ($-C_2H_5$), and amine group ($-NH_2$)—that form the basis of a very large number of natural and synthetic compounds with a variety of psychotropic effects. Drugs in this class may act as anorectics, antidepressants, bronchodilators, entactogens, hallucinogens, or stimulants.

precursor chemical   A chemical used to make some other substance, for example, the raw materials used to make illicit drugs.

prescription drug   A drug that can be purchased only with a medical prescription provided by a registered medical provider, such as a physician or a physician's assistant.

psilocybin   A hallucinogenic alkaloid found in many species of Central American mushrooms.

psychedelic   A substance capable of producing perceptual changes, such as vivid colors and weird shapes, as well as altered awareness of one's mind and body.

psychoactive   *See* **psychotropic**.

psychoanaleptic   *See* psychostimulant.

psychostimulant   A type of stimulant that acts to increase brain activity specifically; also known as a psychoanaleptic.

psychotomimetic A drug that produces psychotic-like effects that may include delusions and hallucinations.

psychotropic Having an effect on the mind.

rave drug *See* **designer drug**.

relapse The return of a condition, such as addiction to or dependency on a drug, which had formerly been successfully overcome.

schedule (drug) A category into which the federal government classifies certain drugs based on their potential medical use and their possibility of illicit recreational applications.

secondhand smoke Cigarette smoke inhaled involuntarily by non-smoking individuals in a closed environment.

serotonin A neurotransmitter associated with a number of mental and emotional functions, including appetite, learning, memory, mood, muscular contraction, and sleep. A number of drugs reduce or increase the amount of serotonin available in the brain, thereby moderating one or more of these actions.

smokeless tobacco Tobacco that is consumed by some method other than smoking, for example, chewing tobacco or snuff.

snuff Finely ground tobacco which is inhaled rather than smoked.

stimulant When used in connection with drugs, a substance that temporarily increases physiological activity in the body, with a number of associated effects, such as increased awareness, interest, physical activity, wakefulness, endurance, and productivity. Physiological changes include increased heart rate and blood pressure.

synaptic gap The space between two neurons.

temporary unrousable unconsciousness A type of coma that can be life-threatening.

tetrahydrocannabinol A primary component of the cannabis plant, often represented simply as THC.

THC *See* **tetrahydrocannabinol**.

tolerance Developing immunity to the effects caused by a substance such that one requires a larger amount of the substance over time to achieve the same results obtained from smaller amounts earlier on in its use.

twelve-step program A program for recovery from alcoholism, drug addiction, and other behavioral problems originally proposed by Alcoholics Anonymous in its 1939 book *Alcoholics Anonymous: The Story of How More Than One Hundred Men Have Recovered From Alcoholism*.

withdrawal symptoms The physical, mental, and emotional effects that an individual experiences when he or she discontinues use of a substance to which he or she has become addicted or dependent.

Index

About the Author

David E. Newton holds an associate's degree in science from Grand Rapids (Michigan) Junior College, a B.A. in chemistry (with high distinction) and an M.A. in education from the University of Michigan, and an Ed.D. in science education from Harvard University. He is the author of more than 400 textbooks, encyclopedias, resource books, research manuals, laboratory manuals, trade books, and other educational materials. He taught mathematics, chemistry, and physical science in Grand Rapids, Michigan, for 13 years; was professor of chemistry and physics at Salem State College in Massachusetts for 15 years; and was adjunct professor in the College of Professional Studies at the University of San Francisco for 10 years. Previous books for ABC-CLIO include *Global Warming* (1993), *Gay and Lesbian Rights* (1994, 2009), *The Ozone Dilemma* (1995), *Violence and the Mass Media* (1996), *Environmental Justice* (1996, 2009), *Encyclopedia of Cryptology* (1997), *Social Issues in Science and Technology: An Encyclopedia* (1999), *DNA Technology* (2009), and *Sexual Health* (2010). Other recent books include *Physics: Oryx Frontiers of Science Series* (2000), *Sick!* (4 volumes; 2000), *Science, Technology, and Society: The Impact of Science in the 19th Century* (2 volumes; 2001), *Encyclopedia of Fire* (2002), *Molecular Nanotechnology: Oryx Frontiers of Science Series* (2002), *Encyclopedia of Water* (2003), *Encyclopedia of Air* (2004), *The New Chemistry* (6 volumes; 2007), *Nuclear Power* (2005), *Stem Cell Research* (2006), *Latinos in the Sciences, Math, and Professions* (2007), and *DNA Evidence and Forensic Science* (2008). He has also been an updating and consulting editor on a number of books and reference works, including *Chemical Compounds* (2005), *Chemical Elements* (2006), *Encyclopedia of Endangered Species* (2006), *World of Mathematics* (2006), *World of Chemistry* (2006), *World of Health* (2006), *UXL Encyclopedia of Science* (2007), *Alternative Medicine* (2008), *Grzimek's Animal Life Encyclopedia* (2009), *Community Health* (2009), and *Genetic Medicine* (2009).